W9-BNT-676

Any Day

HENRY MITCHELL

INDIANA UNIVERSITY PRESS   BLOOMINGTON AND INDIANAPOLIS

Any Day

Illustrations by Susan Davis

The paper used in this publication meets
the minimum requirements of American National Standard for Information Sciences—
Permanence of Paper for Printed Library
Materials, ANSI Z39.48-1984.

Manufactured in the United States of America

**Library of Congress Cataloging-in-
Publication Data**

Mitchell, Henry, 1923–
    Any day / Henry Mitchell ; illustrated by
Susan Davis.
        p.   cm.
    ISBN 0-253-33308-3 (alk. paper)
    I. Title.
AC8.M5758   1997
070.4'4—dc20   97-1356

    2 3 4 5   02 01 00 99 98 97

Book and Jacket Designer: Sharon L. Sklar

Copyeditor: Bobbi Diehl

Typesetter: Greg Delisle

Printer and Binder: Maple-Vail Book Mfg.

Typeface: Sabon

Dedicated to *Elsie Carper*

Thomas Lovejoy

CONTENTS

Contents

Contents

Contents

Publisher's Preface

Henry wouldn't mind if I told a little story to introduce his book.

Long ago, I, a Washingtonian and Easterner, moved to Indiana. Unable completely to sever the cord that bound me to my origins, I subscribed for several years to the *Washington Post*. Week after week I found myself gravitating to Henry Mitchell's Earthman columns, though I was not then a gardener of any sort. This guy, I thought, is something else. This isn't just about gardening, it's life. And an original voice.

Though it wasn't a university press sort of thing, there came a time when the publishing gene demanded action. I asked Henry about doing a book of his columns. Always diffident (his defense against not being Shakespeare), he was sure no one would want his writings in book form. I persisted. He ducked and dodged. Please, I argued, just send us a collection of the columns. We'll organize a book. You won't have to do anything but take bows. He wouldn't help. Didn't want to chance it. Whatever.

Finally, Virginia Mitchell, the Big Hound's wife, did the deed and sent us a box full of Earthman columns. My colleague Roberta Diehl and I quarried a book from this material. *The Essential Earthman* was published in 1980. *The New York Times* called it "the most soul-satisfying gardening book in years."

In 1992 Houghton Mifflin published a second collection of gardening columns, *One Man's Garden*. Once again Henry was his modest self. Virginia Mitchell had to gather the material together and the editors at Houghton Mifflin organized the book. *The Essential Earthman* and *One Man's Garden* are two of the best known and most beloved books of their time.

Henry died in 1993. A victim of cancer, he had gone home from the hospital knowing his days were numbered. In typical Mitchell fashion, he managed a final poignant (he wouldn't have wanted that characterization) gesture by being in his garden "with dirt on his hands" when the call came from the Master Gardener in the Sky.

Besides the gardening columns, Henry wrote numerous feature stories, personal essays, comments on the state of the world, many of which appeared on Fridays under the title "Any Day." Exactly when the Friday columns got named "Any Day" is lost to history. The last official Any Day appeared on October 5, 1984, but the column continued, unnamed, until May 31, 1991.

In the spring of 1996 Virginia Mitchell suggested the idea of an Any Day book. People kept asking her when it would come out. I demurred. It would be a trade book. I wasn't sure we were the right publisher. The material wouldn't hold up over time. She sent me the columns anyway, a box full of three-ring binders, another of loose clippings. I fiddled around. How could I find the time to read through so much stuff? Who would the market be? Gardeners? Everyone? No one specific. Times were tough in publishing. We were trying to bring more focus to our list in response to a dropoff in sales. Zub zub zub.

Then one afternoon I decided to read a few columns in order to confirm my decision to say no. The first one that fell to hand was "Hubbub in the Pew," from December 30, 1977. It begins: "The front bench of the church I know is reserved not for mourners or sinners (specifically) but for members of the women's altar guild, and I will now tell how their ancient territory was challenged on Christmas Eve." There follows a brilliantly observed unique short essay-story about the struggle between tradition and change, men versus women, territoriality in humans, matters of state (in appropriate asides), and God's position in the firmament—all this in under 1500 words. I defy any sentient being to read this story and not fall in love with Henry Mitchell. Or almost any of his stories, for that matter. He will make you laugh and he will make you weep and he will catch you up in the midst of a busy, confusing day and make you pause and reflect: Hey, look at this! He will make you feel good about being a flawed human, and he will even—don't ask me how—make you think that mortality isn't so bad.

There must be well over a thousand pieces to choose from. One wants as many as possible. Hundreds are worth reprinting. I have chosen columns which have integrity as mini essays and which are not bound by time or place or event. Columns that skipped from topic to topic or that dealt with local matters or the headlines of the day have been left out. These are the Any Day columns and other pieces which seem to me to represent the best of Henry Mitchell, the humorist, moralist, guide, writer, and friend.

The essays are presented in the order in which they appeared in the *Post,* the first from December 29, 1973 (Henry was at his best at Christmastime) and the last from April 12, 1991. This approach means that the book does not begin with "Hubbub in the Pew," as I would like, but the "Do-It-Yourself" piece is pretty special too.

When they appeared in the *Post* many of the columns were illustrated by Susan Davis, a talented Maryland artist, and we are fortunate to have been able to include many of her gifted drawings. She did the jacket illustration especially for this book.

John Gallman
Director
September 1996

Any
Day

Do-It-Yourself

An American assembled a knocked-down do-it-yourself machine on Aug. 3, 1908, without assistance, without fury and without extra nuts and bolts at the last.

That achievement, however, has never since been duplicated until this week when, on Christmas Day at 4 in the afternoon, a citizen of this capital singlehandedly assembled a "fireplace log crib" in 17 minutes flat.

"It seems unlikely," said one highly placed source in American business and manufacturing.

"We saw him do it," said two neighbors who understandably refused to give their names, not wanting every reporter of the Western world to besiege them for questioning.

"Yes, I did it," said the recipient of the gift, a handsome man of early middle age with a boyish grin. "It was quite a day."

"I bought the present," said the citizen's wife, "at the World's Most Incredible Hardware Store. I was very scared, because for his birthday I gave him a wheelbarrow that he had to assemble. I didn't know it, I thought it was all put together in the big box but it wasn't. My husband made sort of a scene on the sidewalk at the time. He was putting it together on the sidewalk where it was flat and he wouldn't lose all the parts, but he had a lot of pieces left over when he finished, I remember that, and he sort of raised his voice out there, I remember that, too.

"So I was scared to give him the fireplace log crib when the store told me it came unassembled. Once burned and twice scared, you know. But I had no choice. We need a thing to hold fireplace logs, because my husband never brings them in ahead of time and goes roaring out in the snow and rain when the fire is dying down, and tracks mud in. Once I thought he was going to kick the dog. The store said they could not sell me one already assembled."

The husband, once he was assured his name would not be cited as the freak of the century, agreed to explain how he assembled the log crib:

"The log crib consists of two steel hoops bolted together at the top but diverging at the bottom," he stated. "The bottoms of the hoops rest on two parallel bars. The bottoms are bolted to the bars, of course. Also, the hoops are not assembled when you get them. You make the two steel hula-hoop things (which you later bolt to the bottom bars) by bolting together six arcs to form the two circles. This is all made clear by the directions."

He was asked if the directions were hard to follow.

"No. They were easy. You bolt the arcs together and then bolt A to B and G to H and like that. There are two sizes of bolts; you don't want to get them mixed up."

Did the pieces all seem to be present, one would wonder.

"Oh, yes," said the fellow, known locally as Fermi-Boy. "The wheelbarrow had parts the directions did not show and lacked parts the directions did show.

"But this log crib had all the pieces. Some of the arcs have three sets of holes and some have two sets, so you want to be sure that the three-set arc of Circle A lines up with the three-set arc of Circle B. Otherwise, as any fool would know, you could not get Bolt G through—I mean there would have to be the holes there for the bolt to go through."

Fermi-Boy acknowledged he had bolted the circles together wrong before discovering that, but quickly adjusted.

"The arcs have to be bolted to form the circles and the circles have to be bolted to the bars. Naturally, where the circles are bolted to the bars the bolts have to be the long ones, and not the short ones. The short ones you just bolt the arcs to each other with."

He acknowledged he had used several bolts before discovering that, but quickly adjusted.

"I got plenty of bolts and nuts and I believe two things that look like braces are left over from the wheelbarrow, but this log crib had all the right bolts. Just enough and no more and they all fitted fine. Waste not, want not."

A neighbor was asked if the man cursed while assembling the log crib.

"Oh, no," said Mrs. Teresa Sigler, who agreed to let her name be used since she is moving to the Eastern Shore of Maryland where there are no reporters.

"He just lined everything up and all the bolts fitted and nothing was left over and none of us could believe it."

The proud man said:

"It only took me 17 minutes."

"Well," said his wife, "maybe a little longer than that."

A citizen singlehandedly assembled a "fireplace log crib" in 17 minutes flat.

"Look," said the man, "who's telling the story, you or me. I bolted the &_!%$! thing together, didn't I?"

"Yes, dear," said his wife.

"When I die," said the man, "I am going to leave it to the Museum of History and Technology."

The Smithsonian, which runs the museum, is said to be rather excited at the prospect. "We can give it a hall," a source said. (December 1973)

Patriotism and Dumas Malone

Charlottesville, Va.—Fifty men and women assumed American citizenship here on the Fourth of July on the pretty little lawn of Monticello that was nothing but chaos and wilderness until Thomas Jefferson smoothed it all down to build his house.

A crowd of perhaps 800 was saved by the pouring rain from any show of too-easy emotion, though few scenes have been more moving in the 149 years since the master of Monticello died.

Unlike the usual glorious sun of July, with the last bees trying to explore a few post-season blooms on the lime trees Jefferson was so fond of, visitors saw mists, heard thunder, got their shirts wet.

A fine introduction, some thought, to citizenship and one Jefferson would have liked far better even than the peaceful bees in his limes.

But of course (it occurred to everybody seeing Monticello in mists and rain for the first time) that was why the author of the Declaration of Independence chose this site to live on and dream of (when he had to leave it to be minister to France, Secretary of State, President and so on). Because here there are no bounds, except the weakness of a man's eyes and the distance of God's horizons, to visions. Here it made sense then, and does now, to dream of a vast republic and a society not perfect, but good enough to pass for paradise.

As the skies glowered and the prospect of hot dogs and cakes (prepared by the local Daughters of the American Revolution) faded, Walter Muir Whitehill stood up on the old pavement of the east portico to say we would now hear the eminent scholar and biographer, Dumas Malone, speak on patriotism.

Thus far (though those experienced in adversity were quite certain there was not going to be any picnic on this Fourth) things were routine enough.

The local band played. The new citizens were sworn in as citizens. They promised to obey the republic's laws and defend her against her enemies. Then Dr. Whitehill (scholar, librarian, historian, teacher, author, editor and much else) pleased the crowd by introducing the 83-year-old Malone, newly honored with a Pulitzer Prize for his biography of Jefferson.

As usual Malone spoke without a text. His addresses to the National Endowment for the Humanities and similar gatherings have sometimes been considered masterpieces of simplicity, learning and balance.

But on this occasion he did something different, something he had not planned, something that embarrassed him—he was at a loss for words.

"Patriotism," he had said earlier, "is a great thing, but it can be misused."

It is often the first, not the last, recourse of the scoundrel, as his audience well knew. He spoke a bit to that effect, observing that millions of Jews died under Hitler's brand of patriotism.

He sometimes paused, in between his sentences of even quiet tone, and looked at the new Americans and at the boys in cotton jackets (now largely synthetic, perhaps, but no matter) from the nearby University of Virginia which Jefferson founded, and then he kept looking out toward the Blue Ridge as the mists veiled and unveiled the hills:

"Patriotism is a land. And a people. Will people be able to love the land? It is easy here in Albemarle County. Albemarle is very easy to love. But what of those in ghettos in Philadelphia or New York—it might be hard for them to love the land when they have hardly ever seen it."

But land, the land men love, is not merely pretty real estate:

"It has been said that the great Valley of the Mississippi is the fairest land ever made by God for men's habitation. Perhaps we would be allowed to add Albermarle County, too. All the land of our country."

You start, he seemed to be saying, with the Mississippi Valley, or the Virginia hills, or the Dakota plains or wherever you first love anything, and as you mature your love expands and you begin to see that men love whatever land they grow up in, and which is home to the people and the customs and the institutions they have come to trust.

"It is harder to love all the people than to love the land, because there are so many of them," but the process seems to be the same. You start with the ones you love best and know best and extend the concept from there.

"Now . . ." and he paused longer than usually.

It was a good time to check the visual good order in which Monticello is kept. The pointing of the bricks was crisp and sharp. Jefferson would have been glad to see things were kept in repair.

Mr. Malone (scholars are rarely called anything but Mister in Charlottesville) looked at the hills, and back inside his mind, perhaps, to try to come up with the precise words that would express what he feels of the presence of Jefferson's thought and vision, and what it might mean to new Americans.

He saw the rain falling but paid it no mind.

The audience began to drift toward the shelter of the old limes, or up under the portico, or past the Chinese chippendale railings toward the beech tree or (the faint-hearted) toward the dry roofs of their cars.

"There is so much more I want to say about patriotism," said Malone, very quietly indeed, "but I seem to have lost my way. I should have written it all down and read it to you, but I didn't want to do that. I wanted to just speak to you from what I—but we forget we cannot now do easily what we used to be able to do."

Since he was not out in the crowd, looking toward Jefferson's house and the door (the one with the ingenious weather vane over it and the clock with cannonball weights at the sides) and since he could not hear himself or rightly tell the effect, he was disappointed. "I have let you down," he told a woman afterward. "No," she said, "you did not let us down."

Not wishing to make too large a thing of his own disappointment at not finding the words he wanted, he said:

"There is so much more I want to say. Well. Come see me, and I will think of it then."

The crowd applauded with delight. The Flemish bond of the bricks looked especially good as rain darkened the color a bit, and as people felt the warm rain (which turned into a gully-washer) on their jackets and faces and collars, a sense of adventure set in. There ought to have been some place to jump up and down in the grass, like kids. Of course, one would have lost dignity.

"I have spoken so many times before without notes," Malone said a few minutes after the crowd had all gone. "You get very friendly after a while, with the early fathers of the country. Some more than others."

"Are you maybe not so friendly with John Adams?" somebody asked him, alluding to the person whom Jefferson sometimes found difficult.

"Oh, no, I have got very fond of John Adams," (who, of course, died the same day Jefferson did, on the 50th anniversary of the Declaration of Independence). "I am not all that friendly with Alexander Hamilton."

The sparkle returned to his eye, and he reached for a piece of fried chicken someone offered him.

The new Americans, who had dispersed before this, would not have a long speech to forget. They would have a white-haired scholar, speaking very quietly about patriotism in front of Jefferson's house, to remember. (July 1975)

Mouse Encounters of the First Kind

One holiday night, 50 years after the mice had moved in, and 50 years after endless battle had been done with them, my wife was presiding at a dinner. It was not for the king of England, but somebody like that and heroic measures had been taken to make the old place look as good as possible. (This consisted mainly of turning the lights low and polishing the mirrors and bringing in a lot of camellias from outdoors.)

We had not seen any mice in the kitchen for ages; indeed nobody ever gave a thought to mice.

But from time to time during dinner you could hear little scraping and crunching noises—it could easily have been one of the kids eating peanut brittle upstairs—and houses that are not brand-new have a lot of noises not worth tracking down.

Without much warning some confetti-type material sifted down from the ceiling. A mouse was gnawing happily on a kind of beaver-board that had been installed (for no earthly reason, and at the time I said I thought it was ridiculous to change the old ceiling) to lower the original height of the dining room and to "soundproof" it.

Of course it made no difference at all in soundproofing anything. All it did was make a safe retreat for the mice, who took a couple of decades to discover it. It made a sounding-board, too.

Between the time the Brussels sprouts were served and the time the raspberries came on, the noise continued and the shower of shavings fell.

Nobody noticed it, naturally. In the South, at dinner, you are not supposed to notice anything short of a three-alarm fire, for we all know that little mishaps occur, and we should always be (as Horace said) above them. Not concerned with them.

So the mouse worked on, and nobody paid any more attention than if a platter had dropped in the pantry or a drapery fell off its rod (which happened once), but then to my wife's displeasure, the mouse completed his drilling and stuck his head out, right over the dining table.

It was a shock. Even in our house, where we took things in stride. He got his whiskers through and his bright eyes. Hell, he looked all around at the guests beneath and I thought once he might jump.

"Why don't we move in the other room," said my wife, though I don't think people had finished. Everyone strolled out, as if nothing unusual had occurred.

I was the last to leave the dining room. I looked up at the mouse. I knew I would soon be leaving that house for some hovel in the North where I must make my fortune.

I thought of all those Christmases, you know how that is. Scary.

And all those mousetraps, all that slaughter over all those years. And for what?

God, he was a good-looking mouse. Bright. Full of beans. Great eyes. He was all mouse. There was something (as I knew at the time) between us. (December 1976)

Hubbub in the Pew

The front bench at the church I know is reserved not for mourners or sinners (specifically) but for members of the women's altar guild, and I will now tell how their ancient territory was challenged on Christmas Eve.

The women, insofar as I have ever been able to find out, see to it the altar brass is polished, and that the ceremonial vessels and wine are in good order and (this is a pillar of their front-bench prerogative) that any fainting or heaving choirboys are promptly fetched out of the chancel before they die or get stepped on.

Now the Battle of Christmas Eve was on this wise:

The women arrived 90 minutes before midnight and flung their furs on their front pew, to mark the territory, and disappeared into some mysterious recess where they squirt brass polish, complain that Maude has singed the fair linen with a too-hot iron, and where they from time to time operate creaky cabinets and drawers containing frontals, albs and other curious objects, and all the while they maintain a subdued holy hubbub appropriate to the place.

The ushers, on the other hand, are males.

They took it into their hands (much as Lyndon once took Vietnam into his head) to remove the Guild women from their ancient seat and convert it into an "aisle" for the midnight service, since a batch of violins, violas, cellos, trumpets and drums would occupy the usual aisle.

Now your reporter, as it happened, was sitting quietly in the second pew waiting for the trumpets to gargle, when an usher said would I kindly ask anybody who started to sit in the front pew not to do so.

Well sir, I said, I think that's for the altar-guild women. Yes, he said, but I'd rather have it for an aisle.

At the time I thought, "Brother, that's your project and good luck," but said nothing.

After a few minutes the guild women, who had had ample time to criticize the way the flowers were done and the seating arrangements for the trumpets, emerged into the church and sat down in their front pew. An usher came up and asked them to vacate it.

He might as well have asked the bishop to please hold a basket full of cats. The women gazed at him in disbelief. Could the fool not see the sign that said "Reserved for Altar Guild on Duty?"

Now all these women, and their sistern throughout the world, are descended from those who served at Delphi, Ephesus, Cumae and elsewhere. The average Hun or Tartar or Visigoth (over the centuries) has usually had sense enough not to agitate the local altar-guild ladies, even though it is all right to slaughter everybody else.

But this usher probably had no sense of history.

Anyway, the women rose in a sort of stately controlled fury and marched out of their pew. Some (who knew nothing of how these things work out in the history of mankind) thought the guild had been routed.

I suspected the guild women at that very moment had seized the ushers and snapped all their heads off in the crypt, and was grateful the rest of us did not have to see it.

Sure enough, in a few minutes the women marched back in and sat down in the pew God gave them.

There was no mistaking their triumph. The citadel had been defended.

No sooner were they ensconced again than the trumpets spoke, the cellos lifted their burden, the drums began to roar along with the full organ and the great processional began, complete with torches and crosses and banners.

At first the choirboys came, and as they passed the women surveyed them like a hen missing a few chicks. Each boy was judged on the likelihood of his making a spectacle of himself (the youngsters sometimes get sick at midnight services, way past their bedtimes, for the young cannot take too much glory) but they all looked pretty sturdy and the guild women seemed pleased with the prospects.

As the boys were followed by the men, the volume rose to a tumult and the trumpeters were getting red and the fiddlers sawed for life and the drummer was in heaven for only rarely are the drums allowed to go wild, legally.

In such a setting, who could doubt that God was in firm and certain control of destiny? Strings and winds proclaimed the fitness of order. "Joyful and triumphant" bellowed the tenors and baritones in unison, for a change, and the choir broke into a descant racing around the main melody like a hound in a woods full of possums.

And then suddenly the perfidy of the ushers was seen.

The procession moved like a tide—one of those things no power can speed up or slow down. Surging. Towards the end of the procession came some banners that are not allowed up in the chancel (only the national standard and the flag of the church go up there, it turned out) but of course they had to go somewhere.

They were supposed to turn off from the main procession at the chancel steps, and (according to the ushers) they should use the first pew as an aisle.

But when they got down there, they, of course, saw the altar-guild women occupying that territory and they correctly sensed it would take cannons, not banners, to march through them. So they decided to march through the musicians.

That was wise. The musicians were seated, and therefore relatively defenseless (the guild women were standing) and, besides, the musicians had no ancient, vested rights to be sitting in the aisle, and did not seem ready to do battle, as the altar guild certainly did.

I shut my eyes as the banners sailed through the violins like a mackerel through a can of sardines. When I opened them the musicians seemed still alive, though there is some question why one of them did not have spectacles any more and some of the music racks did not seem quite the same and of course it had been a great shock to the orchestra to have 4-foot-wide banners on poles borne right through them.

The guild women, seeing what confusion and havoc had resulted from not giving their pew for use as an aisle, rose in stately unison and marched out. Relative calm settled on the church and the musicians got on with their Bach and Mozart without further confusion.

And then the time came when the musicians got up and left, and the service entered a new phase which did not require trumpets anymore.

The instant the musicians rose to leave, the women of the altar guild marched back to their pew, as if they were part of the liturgy. I frankly was surprised they had not picked up a few torchbearers to accompany their return, but their demeanor clearly showed that they had been driven from their Jordan, yes, and driven again and again, yes, but here they were, back home and Alleluia.

The ushers were folding up and removing the musicians' chairs, under the full and steady glare of the altar guild. Being men, they were not allowed to glare back.

When the time came for the congregation to head for the altar to

Banners sailed through the violins like a mackerel through a can of sardines.

receive the Sacrament, the guild women were, as usual, the first to ascend the holy steps.

(The ushers, needless to say, were the last.)

For the first time I really understood that otherwise baffling hymn that says, "ten thousand times ten thousand stream up the steps of light."

Of course. A perfect picture of the altar guild victorious over the ushers.

The ushers, having chased the women out twice, probably thought they had traffic under control and may even have thought they were doing things reasonably and right. Thinking you are reasonable and right is a common scenario for disaster, as everyone knows.

It does not make any difference whether you are reasonable and right. It makes all kinds of difference whether what you are attempting is possible. It makes tremendous difference if others are alerted in good time to your project, and it is just as well to spell it out about six times.

Furthermore, if a new route must be carved in the landscape (any landscape) it is just as well to avoid routing the banners through the worst terrain of the entire continent.

Over the roof, possibly, or across the rood beam, or under the choir stalls or through the pulpit—any number of routes were freely available, and always are.

But through the Altar Guild in their immemorial sanctuary on the front pew? Dear Lord, almost nobody is that dumb. And if you try such a thing (in art, in politics, in any other vineyard) you will fail.

You will never budge them, though you may succeed in creating endless confusion for the rest of the world. The daughters of music are the ones who are laid low. The altar guild is right back there where it always was. (December 1977)

A Cure for the King

A grave issue is the provision of expert medical care, not merely to our lords and masters, but to all, and it is too bad that doctors do not more freely share their knowledge with common folk.

It may not be ethical, but I will now share the little-known treatment administered by the very best doctors of England to the late King Charles II, a monarch of quite blessed memory who took care to remember the poor and the weak, even on his deathbed:

"Let not poor Nelly starve," he said, as everyone knows.

Nell Gwyn, needless to say, was a woman of great sweetness who used to sell oranges at the London theater and was later mother of the Duke of St. Albans, which shows what patient merit and plenty of vitamins can produce. Her own mother, who was poor, was cared for by Nell until one day she was called Home. ("Overcome by brandy, Madam Gwyn fell into a nearby brook and was drowned," as a leading encyclopedia puts it.) These things happen. It was a great comfort to Nell, needless to say, that she had tried to make her mother's last days comfortable.

And Charles remembered the sweet girl who sold oranges, before he died, and his son took care of her, and I have always thought it a sweet interlude in the otherwise oft-troublous history of nations.

For some reason there were persons in England who did not love Charles; and historians, who tend to be puritanical and squint-eyed and opposed to raisins in muffins, have been quick to take cheap shots at the good man's name:

"The young man emerges clearly," as the Britannica says in its sharp non-fattening manner, "in precocious maturity, sardonic, lazy, a born dissimulator, skilled in the sort of moral evasions that make for ease . . ."

So much for historians. Snipe, snipe, snipe, especially when the great good king is dead.

It was always said of Charles' father that nothing in his life became him like the leaving of it, and yet Charles II also did all that men can and bore all that men must, and few things affront me more than prying into every . . . but on a more positive note, the good king died in a general incense of love and (as John Evelyn said) of all those dogs he kept around the palace.

The medical profession rallied to his succor, but to no avail, because a higher power than penicillin called him to tend the hounds of heaven and so he passed.

The dedicated efforts of his doctors, though they did not save him for us, are well worth remembering for those occasions when we need healing hands.

The prudent man, while trusting always in the general providence of life, yet avails himself of the friendly cures of the earth and the help of good doctors.

It does not speak well for doctors, though I hesitate to rebuke them, that King Charles' Remedy (which I reprint from an account following Charles' passing in 1685) is so little known to the layman, who might benefit most from it, and which I secured in a roundabout way from the library of a leading medical school where (alas) it is not taught to young Kildares at all nowadays:

" . . . was being shaved in his bedroom. With a sudden cry he fell backward and had a violent convulsion . . . As a first step in treatment the king was relieved of a pint of blood from his right arm, then his shoulder was incised and the area cupped to suck out eight additional ounces.

"An emetic and purgative were administered, and soon after a second purgative.

"This was followed by an enema containing antimony, sacred bitters, rock salt, mallow leaves, violets, beet root, camomile flowers, fennel seed, linseed, cinnamon, cardamom seed, saffron, cochineal and aloes. The enema was repeated in two hours and another purgative given.

"The king's head was shaved and a blister raised on his scalp." (Let me say here that this is one of the very best remedies for rulers, but is less good for ordinary persons.)

"A sneezing powder of hellebore root was administered. A powder of cowslip flowers was given to strengthen the brain. The cathartics were repeated at frequent intervals."

But with an exquisite sense of balance, what the doctors took away on the one hand, they gave on the other:

"A soothing drink of barley water, licorice and sweet almond. Likewise white wine, absinthe, and anise, and extracts of thistle leaves, mint, rue and angelica.

"A plaster of Burgundy pitch and pigeon dung was applied to the king's feet. The bleeding and purging continued (and in addition) melon seeds, manna, slippery elm, black cherry water, an extract of flowers of lime, lily of the valley, peony, lavender and dissolved pearls."

In addition to this came "gentian root, nutmeg, quinine and cloves."

The king did not, however, respond as he should have done. Forty drops of "extract of human skull" were tried and an additional antidote composed of an enormous number of herbs and animal extracts "were forced down the king's throat," and finally, needless to say, "bezoar stone was given."

But then the whole assembly of doctors "lost hope and became despondent," yet they did not fling up their hands and throw in the towel, not at all. They tried "their most active cordial" and some more of that efficacious "antidote" plus some ammonia.

It is nothing against expert and learned doctors, of course, that they cannot in all cases snatch us from the jaws of death, and I for one am still grateful they did what they could for Charles II whose memory is never far from my daily thought.

And I thank God that at least he was spared the frightful death of old Madam Gwyn, all alone and unattended. (January 1978)

Hound Cures

A woman in my family, years ago, knew how to fix washers on bathroom faucets and it was the sensation of the family for years on end.

"Katherine," they used to say, "can do anything. She fixes faucets and everything."

In plain fact, the only thing Katherine was good at was changing washers on handbasin faucets and shooting rats with a .410 shotgun, which she used to do from a second-story window in 1909. "She can shoot rats," everyone in the family said.

In those days, nobody knew how to do anything useful about the house, so Katherine was the marvel, and had this enormous reputation for practical skills based entirely, as I say, on the rats and the hand-basins.

We can fix kitchen sink drain-traps, we can start stalled Volks-wagens (not Volvos, of course), we can get rid of carpenter bees, we can write wills without lawyers, we can fold our own parachutes, treat the hernias in our own hounds, and—in brief—we are as happy as Leonardo ever was, if you take us all together.

I think back to the time when Katherine was the only member of the family who could even replace a washer.

And yet there are days I question whether we have entered a Renais-sance or a collapse. I do know that (for one has a minimal honor to defend, at least) nobody in the family will stand in line for restaurants, theaters, art galleries, and that nobody will join those standing ova-tions that are given, willy-nilly, to everybody who paid his grocery bill on time. But apart from those two idiosyncrasies, we are a totally typical American family.

It was only today, however, that I learned to practice medicine without a doctor. My father, uncle, grandfather, great-grandfather, etc., were doctors, so it used to be the family view that you called a doctor when you were sick or injured.

Thanks to a postnasal drip—this is so grim I am not going to bother you with the details—I have a raw nose, and in the ordinary course of events I would ask a doctor about it.

But doctors lately have been reminding us they are not God—a sharp change from the doctors in the family in years past, I can tell you—and that most things sort of cure themselves.

And yet my nose bothered me. Imagine my luck in finding, while searching for nail scissors in a drawer, some miraculous ointment made of ground aloes that a vet administered to Luke (a hound) in 1970. March, 1970, in fact.

Poor Luke got a severe skin burn on the lower portion of his body from being boarded in a kennel up here where they did not wash the floors of the pens. The vet said at the time there was no other way he could have got such a burn. Anyway, we got this tube of stuff and it was the most wonderful relief to Luke.

So I thought, upon reading the label, there was nothing in it to harm man or beast, so I tried some. Needless to say, I never threw away Luke's ointment, which was right there in the drawer of the bathroom table (though the nail scissors were not).

Stopped the burning instantly and my nose is neither so painful nor so awful to look at as it was. I do not recommend the hound's ointment for anybody else's nose, but it certainly has worked on mine. Of course, if I drop dead of hound poisoning at 6 p.m., the doctors will all say that's what you get for not consulting them, but you can also drop dead after seeing doctors.

There is a fellow right here in the office who said (he is part of a Renaissance or do-it-yourself family also) he wished he had known about my nose rawness:

"I could have given you some of that wonderful ointment my father uses for the cows' udders. Works like a dream."

I once knew a business manager for a magazine and she had grievous kidney complaints and I noticed she was taking some red pills that looked exactly like the ones Bass (another hound) was taking for her nephritis.

But Bass was also taking some big brown pills.

The business manager's ailment was not fully alleviated, but the hound's was.

"Nancy," I said, "ask your doctor to give you some big brown pills, the ones the size of an unshelled peanut, along with the red ones. That's what Bass takes, and it's cleared everything up for her."

Well, you know how conservative business managers are. She stuck with the red pills alone. Still suffers. I even offered her some of the dog's pills once Bass didn't need them; but no, she'd rather stick in the same old rut, however ineffective for her kidneys.

Other things people need to learn to be are an accountant, tax lawyer, tree surgeon, theologian and carpenter.

So much to learn, so little time to learn it in.

We are like those infant sea turtles that hatch at 10 a.m. and had better know how to get into the sea by 10:30 a.m. or they're goners. And once in that sea, they'd better know how to do everything that needs to be done.

Nobody in the family knows how to do income taxes. These things take generations, I suppose.

But I laugh, and I am not without smugness, when I think of the family 30 years ago when nobody knew how to do anything except Katherine could shoot rats with a .410.

We've come, as I said at a recent gathering, a long way, baby. (March 1978)

The Quality of Food

If you're hungry, I always used to argue, anything tastes good, and if you're not hungry, nothing does; therefore, the quality of food is irrelevant.

I am a Group A consumer—I expect nothing, require nothing, and the American food industry is built on me.

At home I am a tiger, however, and fodder there is of surprisingly high quality.

Naturally, if you eat at somebody's house, you can't very well say the rice is a slimy pitfall, nor can you bang the table if they slop chemical "chocolate" over the ice cream.

This natural politeness extends to restaurants, where I accept, like everybody else, the overdone asparagus, the underripe avocado, the hamburger that was okay last Tuesday.

I was in London last week where I ate as badly cooked a piece of lamb as ever saw a plate, even in England, in one of the most expensive places there.

Did I complain? How could I, being a foreigner? The English, like me, eat anything that's warm, hot or cold and no questions asked.

But I also had a cup of coffee at the Montcalm Hotel, and it was splendid. Of course it cost $1.20, but it was real coffee. It has opened my horizons, and I think I am about to become a member of Group B consumers.

They are the ones who expect food to be perfect.

My mother-in-law, of revered memory, was a Group B. She ate very little, but what she ate was flawless.

She lived in a small town in Virginia, which did not have very good markets. She had strawberries out of this world, and even cream that you spooned.

Sometimes she had a baked stuffed mackerel or a plain shad—it made no difference, it was always the best you ever ate anywhere.

Because she was a Group B you could have plopped her in Butte with a sack of pig knuckles and in an hour or so you would have had a feast. Wherever she spread her table you found two stars and well worth a detour. (I mean those oldtime restaurant stars when two stars means better than anything in Washington.)

She was not without guile, of course. It took her five years to negotiate the cream. Mr. Traherne taught some subject or other at a school and had a Jersey cow.

Five years of courtesy and small attentions and behold, she could buy cream from him.

The ordinary group A consumer could never stay the course or live so long to reap the great reward. But when my mother-in-law set her mind on cream, she got it.

"And shall not grace find means?" asks the poet Milton in one of his supreme passages. It always reminded me of my mother-in-law's grocery shopping.

She found the means of cream. And of orange cakes. And of butterbeans and corn. There were tiny squashes, infant string beans, barely laid eggs, wine jellies quivering just short of collapse, while the town around her was mere mush and burnt. Except Charity's house. She was a Group B, too, but then she had nerve, and if the butcher didn't do right, she got a cleaver and cut it herself.

All this came back to me with the Montcalm coffee. Earlier that very day I had had coffee at the Cumberland, which is one of the few places in London you can get coffee as bad as an American bus stop.

When I drank the great cup, it almost switched my group. But then I fell back, and settled once more into indifference and courage and cynicism.

One great coffee does not a Group B make.

And in the past few days I have, as always, drunk whatever gloop the office machines dispense, or whatever came my way. Without hope, without anger.

Only today I was drinking the "coffee" from an office machine and a reporter nearby said, "Want some cream?"

"You carry cream around with you these days?" I asked. Not really surprised. Not at that one.

"Sure." And he reached into his investigative satchel and got out a whole quart of cream. You had to spoon it.

It helped the coffee. Needless to say.

Most of us somewhere got going wrong. It has always been possible to eat well. The old woman in the town who knew where to get the vegetables, the great veal, the Jersey.

And here, not 10 feet from my desk, is a fellow who carries around Devon cream with him in a sack.

I would have always said it's not possible, in this day and age, if you're just a reporter, to eat well. There is not time, there are not resources.

But there was another reporter—of course it was a jolt—who carried the quart of cream around with him. Probably got it from the same Mr. Traherne my mother-in-law did. Don't ask me what he does to keep it fresh. Probably drinks it all within four hours or something and starts fresh the next day.

It's not time and it's not resources. It's being Group B. Born to strawberries (Fairfax, not Blakemore—only the really great strawberries will do for Group B).

Lord, my heart is turning over. I want to be a Group B, too. I'm going to find me a Jersey if it kills me. (June 1978)

Miss Furbish's Lousewort

A civilized man never knows when he may be called on to defend the citadel, so to speak, against the next charge of the barbarians with their odd cries and stone hatchets.

So it is not one day too soon for us to contemplate Miss Furbish's lousewort and what it means to this nation and how we must order ourselves in the struggle.

Miss Furbish's lousewort, as everyone will soon become aware, is a rare plant facing extinction along the banks of the St. John River in Maine. There seem to be perhaps 800 individual plants in the world, and most of them would be lost if nothing were done to protect them from the projected ruin of their natural home.

Two dams are proposed there that would obliterate Miss Furbish's lousewort's habitat.

The law of this republic forbids the use of government money for any project that would grievously damage a plant so rare as this lousewort.

But there is good news today. The Army Corps of Engineers (the dam or the goddam people, depending on your point of view) themselves discovered the existence of this rarity in their path. They themselves called attention to it, and asked the Fish and Wildlife Service (guardian of threatened louseworts) how to proceed.

This is one of the most complex situations that has come before the government in administering its laws on endangered life. Through a miracle, you might almost say, it seems probable that the Engineers will be able to save the lousewort, through propagation and transplanting to another site, short of a constitutional crisis.

Mind you, it is one thing to talk about "another site" and quite something else to find a site and establish a rare plant there so that it continues to breed.

It is enormously important, though, that the Engineers faced the problem straight, without subterfuge and lies, and the guardians of endangered life are little less than thrilled at this example of cooperation in fulfilling the law.

As things stand now, the Engineers commit themselves to finding the means to preserve the lousewort in another location. The enforcers of the law will study the solution that the Engineers find, and if all goes well, as it is expected to, there will be no objection to the dams on behalf of the lousewort.

So far, so good.

Unfortunately, the know-nothings and rooty-toot lunkheads of the continent—a species in no danger of extinction—have seized on the delightful name of the plant to make sport of the law.

We may hear much from them in the months ahead.

They are sure to point out this plant is not very handsome and has no known economic, medicinal or especially esthetic use. It could vanish completely and we would not be the poorer.

Just yesterday I noticed one of those he-man type articles on the editorial page of The Wall Street Journal saying, in effect, we have lost our minds in American law.

Snail darters, Miss Furbish's lousewort, anopheles mosquitoes and diamondback rattlers (it goes on) could vanish utterly and the "average voter" would say good riddance.

It is possible that the average voter would in fact say good riddance, if he relied only on a press that said the whole business of endangered species is a bucket of nonsense.

But the average voter is also the average American, and is quite capable of giving attention to something he formerly paid no attention to, and quite capable of changing his mind on Vietnam, Watergate, snail darters and louseworts.

This may be the place to mourn that four-letter Anglo-Saxon words are now so unfamiliar that "wort" is commonly mispronounced. It is like all those other words spelled with an "o" and pronounced with an "u." (Work, word, worth, whorl, worm, world and so on.) It has been in the language for only 1,100 years—too new for us to have the hang of it.

A wort is a plant.

There are many sorts of louseworts (the name, by the way, was given by shepherds who noticed that fields where this plant grew were the same fields in which their sheep had lice. It is likely that all their pastures had louseworts, or else that all their sheep had lice, no matter what the pasture; but shepherds are always looking about for something to blame their vermin on).

Many louseworts are common. You could build a dam and never

give them a thought. It is just Miss Furnish's lousewort (*Pedicularis furbishiae*) that is endangered.

Why, one might ask, should there be any effort to preserve a plant with no known use beyond the production of infant louseworts?

There are several answers:

1. Our own vast ignorance of this lousewort is no guarantee that it has no "value." The rubber tree only recently came into practical economic use. The penicillin mold was not much esteemed on cantaloupes and its remarkable properties were long unknown.

2. Apart from important human uses that might be disclosed in the future, a plant of no known use to us might be of considerable use to some other creature. If there are only 800 of these louseworts, it is hardly going to turn out that the snail darter, say, desperately requires them for food. But the principle is sound, that life does not exist in a vacuum (except in the immediate vicinity of some typewriters) and what affects the plankton eventually affects the osprey.

3. Even if the plant is of no use to man or beast, there is the esthetic question of the richness and variety of the natural world. Who would want a world without tigers and rattlesnakes, lambs and leopards, Wall Street Journals and Hustlers?

As individuals we may find it possible to live out our lives in such biological and horticultural and faunal slums as downtown Manhattan, but even there the normal heart rejoices to think of wolves and quetzals flourishing in the great world, if not in the restricted prison in which some men are content to live their poor lives.

4. There is the matter of genes. They can combine and segregate in astounding ways. What the lousewort's genes may be worth, a million years from now, we have no way of knowing, but we do at least have the sense to know that once lost there is no way to recreate this stuff of life. If it is argued that men will no longer walk the earth then, that is beside the point.

5. Finally, there is the matter of human honor. Whether it is honorable to bang through the world oblivious to every thing and every creature that does not seem immediately useful for our advancement in our own poor notions (notions all too likely to change as we increase in wisdom) of what "advancement" is.

Or whether it is honorable to brood over the treasure of life and sustain and promote it, to shelter and celebrate it.

Give any man the choice and he will choose, despite his moments of insanity and natural aptitude for going bananas now and again—he will prefer the side of grandeur and richness to the narrow rigid keyholes of locked compartments.

Whether life is a rat race or a garland is a matter of some consequence.

What we conclude, on such questions, affects not merely the lousewort, but the respect with which we hold ourselves and the way we go about doing everything we do.

Nobody is likely to argue that all life must be preserved at all costs at all times.

There may even be occasions for fights of one kind or another that do damage of one kind or another.

With the lousewort, we will hear the argument that we have a choice between a few worthless plants and two vitally important electric generating plants. But as it happens in truth, it appears we can have both the lousewort and the electricity, provided we think ahead and do not just sit on our butts making wisecracks about forms of life we know nothing of.

Sooner or later, needless to say, there will be conflicts far harder than the one presented by Miss F's l.

How we acquit ourselves then depends on how we have trained ourselves. Wars are won, they say, on playing fields at schools.

Whether we come out on the side of life or the side of electric can openers—a choice that goes to the center of what our own lives are worth—defines a great deal in the way we get on with others and the way we get on with ourselves inside our own hearts.

Some say barbarians will win, and it is worth noticing they have already put rattlesnakes on the worthless list, and no doubt tigers, bears, dogs will soon follow.

There have always been savages at the gate. The question is not so much how savages behave as how we do.

The center is going to hold. One more round. (July 1978)

Hank as Hero

You should be naked, as a rule, before plunging into the great fountain basin of the Tuileries Garden. The water there is none too clean, and it stains white flannels and ruins your passport.

But on that day there was no time for getting back to nature. There was only time for American culture and honor to operate in a flash.

Our topic today is, as you will have guessed, the nature of heroism, and the nature of cowardice also. This account is from my uncompleted book, "Hank's Guide to the Heroic Life." And now back to the facts:

The sun was soft and the sycamores shivered deliciously on that summer day, and our hero-to-be was proceeding across the Tuileries to meet a Scotch girl.

She was staying at the Hotel Wagram on the Rue de Rivoli, not far from the great monumental stairs leading out of these famous gardens.

Our hero was in his early 20s and was sauntering through the trees like a unicorn crowned with roses because, as he reflected at the time, he looked pretty damn good and his white flannels were decent in the waist but tight enough around his legs to show off his calf muscles, the reward of some years of running about on track teams.

He approached the great basin, with 200 Parisians sitting on little chairs fanning themselves against the frightful heat. It was 82 degrees and the French, in that summer of 1947, enjoyed falling unconscious from the heat on every sidewalk.

On the foot-wide rim of the basin a baby sat, aged five months perhaps, with his teen-aged sister standing on the ground, her body touching the raised basin and the baby.

The baby started to crawl—his first crawl, most likely, and almost his last—and fell in and went down like a rock. You would think babies would float a little, being puffy, but this one went down as if shot.

The young woman gazed. Her eyes were fixed on the little creature under water. For the longest kind of time she stood there—maybe three whole seconds—and said nothing, screamed nothing, did nothing.

The people in the chairs kept on fanning themselves, looking idly about. Most of them did not see the baby, and the ones who did see him assumed his sister would simply reach in and fish him out.

Our American hero, roused from his continuing reveries on his sharp appearance, sprang.

He was 80 feet from the basin, but he alone was on his feet and had a perspective of the baby falling in, and he alone perceived the young woman was unable to budge. Like a story, people really can freeze.

"I am going to look like an ass," he thought as he began to sprint. No second is too split for a young man to think about himself.

Into the basin he leapt. The baby was on the bottom, not moving. Our hero fetched him up, set him on the rim, and the sister came to life and began to cry, snatching the baby to her arms.

By this time the people on the chairs were roused and all began to talk. "Alors," they said, with that splendid French intonation of alarm and contentment at once.

Down the monumental stairs, once it was all over, came France's finest, their uniforms touched with scarlet, and all of them blowing whistles and prepared to quell whatever the riot was.

Our hero climbed out of the basin looking, as he had foreseen, like an utter ass, the water oozing from his shoes and his white flannels not only stained but reeking like a sheep fetched out of a thunderstorm.

He took the subway home. His fellow passengers withdrew from him as much as possible. He wanted to say:

"You prissy jerks. I have just saved a citizen of France at enormous risk."

Instead he just got off at St. Philippe de Roule and earned a fishy look from his concierge.

His flannels were the sort no longer made, a quarter-inch thick. A youth could be a real slob, but in flannels like that he looked like something.

The Scotch girl, who for some reason had been unwilling in previous days to have a date with our hero, had of course succumbed to persistent urging, and the flannels were the item calculated to end all resistance once and for all. And they would have, too.

Well. He got dressed again, took the subway back, crossed the Tuileries Gardens once more and the Scotch girl flat refused to see him, after her two-hour wait, and would never even talk to him on the phone.

To say nothing of the cleaning bill, and the commotion of the passport. Our hero was to leave the next day for Geneva, and his passport was sopping and all the ink had run and the little sticker came off.

"This is no good," said the Swiss at their Paris office.

"The American Embassy says it's okay," our hero lied.

"Well, it's not," said the Swiss, "but if your government wants to recognize a ruined passport it's no skin off my nose," and he glued in a Swiss sticker.

At the American Embassy the man said:

"This is no good."

"Well," he said, "the Swiss think it is, and they've put their sticker on it. If it's good enough for them why isn't it good enough for my own country?"

So he said well all right, and made some magic marks and the prince went right along with a passport full of run ink, water-stained pages and vanished stamps.

One reward of heroism, in some cases, is a dazzling insight into how governments work.

But our hero, back to him, thought a lot about why nobody else did anything, though they were closer. And the answer is clear:

They did not think there was any danger.

There was no noise, no screaming. The sycamore leaves shivered as usual, and the cherries in the paper cones were being dutifully plopped into the mouths of those sitting near the basin.

And just as our hero thought of his flannels, the Parisians were thinking of similar things. I do not doubt that more than one inner conversation went like this:

"There is a baby in the water. Someone must pull it out. Many can do so. I, on the other hand, have to catch a bus in five minutes."

Things are not presented to us as moments of enormous crisis. Dogs continue to race about on the grass. Pigeons keep doing their necks. The old lady keeps on poking at her lemon ice with an inadequate spoon. So how is one to know that now is the time to act?

And who can seriously believe the difference between life and death amounts merely to some undignified act like jumping in a basin of water and ruining your flannels?

If a house is afire, one might brave the flames to save a baby. In such a case one would know that bravery was called for, and that every second counted.

But on a summer day, in the gardens of the Tuileries, one had no such clues.

My observation of years is that men will risk death, when the case is clear.

They will not, as a rule, risk getting their pants wet or making a jackass of themselves in public.

There was that case in New York, where a young woman was murdered on the sidewalk and nobody did anything. All anybody had to do was pick up the phone and call the cops.

Exactly. It was because so little was required, and because so many hundreds could have done it, that nobody thought of doing it himself.

There was no callousness there, no fear of being involved. What, after all, was there to fear?

The ordinariness of doom, I suspect, is what threw everybody off. Those same bystanders, given clearer clues, would have risked life itself for her.

No man is a hero while brushing his teeth or clipping hair out of his ears. He needs some kind of warning that this is the moment to act. He has to be in a position of dignity. He has to be sure everything's zipped.

Life does not always give that warning. The dogs still trotting about sniffing the trees. A day like any other day. How could he know?

Then there is normal fear. Our hero in the water basin did not have to face that. But fear is normal, and a man needs a minute to deal with it before he goes past it. And often life does not give him that necessary minute, and he wonders the rest of his life if he is a born coward.

Usually he is merely a guy who needed a minute more than he got. And the gungest-ho heroes can behave poorly if they are caught off guard.

Next year we shall deal with another sort of hero:

The jerk, say, who is scared of dogs but behaves brilliantly anyway. And the one that can't take loud noises, but gets on with it all the same. And the one who is sort of at the bottom of the totem pole, as far as respect and stroking are concerned, but who does not accept the case of Scotch anyway. Not because it's beneath his dignity—nothing is, the world would think—but because he is on his way up and is reaching for virtues he does not yet have.

Courage over the long run is something different from our fine hero of the fountain basin. Tune in next year. (December 1978)

Prudence

There is often either more or less in the eggnog than the sipper supposes and our theme, therefore, is the value of that great virtue. Prudence.

Last week in this space we dealt with heroism, an inspiring and gaudy subject, which was all very well for the festival of Christmas, but now as we face the new year we must salute prudence, which gets more people through the world than heroism.

Now there was a woman named Felicity Wells, daughter of a substantial dowager in one of our provincial capitals, and old Mrs. Wells was comforted (and kept alive) in her last days by discreet doses of eggnog through the day.

The Wellses were a teetotal family, at least the women were, so as a matter of delicacy the old lady's medicinal bourbon was kept in a blue china bottle labeled "Shampoo." The nurse would shake some into a cup and the old lady was fine for two hours.

This wholesome posset rendered equable an otherwise irritating bed rest, and stimulated an old heart disinclined to beat.

In time, however, old Mrs. Wells left for those fields of light and was largely mourned.

A few months later, of a Saturday night, the daughter Felicity was preparing her coiffure for the Lord's Day and ran out of hair tonic. She seized the blue porcelain tonic bottle of her late mother's and gave her scalp a great swig.

Her nephew Henry informed me later that water ran in the Wells household way past midnight as Felicity Wells tried to wash the demon rum out of her hair, to no avail. The foul (as she thought) scent persisted, and she missed church the next day for the first time (it was widely said) in 40 years.

We see, in her example, a failure of imprudence and the common cost of imprudent action.

A flighty young girl might have assumed that stuff in the hair tonic bottle was hair tonic, but a woman of Felicity's years and experience in the world should have been skeptical, and tested carefully before slopping it all over her hair.

The nurse, after the old lady's death, also failed in prudence by not drinking the rest of the bottle, but leaving it to ensnare the innocent.

A different test of prudence was presented by the part of Cletus and Rebekah Ffould, good citizens of that same city, who were not blessed with any great wealth, although the lady was connected by birth to the High Sheriff of McNairy County and was, therefore, a woman of the better sort.

The Ffoulds thought there should be an eggnog party at their small house every year about Dec. 28, and 175 people came every year, and because the house was so small most of them left as soon as possible. Eleven minutes.

Old-timers said that in years past the Ffoulds had regular eggnog, more or less drinkable, but with rising costs everywhere, they began to "improve" their eggnog, to the point that by the time I was old enough to attend, they were using artificial cream, artificial eggs, artificial vanilla, artificial rum and some mysterious ingredient widely believed (by regulars) to be the base of milk of magnesia.

Fortunately they had a lot of window sills. People would accept a cup, take a sip, and set the cup down on the sill. By the end of the first hour the sills were solid with brimming cups, and at the end of the party Rebekah threw everything out, pleased that everyone had come to her party.

"And nobody got tight," she often said. (Nor, for that matter, she might have added, do lobsters fly.)

I failed in prudence the first year, drinking a whole cup.

There was no booze in their eggnog, yet one could get rather sick on it. It made you feel like a trilobite buried in a chalk cliff.

We can learn, however, and I never had any more in following years. Prudence may fail once, but operate thereafter.

Now there was a Navy man I did not know, but I know this thing is true:

He made eggnog and felt it should cure for several weeks. He made up the batch and funneled it into gallons and then set them in a cold attic. All the booze had to marry all the eggs, he said, and this took at least two weeks.

One year he lacked one top for a jug. He put regular screw tops on all the other gallons, and put waxed paper over the one that had no top.

In due time he retrieved the gallons, all in good shape, except the one with the waxed paper top. A mouse had gnawed through and had met a terrible death amid the cheer, so to speak.

A fellow who worked around the house said:

"Lord, if you're going to throw that gallon away, I know some people who could use it."

"Well," said the commander, "I just don't know, I'd hate for anybody at all to drink eggnog a mouse has drowned in."

However.

A few days later the Navy man asked Josh how it had worked out.

"We were real satisfied by it," he said, "and when we finished the gallon we fried the mouse."

We see here a failure of prudence in not mouse-proofing the top of the jug. At the same time, though, we see that errors of prudence can turn out—thank god—better than anybody would have thought. (December 1978)

They Took Their Stand

Nothing is so heady as sounding off when you're a kid, then coming back a half-century later to say "I told you so."

And this most delicious of all duties has befallen three gentlemen, now well into their 70s, who have utterly enjoyed a three-day backward look at their alarms of a half-century ago and pronounced themselves not merely right but right in spades.

Seated behind a table, their snow-white heads luminous as lightning bugs in a twilit June garden, the three men peered contentedly out at a packed auditorium at Vanderbilt University to see many turned away, so crowded was the hall. Television monitors were installed elsewhere so the overflow crowd could watch the proceedings in another auditorium.

The three men, all figures of consequence in American literature of this century, were Robert Penn Warren, Andrew Lytle and Lyle Lanier. As everybody knows, Warren is up to here in Pulitzer Prizes ("All the King's Men" and his collection of verse called "Promises") and he founded the Southern Review, along with Cleanth Brooks, and together they also wrote "Understanding Poetry." That book, to be plain about it, is the best thing of its sort ever written.

But Lytle, not so well-known as Warren, was an editor of the Sewanee Review and is known as a superb spinner of good stories, and his novels are often considered beautifully crafted.

Lanier is executive vice president and provost emeritus of the University of Illinois, but have no fear, he is not a Yankee but was born in Tennessee and like the other two was graduated from Vanderbilt University in the 1920s.

Now when these fellows were young the Scopes Trial took place. A young teacher had been fired for teaching Darwin and such heathen gibberish, and Clarence Darrow defended him, while William Jennings Bryan took the opposing side and maintained sufficient nonsense that the civilized portion of the republic began to laugh mightily at the backwoods state of Tennessee.

If you've never lived in the South, you have no idea how annoying it is for the rest of the country to assume you never had a pair of shoes, can't read the label on the box of grits and can't perform any craft or trade except making moonshine on still nights.

Anyway, these young fellows, virtually all at Vanderbilt, which is an independent school in Nashville, the capital of Tennessee, all smarted together and got rather defensive on behalf of the honor of their homeland.

The more they thought about it, the more they agreed that not only were Tennessee and the South not so bad as the Yankees said, but also it was (or could be) the savior of the nation. The South deserved praise, not shame, for maintaining traditional values. Including religion, by God.

As Southerners tend to do, they attacked. Instead of arguing that there are loons everywhere, as well as in Tennessee, and that the state and region ought not be judged by the anti-Darwin rabble, they took a different tack:

The very poverty of the South, the very nonsense and viciousness of much religion practiced in the South, the very backwardness of Southern agriculture and education and so on, were in fact virtues. Not only were all the shortcomings of the South really virtues in disguise, but if the North didn't return to those values the republic itself would fail. And what's more, if the South ever were seduced by such Babylonish whores as industry, the South would herself collapse and be as frightful as the North, and then there would be no hope, ever, for America to become truly great.

This set of notions naturally struck most of the world as somewhat insane, but at Vanderbilt, of course, and among literate Tennesseeans (however few of them there may have been) they found some acceptance.

Now the writers of these notions—their book, which has scarcely ever been out of print since 1930, is called "I'll Take My Stand"—were not insane at all, or at least they have never been locked up for it. Instead, they were merely young and more than a little indignant at the laughter the rest of the nation commonly directed to the South. Not only was the South poor (entirely as the result of Yankee turpitude, all Southerners knew) but she was laughed at as well. Sneered at. So it was the task of any red-blooded Southern intellectual (most of whom indeed have red blood and are not without ginger) to come to her defense.

I should say this is not necessarily the orthodox view of how this

Agrarian (as it is called, in allusion to the distrust of industry and the celebration of Southern rural life) movement came about. But I feel I should explain the truth of the business.

Since the young writers were not blind to some of the South's actual shortcomings—never mind the North, but the South did have a few problems if not indeed actual faults—they had a hard row to hoe to work themselves around to making virtues of what were apparent vices.

The oppressed condition of Southern blacks, for example, could hardly be ignored by Vanderbilt intellectuals. Nor could the appalling ignorance of so many uneducated, and indeed illiterate, Southerners. As far as that goes, it was hard to exalt and celebrate and sing hymns to the general lack of electricity, central heating, good plumbing, good roads, and so on forever.

Fortunately all the Agrarians, including the three who still survive, were literary types and understood poetic paradox well. As when the poet Browning wrote:

"All I could never be, all [that] men despised in me, this was I worth to God, whose wheel the pitcher shaped."

In all my life I have never yet met a true Southerner who did not cherish and totally comprehend the notion that the first shall be last, and the last first. Everything that the world calls despicable, everything the world sneers at, still has within it the possibility of glory.

Shakespeare himself spoke of the toad, ugly and venomous, but with a precious jewel in his head. As much, surely, could be said for the Southern Baptists?

When everyone remarks on the pervasiveness of religion in the South, nobody means that charity, compassion or any such thing is detectable there, but only that some aspects of Christian teaching are ingrained. Especially such nuggets as, "He hath scattered the proud in the imagination of their hearts, he hath exalted the humble and meek, and the rich he hath sent empty away."

And if there is one sacred text in the South it is bound to be this:

"The stone that the builders rejected, the same is become the chief cornerstone."

So these young writers, backed by Shakespeare, Browning and the Magnificat, gazed with all their might at their poor beloved South and not surprisingly found the jewel amidst the uglitude.

With industry comes more money, yes. But (as one of them rhetorically asked) what is the point of more money if you lose all the good things of life in acquiring it? How shall it profit a man to gain the whole world if he lose his own soul?

The argument is specious. The argument is little short of insane. But it was their argument and they have stuck to it all these years.

"The only thing I've gotten from this seminar," said a youth who had stolen out to the hallway to smoke a cigarette with other sinners while the litany rolled on the auditorium, "I read on a ——house wall today. It said [unprintable]."

I quote him, at least partially, to show there is some resistance to a movement that celebrates the small farm and the supposed virtues of rural life, such as the network of extended family, the solidity of unquestioned moral rules, the independence of the man not a slave to money, the nobility of pursuing Adam's profession to secure the good fruits of the earth in due season, the bond between man and horse or mule, between man and dog and dog and fox and fox and coon, etc., etc.

"I grew up in a small town in Tennessee where my father was a preacher. I used to think he was a [name of denomination] son-of-a-bitch. Now I just think he is a goddam bastard. They won't have him in heaven, when his time comes, and they won't have him in hell, either. But hell will probably give him some extra brimstone to go somewhere and start up his own hell."

"You're a very young man," he was told somewhat sternly.

It does seem to me we have enough trouble in the country without young whippersnappers speaking disrespectfully of their fathers. Even if the whippersnapper is basically right.

"Things may not go so badly with your father as you think."

"You know what this Southern religion is?" he said, blasting forth a cloud of tobacco smoke. "It's nothing but fear. You live on a cruddy little farm and you can't control the weather or the sale price of cotton or anything else, and you pray like hell you'll survive."

"Yes," he was told. "And if there's an ounce of grace in you you're grateful if you do survive."

"There's one more thing," he said, eyes narrowing and burning somewhat, "this religion is about a guy that got crucified, which gives you the right to go out and crucify everybody else, or at least everybody else that gets in your way or doesn't agree with you."

"Well," he was asked, "you probably won't go back to live in your small town again, from what you say."

"——, no," he averred.

All the network scattered, all the circle broken. What about the old mule, the contentment of arising at 5 to enter the field and chop through the long sweet day, the egrets white in their dusky cypress trees, the water snakes dozing (they often wander up from the bayou and for a time sleep in the tangled growth at the end of the field). What about the redbone hound, the cries like bells on November nights, the faint sounds of birds as they are flying?

S— no, s— no.

Unfortunately, if you write a manifesto (as the Agrarians did on behalf of "traditional" Southern values), you either mean something or you don't.

You can say, as they did, that of course they want to see oppression of blacks stopped, want to see blacks educated and equal before the law. You can say, as they did, that of course there is a place for industry (the Vanderbilt intellectuals were aware they used electric lights and books printed industrially). You can hedge and hum and haw, as they all did. But in a manifesto you sooner or later come down on one side or the other, else you don't have much of a manifesto.

And they did come down, unanimously, against the corrosive acids of modernity, against industry and a society based on the money that works industry.

The South, for her part, always seemed ungrateful to her intellectual Agrarians. The South is like some lovers, she's faithless. The instant the Agrarians turned their backs, the South was fetching new lovers in the doors, down the chimneys, up through the floor boards.

No industry has gone uncourted by the South. No modesty has restrained her in her shameless pursuit of industry and dollars and technology.

While the west end of Nashville (Vanderbilt) was thundering forth the ancient call to hold fast to the yeoman virtues of the farm, the mule, the small school where the benches were hard and you learned Virgil, the center of Nashville was singing quite another song:

The very alleys were bursting with nightclubs, girls dancing naked and God only knows what all, with spiritous liquors abounding.

Instead of Juvenal and Horace, the poetry is that of Grand Old Opry, and for the image of the Southern matron (who is supposed to be reading the Good Book and drying sassafras roots when not bent on errands of mercy and medicine for the happy-go-lucky blacks that would die of diphtheria except for her ministrations)—for the image of that matron you have comic female stars whose clothes are like a scarecrow's and whose voice is like a strangulated pig. Minnie Pearl, for example. (Herself a matron of Nashville, and a woman of refinement. But the product she sells, the voice she sells, is the image that sticks.)

At the very moment of the three-day seminar of lectures on the Agrarians, the state of Tennessee and her governor were all but incoherent with all but climactic joy that a Japanese auto manufacturer is going to move into the little town of Smyrna, out from Nashville. Three hundred million dollars invested, and 2,200 jobs, with an average pay of $20,000 per worker.

The governor (not the former governor who has been indicted for being a crook) speaks with ecstasy of what this influx of money will mean.

It is the very temptation the Agrarians have been warning against for 50 years.

Everywhere in Tennessee people say the new plant is the beginning of a "new Detroit" right down there in Dixie.

Only a few voices are saying, "Have you been in Detroit lately?" Only a few voices are asking what the new car factory will mean in the formerly recession-proof boundaries of Rutherford County, or whether the $10 million tax concessions (for the company will spend millions of its own money on facilities) are all that wise. Or what new schools may cost, or what may happen to the cost of living, or what will happen to the small farms as young men leave. What will happen, for that matter, to the redbone hounds and the cries of November nights.

The terrible thing, in a way, is that the South is "better" than it was. There is more learning. Blowhards spouting venom from pulpits are rarer now than they were. Individual freedom is greater, far greater, than it was in 1930. There are more choices—it's easier now to call your father a son-of-a-bitch than it was—and there is more art, more food, more reading, more social intercourse. Instead of ruining Tennessee, it's clear, at least to me and the millions like me, that Tennessee is the better for the coming of the modern world.

Men like the Agrarians, highly educated by current standards, would naturally deplore the idiocy of television, the depressing ugliness of parking lots and shopping centers where once there was rich farmland, and when all is said, theirs is an elitist position that runs directly counter to the American choice for more industry, more

Detroits, more bankrupt New Yorks, more people utterly dependent on the state or a corporation for their very lives.

For the time being, at least in Tennessee, in Southern cities like Memphis or Atlanta or Nashville, you see the burgeoning of wealth, of arts centers, and it all looks like a vast improvement over 1930.

How much farm land do you donate for asinine suburbs and centers before it really makes a difference? How many girls with dulcimers go down the drain in favor of jukeboxes (though my own view is that much of American art is to be found on jukeboxes) before some quality of life changes for the worse?

The traditional value that the Agrarians pleaded for—not altogether rationally, not altogether accurately—is easy to make fun of, and the temptation is irresistible when they take themselves so solemnly.

But what they also, and chiefly, stood for is something a bit more profound than adoration of the mule.

A society that thinks chiefly of quantity, not quality, and of creature comforts rather than intellectual and spiritual values, is not going to last.

Furthermore, a society that regards a man as a unit of labor, who can be moved about or dropped or left to starve if that unit is not needed for the moment, is not going to last.

And besides, it is wrong to ignore the effect on a man's integrity and independence of a system in which he is totally at the mercy of an employer or the generosity of a government. A few generations of this, and how readily will you find men able and competent to speak their mind boldly, how easily will you draw volunteers to defend the state when necessary?

When everything yields to the needs of industry—hell, give them tax breaks, give them land, use every resource of government to make their way easy—and when all the old patterns of family loyalty, families that are friends generation after generation, are at last broken, what are you going to be left with, except maybe the freedom to drink yourself dead at a singles bar?

There is a level at which the Agrarians are not so stupid as first appears. There is a level at which Shakespeare was right about the toad, ugly and venomous, with the precious jewel, all the same.

As any Southerner darkly suspects, the stone the builders pitched out is maybe the crown and glory of the arch, after all. (November 1980)

Courage

There isn't time to think, is there? She's going under and if the water doesn't kill her, the ice will.

Some of us didn't watch the television coverage of the plane wreck in the Potomac. But the set was on, and I happened to be walking in front of it when the woman lost the life ring and began to sink. I saw the guy leap and swim over to her. I knew I had seen all there was to see.

But you can't think of those bystanders, those cops and firemen, those gentlemen in whirlybirds, without a sense of wonder that there wasn't a slob among them.

Courage is the most private of all human parts, and there is some vulgarity, I suspect, even to gaze at it, let alone to talk about it.

But then it's everything. You remember the story of Lord Jim, Conrad's big novel about the sea captain who saved his own hide while all his passengers drowned. The problem there was cowardice, and the trouble was the guy was caught off guard. If there'd been time to think, he would have done it differently.

So you wonder, if you see heroes, were any cowards there? You keep looking at them. And everybody translates the sight into the same question: If we were there would we be heroes? Or just on our duffs trying to figure it out.

There was a fireman back in my country, name of Billy Burrell, who went to a routine fire that stopped being routine. It was a cruddy little house and there were people in it. Burrell raced in. The doors, even, were on fire, and the metal of the windows was running down like the lead kids make toy soldiers with. Nothing could live in that fire and nothing did.

Burrell came staggering out. He was on fire. They squirted hoses on him. Then an astonishing thing happened. He dashed back toward the burning house. It took more than one guy to hold him.

He might as well not have dared those burning doors in the first place. He certainly brought nothing out. Except, of course, a prouder name.

There are days you think bad of your country. But the land has had some things happen on it, sufficient to consecrate the average field.

Courage

It may be we don't see heroes much nowadays. But then you already know why that is.

It's a plunge inside and no camera catches it. Even if there is an outward and visible sign, the camera is not usually around to bear witness when the big gift is given.

The first time I ever read that poem of Spender's there was a typo in it, where he speaks of those who leave the air signed with their honor. My copy said they left the air singed with their honor. As if honor burnt like a coal so that even the air was singed. I like that typo.

There's that big opera they sing in the theater about the guy who first has to go through fire and then has to go through water so dense and whirling there's nothing else. He has to do that because that's what he has to do to make the music come out right, and all he's got in the way of protection is a flute his girl gave him that's supposed to be magical. So he toots off through the fire and then the floods trying to remember to sound his music.

When he comes out okay, you can't take much more. Glory is best beheld in brief and regulated flashes.

Sometimes I think about Billy, the one at the burning door, and wonder how's he doing. Not that I ever knew him. He'd be surprised I know his name.

I wonder what it's like. Maybe it's like those winners of the big race that Pindar was forever celebrating in the stuff he wrote. The victory was so dazzling at 18 that those runners never had a normal life again. The early glory so overshadowed any other possibility that I wonder if they ever regretted it. Glory, I imagine, can be a gold-crowned mischief.

But I don't think it was for the fireman I mentioned. He was so modest he never even knew glory had hit him. He had just seen the fire and heard 'em hollering and did what everybody would have done.

The gist of it is bound to be separate from whether anybody is helped. The fireman never brought anybody out. The readiness was all.

They say the gods pull our wings off, like flies, and torment us for their sport. Nothing is going to change that. That's what they do.

To see some helpless mortal wheel around and snarl defiance at what is fated is a highly refreshing thing. Billy Burrell, I well remember, had a whole damn town in his debt once, not because he helped anybody out of the fire, but because he lived right there in the same town we did. Like having Achilles right down the road a piece.

We have great faith in time, most of us. Some things are best to deal with at a little distance. Not trying to make sense of it all at once. Getting at it gradually and somewhat sideways.

On the bus you probably saw those kids raising merry hell on the seminary's hill—I did, coming to work. The ice was great from the packed pressure of the snow, and the garbage-can lids took off like outer space. The kids outdid themselves in a flurry of red mittens and delicious squeals.

There was a mother there, stalking over to one tot and the bus rolled on before I could hear (what I know she said) that Early Wayne had better come rat cheer, don't you make me come after you, you know your daddy told you to stay right off of that hill, etc. etc.

The visions come and go so quick. You see them for just a few seconds. And thank God. (January 1982)

The End of Chivalry

Someday I suppose a war will be lost on the Astroturves of Houston or the playing fields of Unicorn U. The idealism and chivalry that are nurtured by manly sports and right thinking have much to answer for, when the bill of human grief is totted up. Nothing is more dangerous, or more likely to result in widescreen horrorcolor, than the notion that one is disciplined and fit, that one is noble, that one is a faithful servant manfully to fight under God's or St. George's or the proletariat's or the ayatollah's banner unto death.

"Is there a sense of chivalry in the United States?" demanded Mark Girouard, who has written a marvelous book called "The Return to Camelot," which deals with the revival of chivalric notions in the 19th century.

"You got me," I said honestly. "I don't think so. I don't know. It depends. But I don't think chivalry, in the sense of vigils and damsels and despising money and all that."

But then I am the last guy to ask. There are days I think I must be French, I am so realistic and plain and devoted to simple drudgery. Even as a child, I assumed the large ostrich-plume fan in the portrait of Aunt Marie was a feather duster for reaching the ceiling.

But this is one of the supreme questions of human life, as I see it— not the nature of Aunt Marie's fan, of course, but the role of idealism versus bald reality—and it is more important than most that one wrestles with. And has no answer.

Like many of us, no doubt, I am not chivalrous but then I am not anti-chivalry. I grew up with the stories of King Arthur and once I went to Grenoble especially to see the tomb of the Chevalier Bayard, and I never could help noticing in the big funny novel, "Don Quixote," that it was as beautiful as it was hilarious. The knight of that story, you recall, had his poor brains addled by reading romances of knights, and he set out to be one, and did endless mischief because, as his sensible niece once observed, he always wanted better bread than is made with wheat. And the great novelist who tells his story shows how much misery he won, thereby, for himself and for others.

All the same, when that crazy knight dies, you are grateful he once lived; and even Cervantes, the author, who points out all his follies, is half in love with him and probably is standing yet at the vigil of his bier.

But when this great revival of chivalry took place, especially during the 1800s in England, the code took hold. Never mind that kids slaved in factories and beat old horses drawing carts, chivalry was nevertheless in the air.

Walter Scott wrote about knights. A whole batch of painters took to painting knights. Queen Victoria had a memorial to her dear Albert carved with his effigy in full armor like a medieval knight, in flawless marble, with his favorite hound, Eos, at his feet, also in marble, of course. And the duke of Clarence, the one who was not quite as bright as he might have been and whose sexual appetites were as you might say especially gifted and who died at the age of 28—never mind, there he is, too, carved gloriously in the manner of a knight with a kneeling lady angel holding a crown of glory over his head.

And at schools then, boys learned to take cold showers and to be pure. And to reverence women and to bow when they crossed before an altar and to take what came: never to push themselves, never to be devious and underhanded, never to fake friendship or approval when they didn't feel it; always to be ready to fight a slur against their honor, and never to complain or make a lot of excuses when the world went against them.

This was all in the air. Men often failed to live up to the standards they set for themselves, but they believed in the standards.

Once there was a great tournament held at Eglinton, a country house, in which modern knights showed up in medieval armor to joust and tilt before the Queen of Beauty. (It poured rain and ruined the tournament and everybody sloshed around in mud thigh deep.) And Queen Victoria attended her own great fancy dress ball as Philippa, wife of Edward III (it was this queen who introduced rosemary into England, you recall); and there was a terrific renewal of interest in coats of arms and old castles, and on and on.

One result was that when World War I approached, virtually all England responded with a head full of cavalry charges and visions of knights defending their lady's honor and all the rest.

The Great War of 1914 to 1918 put an end to that nonsense. For four years men lived like rats in trenches, advancing a mile this month, losing and retreating a mile next month, and nothing to show for it except the slaughter of millions.

How far do we accept "reality" before we die inside as men ...

It was a jolt. It turned out there were not going to be any cavalry charges on spring days with the temperature at 65 degrees and the meadows in bloom and the trumpets inspiring and an archbishop blessing the horses and a regal voice declaiming the great lines of King Henry before the fight of Agincourt. On the contrary, the war was a matter of mud and excrement and prolonged screams and barbed wire and, worse than any of that, the inescapable revelation that nothing whatever was being accomplished. And nobody, least of all the general staff and the government and the church, had the least idea how to stop it, once it was started.

For a long time, every response to senseless death and suffering was an appeal to the gorgeous imagery of St. Michael the archangel, and to Galahad and Lancelot and Perceval and the great knights of our literature.

But despite the heroic efforts of poets and hack journalists to interpret the disaster in terms of fair knights laying down their lives for the sacred brotherhood, it became impossible to sustain any such lie, and at the last all England knew (and the Germans and French and Austrians and Americans knew) that the truth was that nobody knew what the hell he was doing or why. And it was not in any way like a brave cavalry charge on a sunny day with the trumpets blaring and the archangels hovering.

It was ordure and worse, and once this dawned on the great chivalric empires, the world has not been the same since.

If men and women had not come to 1914 with their heads full of fantasies, if they had not miscast themselves as knightly heroes, if they had learned a less exalted and more humble and more truthful vision of themselves, then they might not have rushed with such a head of emotional steam into a world disaster.

No later wars were terrible in the way the Great War was. No later wars were fought by nations infused from border to border with visions of the Grail.

Girouard and I laughed and talked through an afternoon, about the chivalric revival, admiring the occasional beautiful pictures in his lavishly illustrated book, and not quite wanting to laugh at the hilarious ones that were meant to be serious.

So notions of chivalry can be very funny, very dangerous. As, God knows, Cervantes pointed out centuries before the silly airs of would-be knights in the period before World War I.

But you can't help asking if things would have been better then if instead of a dream of chivalry they had had the dream we have: that nothing is worth much, except in terms of what gets a man or a nation "ahead."

It would have been as bad, probably, and there wouldn't even have been the illusion (however brief) that one was a warrior for God.

Like most moderns, I yield to no man in my admiration for Cervantes and his funny parody of the glories of knighthood.

But the other extreme, the notion that we are merely what our drudgery reveals us to be, and that we are nothing but creatures collecting laundry, remembering to fill up the gas tank, and devising ways to stay even with or ahead of inflation—that is no guarantee of peace or honor, either.

A balance must be struck. And no man born of woman is ever sure where the true and right balance lies. How far do we beautify life before the images become an obscene lie. On the other hand, how far do we accept "reality" before we die inside as men, and become some stupid cog in some stupid computer system.

I know as well as we all do that something went wrong in the Great War. I also know it was not entirely dumb to kneel after a long dusty ride on the smelly bus on the clean cold stone of Grenoble. So where does that leave us?

Where men have always been. Ignorant, uncertain, beastly, vicious, noble, filthy and little short of angels. We're supposed to be grateful, I gather, that we even see the tangles and know how tangled they truly are. Nobody but a supersaint or a superimbecile expects, anymore, to ravel the tangles out.

We are no closer than the first cave men at living life on the level we suspect human life might be lived. We may be able to boast—big deal— we fool ourselves deliberately a little less than our fathers did. (February 1982)

Goodbye, Little Sheba

I overcame grief at the age of 8 and have never suffered (worth speaking of) since then, and it seems to me that grief, like mumps, is best got out of the way early in life.

My dog Jack, in those days, was the magic of my life, since in my country it was common to grow up in a rather austere or cool house. This was in the days before it was known that kids should grow up in a warm heap. A dog was not austere, however, nor oracular nor overpowering, so for a kid a dog was a great treasure.

One day another kid, a great buddy of mine, told me with the relish that only close friends can dispense, that Jack was squashed a couple of blocks away under the viaduct. I got up there, and sure enough. It was hard to get him home to bury him beside the garage.

Time, that takes away everything else, took away the misery. Of course as one bounds along life's highway there are occasional sad sights. The first day I was in New Guinea I saw a fellow running about burning to death, and I have had my share of pulling people out of car wrecks dead or dying, and these things do nothing for cheer.

Brightness falls from the air, queens have died young and fair. So I do not trifle with you by seeming to argue that life is altogether brisk, but I do mean that losing a mutt is an exponential mode of pain. Precisely as minor ear infections hurt worse than many terminal ailments.

Still, if you live through it at the age of 8, you never have to hurt quite that way again, and you do learn eventually that pain is no excuse for withdrawing from the fray, or for over-arming the heart against hurt.

"Never again," some say, not wanting to "go through that again." But they err.

Now we have lost our middle mutt, Sheba. I knew, when the tail started describing 180-degree arcs instead of 360, that something was wrong, and at the last, when the tail did not move at all, I knew she was dead.

Of course the vet warned of this six years ago.

"Don't get fond of her," he said, "because I doubt she will make it six weeks. Never saw a dog so abused."

She was new to us then. She had been abandoned on Third Avenue by an owner who simply wished to walk away and leave the dog in the mad traffic, thus earning a permanent berth in hell quicker than most.

Sheba had a broken back and not very good teeth and about as much charm as a wet sock. She was shipped from New York at heinous expense in a Pullman bedroom, etc., etc., and for some days she did not walk but sat expiring quietly on the sofa between enforced excursions to the back yard.

Then it occurred to her she was not going to be beat with a stick. She perked up a little, though still unable to manage to climb over a curb if you walked her on the sidewalk.

But with time she eventually learned to go up one step, learned to run with surprising speed without (what she clearly needed) a gyroscope.

My wife said, when the vet said not to get fond of the animal, that the vet was nuts. Why there were years in that dog (she said) not having any faith whatever (I have often noticed) in expert opinion. She forbade the mutt to die, and the dog decided (as others have often done) there is no point arguing.

Sheba, a few years later, adopted a basset pup. The pup, no matter how hard Sheba tried, became less and less like a Lhasa apso every week. To her dying day, Sheba never gave up working on the hound— a corrective growl here, a firm nip there, and she never wasted time wondering where she went wrong.

The years passed. The original vet was probably right about not getting too fond of the beast, but Sheba was the most subversive dog I ever knew. Diabolical. Rightly was she named for that queen that seduced Solomon.

Until we had her, no dog had ever brought those nuggets of dry dog food into the living room. We forbade it. Sheba rarely cared what we didn't allow. Brought her Purina in, anyhow, and guarded it by the hour with ferocious snarls. She weighed 10 pounds, I would say, and she had her way in all things, cowing the other dogs. The hound could have tended to her in one mouthful, but of course kept a very respectful manner in Sheba's presence.

She visited the vet for some intravenous stuff to keep her comfortable and died without apparent discomfort at home in human arms, signaling by a cessation of tail centrifugally that the day was done.

She had some years the vet never thought she'd have. She gave some pleasure we never thought we'd have, since she came to us a total burden, yet left us substantially in her debt.

She was, as one of our great wits said of Cleopatra, a creature of similarly gaudy nights, a lass unparalleled.

It is precisely because almost every American can report the same facts that I mention old Sheba in the first place. A few tears aren't going to kill you, when you lose your mutt.

Now some people cannot have dogs. But others bow out, fearing the day the dog will die, and not wanting that particular mode of discomfort. But for me, I would hate to die myself without a mutt or two racing around the place extremely interested in the funeral baked meats. This, I have always imagined, would permit me to holler (at whatever chariot swang low) the excellent roar of the great Sufi mystic who had a wisdom rare among saints:

"Not without my dog." (April 1982)

The Lure of Klondikes and Cheetos

I have taken to eating Klondikes, an ice cream square encased in chocolate. They are much like the Eskimo Pies of my childhood, except they have "nuts" in the chocolate coating which (upon investigation) turn out to be cereal ground into small fragments. They give the same effect as nuts.

Somewhat similar are confections called Polar Bears. I do not care much for Polar Bears since some my wife bought had melted slightly on the way from the store to the home freezer, and they were icy upon being refrozen. It is clear this is not the fault of the confection itself. Still, if you take against bears, there it is.

What I want the government to investigate is the last bite of Klondikes. I have tried eating them different ways (you hold them in their tin foil wrapping and skillful connoisseurs eat the last bite before they melt all over your shirt) but no matter how I do it, the last bite has some addictive additive in it.

All the other bites are okay. You just eat along, pleasantly and contentedly, but without (I should say) anything approaching foudroyant enlightenment.

But the last bite, no matter which corner is last, has some addictive property that triggers deep responses not only in the soul but in the body chemistry, a sort of imperious command:

"Get another one."

On my good days I eat one, or at most two. On other days I have eaten four. They cost 86 cents each down here, in our elegant Post lunchroom, plus tax, and the cash register official gives you a hard look after the second and third trip.

They say the Food and Drug Administration, which used to investigate odd things in the national fodder, has been gutted; otherwise, it would be the right outfit to look into this addictive last bite.

Another junk food (junk food is food that has other things besides food in it) I am semi-addicted to is Cheetos. These are "cheese-flavored snacks," which does not give you much idea. Actually, they are crunchy elongated things rather like worms caught at Yucca Flats and turned crisp and orange in a nonce.

...a sort of imperious command : "Get another one."

Like the Klondikes, they eat along very nicely until you get to the last three, all of which are irradiated, I suppose, with something like opium, heroin, or whatever may be the most addictive substance upon earth. On my worst day, I have eaten five bags of Cheetos.

As everyone knows, modern technology is wonderful and corporations keep bringing us better things for better life through chemistry.

I assume that Klondikes and Cheetos, like everything else, are the fruit of research at du Pont, General Electric and Mobil Oil in tandem.

It is better to eat four Klondikes than four bags of Cheetos, because the Klondikes leave no telltale signs except an occasional spot on the shirt where the brittle chocolate breaks off and falls down (and you smudge it, brushing it off), whereas Cheetos turn your fingers a rich (and conspicuous) Day-Glo orange. Cheetos also give you 1,300 milligrams of sodium if you eat four bags of them, as I do, and sodium is the big new killer bee of the American diet, of course.

Besides, Cheetos not only turn your hands and lips orange. They also have something in them, silica, possibly? Or diamond dust? That cuts the sides of the mouth where the upper and lower lips join. The salt gets in these cuts and (unlike other addictive substances) Cheetos are therefore self-limiting. You have to wait a couple of days before starting on them again.

Now I do not believe the addictive substance in Klondikes and Cheetos is ferrous sulfate or thiamine mononitrate or the other things listed on the Table of Contents.

For a long time, I feared that I alone was addicted to these two products, but my daughter tells me they now sell Klondikes bold as brass right out on the sidewalk in New York, and I have seen too many empty Cheetos sacks in this capital to believe any longer that only I am hooked.

All I am asking is for Johns Hopkins (since the government probably no longer cares) to find out what is in the last bite of these otherwise dissimilar confections that causes the Pavlovian dash for additional supplies.

This should be done (and the substance banned) before the nation becomes a republic of enslaved addicts and before I go broke. (June 1982)

Self-Praise and Ruin

A change has occurred in the American New Year. It used to be a time for soul-searching, and (perhaps half-hearted) resolutions to straighten up and fly right.

Recently, however, it has become a time for self-congratulation, and you may expect tomorrow to hear every windbag on the continent gas on about the glory of our state, following (I suppose) the lead of the White House.

I used to think, by the way, that the presidency could be filled perfectly well by drawing lots; that one man would do about as well as another, but it is increasingly difficult to maintain this hopeful view, which I now amend to "anybody except maybe movie actors."

When the Roman Empire collapsed, it was not generally reported in Rome, or even much noticed there. It was only later, looking back, that her ruin was apparent, and it is that way with us, too.

You will have noticed the secretary of transportation has gone on to higher endeavors, leaving the government for cable television. Which may remind you, as it does me, that the government of this nation sat placidly while its passenger railroad system fell into ruin. You can't even get to Charlottesville nowadays, out in the capital's suburbs, unless you pay an exorbitant fare on a plane, or venture out on a highway full of drunks and hopheads, or ride the bus from a typical Calcutta-gutter-rat terminal. A government that allows a train system to disintegrate has no mandate, and no right, to govern. Elsewhere in the world trains scoot from town to town at 125 mph, and plans are far along for trains at 300 mph and more. But just try to get to Cincinnati or Chicago or Topeka or anywhere else from this capital.

In the town itself, for some years, it has been clear even to nincompoops that the population has quadrupled and more, though the city has not expanded geographically. We have the same streets. They are packed now. Furthermore, for some years it has been clear, though not necessarily clear to nincompoops, that oil is a problem now and will be an even greater problem tomorrow. This would be a signal, you might think, to develop a mass transportation system with the greatest possible speed.

Self-Praise and Ruin

Instead, the Washington subway, years late in conception and execution, still drags along as if it were some project for a museum
honoring Garfield (president or cat, makes no difference).

What kind of government cannot get a subway built within 10
generations? What kind of competence is suggested by the decision to
buy subway cars from Italy, of all places, that nation that may or may
not still have running water in its capital?

The truth is, of course, that politics is staffed—has anybody, by the
way, ever run a table of the IQs of the Congress which seem to hover
about 108?—by men at their wits' end, who are pleased and doubtless
surprised to have landed on their feet after all. For this reason and this
reason alone the subway has not been completed, the incompetence of
local politicians.

If anyone wishes to say that in a country so large, it is natural to
develop the airlines rather than the trains, he is invited to look at the
airlines network of America, which is outrageous and outrageously
inconvenient. Apparently the only solution is for Pan-Am and all the
others to go bankrupt and for the nation to start again at Square One
to devise something better for getting people moved.

Transportation is so basic, and we are so used to wretched arrangements, that we almost do not notice it any more, unless we visit a
nation in which transportation is well managed. Which is to say, I
increasingly believe, almost anywhere else except the United States and
Mexico and places like that.

To branch out a bit, infant mortality is too high. Furthermore, there
is a decline in the number of physicians entering research, since they all
wish to be millionaires dispensing antibiotics and assuring old ladies
with intestinal obstruction that they probably have a "bug" and should
take a Tylenol.

American art and letters are ludicrous. Journalists are shockingly
overpraised, novelists of quite moderate talent are turned into lions,
and poets (while nobody, quite sensibly, reads them) spend much of
their lives getting together to praise each other.

American industry—well.

Crime spreads. In this very office a friend of mine fretted that people
kept stealing his ashtray. He got a heavy metal one, drilled a hole in it
and attached it to his desk with a cord. Within two weeks somebody
cut the cord and stole the ashtray. He now has a huge one weighing 23
pounds and shaped like a great scallop, probably in the hopes that this

It is a superb example of the combination of American monetary extravagance and spiritual poverty.

symbol of pilgrims will protect it somehow. Ha. Within a week somebody will make off with it and write a story about the world's largest mess of coquilles St. Jacques which will be widely admired, and never mind my poor old colleague without an ashtray again. There is a pipe that burns dragon dung.

The president has gone out West to holiday with a fortune made in—God save the state—a thing called TV Guide. In every direction, the American tension has slackened, except among the down-and-out, who are tense enough still.

Every luxury operation in the nation is flourishing. Chocolates that cost $1.25 per bonbon. Absurdly expensive restaurants, in which the food is utterly routine and uninspired, are packed.

Madalyn O'Hair inquires on holiday television where the Holy Ghost "kept his sperm," and you wonder if she may have missed a point or two of theology along the way to her numerous advanced degrees, but then it occurs to you there are plenty of fundamental types who are prepared to inform her, so maybe it's best for them to holler each other into the ground.

Then there's a fellow named Christo, who has neither a first nor last name, but who manages quite well with just Christo, doubtless in allusion to the count or the God, who is now hard at work on an heroic task: He will wrap several islands in Biscayne Bay with pink plastic; that is, he will attach a sort of skirt of pink plastic extending for 200 feet from the shores of these islands. It will cost $2.5 million. It is a superb example of the combination of American monetary extravagance and spiritual poverty.

It would probably never have been noticed, except it seems a symbol of American wits at the moment or something picked up at a California party. And something that the nation at large is (as usual) a bit baffled by, but not really surprised at. (December 1982)

Song and Spirit

So once more when we got to the place we all knelt down, in the face of death again, as all men everywhere have always done, and said our prayers each one according to his way, for the lamb of thine own flock, the creature of thine own redeeming.

The tremendous-throated pipes roared their defiance which was brave, but we were only on our knees and we were silent. We got up and the procession entered from the north transept without any sound at all.

The cross and the torches, the choir of boys, all mute, and they got to the rood screen and passed through but we stood on the other side in the big stone nave where we belonged.

"Out of the depths," the human voice began, "have I cried unto thee, O Lord. Lord hear the voice of my supplication."

The music began and the boys sang.

When the Black Prince died, who had been the great English model of knighthood, he wanted to be buried in the church basement, beneath the choir, where forever the boys would sing above, but his fellows wouldn't hear of it and buried him up by the altar, which was not what he wanted at all. But over the centuries so many people touched and wore away his tomb and his trophies in Kent that they had to move him back down to the crypt, and there he is till now, where he wanted to be, and the choristers still sing above his stone.

Well, anybody who ever heard them sing can comprehend the prince's wish, to have that music envelop his very skeleton always.

But on the day this week that I speak of, it was not the Black Prince but our friend Frances, and I would not dream of mentioning a private thing, except it is not private or particular but is common to all. Nobody ever lived long enough to read this who did not have a friend die, someone (as George C. McGhee said in an appropriate and beautiful short talk) remarkable and joyous, and now dead.

In pastures green (the kids sang on) he leadeth me, the quiet waters by.

Everything depends, in these matters, on singing right. It has to be full without being pompous, full of decent pride without being vainglorious, full of tenderness without being false: and I marveled that mere boys could do it.

Song and Spirit

The woman whose life we had got together to praise God for had a soft voice and tended her household. She cooked a dish she called Spaghetti Bolognese which she had adapted to the English palate. On the other hand (she was endlessly domestical, and it is right to mention the food she served) she was beyond compare with little half-dollar meringues glued together, flat side to flat side, with Devonshire cream. I wonder how many men fell forever in love with her for these.

Well. This was in Washington, the organ and the choir, and she is in the earth near Winchester, near the River Itchen along which she and her husband so often walked like silly lovers, and not far from the old cottage where they lived, with the yellow rose around the door.

She had lived for a while in Washington and made a great warmth among those who knew her. How many do this in this capital for a little while, some with circles of friends far smaller than hers, some with perhaps even more, and when it touches you it is irrelevant what her influence is or what her station is. A good woman is above rubies, whether her life touches three or three million.

Themistocles once observed there are those who have no memorial except the air we breathe. Socrates used to say a woman needs no perfume, she herself smells sweet.

Thy servant Frances whom we commit. All the day long till the shadows, and peace at the last.

My car was way outside the church, by the gnarled old Glastonbury thorn that has grown there for a long time, and I poked about, minding the thorns which are surprisingly efficient, to see if it was in bloom. It often is in winter, long before spring, and at first I couldn't find any flowers on it, then I did, just two, and they were as good as an April floraison. So I got in my car and slammed the door and usual-life began again.

The bells in the tower rang but were muffled, the louvers closed, lest they upset the neighbors of the church who, no doubt, would all drop dead if they had to hear a true bronze voice above a tin racket of the streets.

So now it's dark and time for supper once again. And I'm glad I went to the place where they sang in the day. And I'm glad I knew her in clear days and I thank God every man is born into the net of affection and happiness in a human world, no matter what ever comes, no matter how short the term of summer's lease.

O Israel (as the chaplain so wisely put it) trust. And he shall redeem

Israel from all his sins. And as the kids sang—not even being men, how can they know the sharp knife of what they sing?—My head dost thou with oil anoint, and my cup overflows. Comfort is not far from taunting, as affection is not far from teasing.

It's good when the 32-foot pipes of the organ (that's four stories nowadays) snarl in defiant volume against every insult to mortal breathing. Even if you're on your knees. For this purpose music came into the world, to fight what we cannot. And it's good, softer, when it's less inflamed and more like the comfort you once heard as a little kid and got hurt. I know, I know, poor tiger, and it's going to be all right, and you believed it then and still do now. (January 1983)

The Reality of Images

The odd thing about life is its images. They should be taken seriously. One interesting thing about an image is that it's beyond control, so there is no point trying to develop one of one's own.

I used to think that content, logic, substance (as it is called) were the big things. I now think images are bigger—not that they are ever divorced from the substance, the style or the soul of a thing. That's why they are powerful.

The person or institution or thing that provides the image has no control over the person who perceives the image. We may get the image all "wrong," but that does not keep it from being effective, as far as we are concerned.

Once I was standing about as Golda Meir got out of a car to enter a building. She was old and sick. She had had years of political work behind her. Our eyes happened to meet. Nothing was said. Her eyes were five miles deep. Her face registered nothing; there was no movement there. She was like a piece of sculpture, permanent, and beyond adding or subtracting some pleasant novelty of line. She seemed sad, or drained, but not tired. She was ready to go on, to whatever god-awful reception awaited her.

The thing that struck me was that she was not intentionally projecting anything. She was just getting out of a car. If her mind was on anything, it was probably on whether her cat needed a low-protein diet back in Israel. Or who knows. Of all the thousands of times she wished to convey through her person a particular image, this was one time she almost certainly did not wish to convey anything at all. But if I think of her, it is the first image that comes to mind. Odd.

Sometimes I watch late-night talk shows. A character actress told Dick Cavett she always watched his show, which (she said) was often "crappy." True. Sometimes you marvel at the world, which has so many asses in it.

I have tried to think why I was so churned up seeing Janet Baker on the Cavett show. She sings, of course. She sings gloriously, everybody knows that. But then so do a handful of others. What happens, when one is all but shattered by an image—in this case simply Baker standing up singing a song of Ben Jonson's—is the coming together of maybe 40,000 things, most of them half lost in the memory, but a sound, a scent, a human figure, a mere accident of light, can call up all that is forgotten, not in any tiresome detail, but with the original force intact or even amplified.

I went to a lecture at the Smithsonian, the Frank Nelson Doubleday lecture with a bunch of southerners (Eudora Welty, Walker Percy, C. Vann Woodward) speaking about a bunch of Yankees (Melville, Hawthorne, Parkman). There were some facts new to me, one or two things I had not thought of, but really you don't have to get done up in a dinner jacket and race about town just to find something you never thought of before. You can do that just answering the phone.

The thing I remember most vividly is Welty in her amazing green dress with big purple stars that had mirrors in them. A sort of Merlin costume, I thought. The colors of the grape vine. Her voice was soft but standard; she has made an effort, I warrant you, not to sound to melting, too southern, or in any other way extraordinary; she could have learned to sound grand and I am not sure how she escaped it, which is why I think she has given more attention to her voice than most people would guess, wishing it to be firm, standard, unexceptional, modest—and in the voice, this usually leads to distinction of tone, so that anybody would recognize the Welty voice, or what may be called the Eudoran timbre, anywhere.

I was much moved. I wonder if people often think they are bizarre, as I often wonder about myself, when they find themselves continually being moved greatly. All people are so similar that we rarely have any idea whether we are strange or standard. Both, probably.

Then one night I was up on top of the Federal Reserve Building at a supper benefiting a charity, Recordings for the Blind, Inc., and I had noticed Rose Fales, one of the wheels, in great tension. There had been a crisis over the tablecloths (they didn't show up) and she had missed a cocktail party at the Bushes, to which she had been asked, and one way and another she had been going full steam and full of anxiety. I saw her late in the evening, over at the side of the room, her head thrown back, laughing. Rose in triumph. I still cannot think why I was so enchanted by that fleeting moment, or why I remember her that way. Odd.

But then images are. But then people are. But then we are. (May 1983)

Story Telling and History

Now you take "Cinderella," a story that is never out of the news for long. Someone has asked my opinion of that glass slipper, which raises the fairly cosmic question of what stories are all about.

The slipper may not have been glass, to begin with. The French word is *verre,* but the word for ermine is *vair.* Hence ermine becomes glass.

Odd, of course, that only Cinderella's dainty hoof happened to fit, even though common experience shows that when you try a shoe on 600,000 nubile maidens there will be more than one foot that squeezes in. The conclusion is plain enough—the prince wanted Cinderella and no other. Why not just claim her? He may not have been free to choose, without a competition, even though he controlled the contest.

But the point of the story is simply that two dandy young creatures found each other in spite of hostile circumstances.

Which brings us to a thought that applies not only to fairy tales, but to histories, myths and the legends of nations, corporations and families: you start with the desired ending, and construct a story to reach it.

In histories, of course, the writers and editors are scrupulous to tell the truth. All the same, histories have a way of resembling fairy stories and myths in some ways, and the question can reasonably be asked of any writer, what is truth?

Take any war, any assassination, any astonishing crime, and you will see that the result you get depends a good bit on which facts are thought important, which are thought true, and of course it makes a difference who does the thinking about these judgments; in other words, who is the writer?

Such is the richness of life that millions of facts touch even the slightest human actions and they cannot all be dealt with, even if all could be known. Besides (as every writer knows and deplores) one fact contradicts another, and how are these to be sorted out?

Take King Solomon. It did not occur to the many writers of his history in the Old Testament to question his legitimacy to rule over Israel. That was not their task, yet in their accounts they consciously or unconsciously did all they could to establish his right to the throne.

And they had their work cut out for them, as any writer does who is bound by religious principles and a moderate regard at least for what seems the truth.

Solomon's throne was divinely ordained, and, for that matter, Israel was chosen among all other nations to be, as it were, the people with a favored and special relationship to God.

The only reason they had their land, according to their history, was that God gave it to Abraham and his seed forever.

Already, before the time of Solomon, enormous difficulties arose. Any non-Israelite neighbor might say the Israelites simply conquered the land by military force, just as David conquered Jerusalem by strength of arms and moved his capital there from Hebron.

Still, if God gave Abraham the land, then why did he think it necessary to buy from a Hittite land given by God, or why did David buy the site for the temple in Jerusalem?

Title to land was through inheritance only, from Abraham.

There were also divine laws against incest, but incidents figure in Solomon's ancestry. On the surface, these might be thought to cloud his claim.

Another iron law regulated marriage, which in theory could occur only within the tribe of pure descent, not with foreigners. Still, some foreigners were more foreign than others. But Moabites and Ammonites, for example, could never become part of the congregation of Israel even after many generations. Solomon's ancestry, however, includes foreigners who seem on the surface of it to violate this central law, and he himself married women of the Egyptians, Moabites, Ammonites, Edomites, Zidonians and Hittites.

Marriage with foreigners simply occurred, for all the thundering of the prophets.

There are centuries of learned analysis of the Old Testament to this day, as well as continuing interest in such figures as Solomon. "The Legitimacy of Solomon" by the social anthropologist Edmund Leach (Cape, 1969) considers the question of how the Old Testament historians worked out some of these contradictions, that seem open violations of the most serious law, but which in the end do not affect the legitimacy of Solomon's claim to the throne.

None of the writers of the sacred history, it may be assumed, dared tamper with the facts as known to them—they do not disguise incest, exogamy, etc.—and the Lord knows they are withering enough in their examination of their kings.

Can incest, a crime, also be a good thing? Can a foreigner be turned into a nonforeigner? In a narrow sense, of course not.

Still, there a nation is with a throne to be filled and there the historian is, unable to tamper with the facts of Solomon's ancestry.

The wonder is that things can be worked out.

But within limits they can be. Never underestimate human ingenuity and dedication to the task. If you require airtight logic and have no truck with legal fictions, ingenious laws, mercy, special interventions and so forth, you are in large trouble, not only as a historian and writer but as a man, for human life is full of irreconcilable contradictions that nevertheless must be reconciled somehow if life is to go on with any cheer.

All the same, the conscientious storyteller's lot is not an easy one, doing his best to bring order out of chaos.

"Cinderella" is not a bad place to begin gently teaching a child that there are other things beside common sense and logic, and a bit later on, the story of Solomon may advance the lesson, so that in due time one is perfectly at home in Washington. (September 1983)

Lincoln, Mozart and the Mysteries of Art

I shall not explain either Lincoln or "Cosi fan tutte," but for years I have thought before dozing off on great matters such as the central mystery of art.

Lincoln's Gettysburg Address was delivered 120 years ago tomorrow and is a fair sample of words that are more splendid than their surface shows. He twice uses the word "devotion" even though he knew better than any other American president the danger of words longer than two syllables. No other president understood so well the grandeur of monosyllables, yet here he rumbles along with "devotion" twice in one sentence.

He also begins with the archaic, and really silly when you think of it, opening phrase, "Four score and seven years ago," which was risky beyond measure. In the first place it did not make any difference whatever whether it was 87 or 88 or 89 years ago, and to give a date that emphasis carried the danger of seeming simply foolish.

There are a couple of other places in the talk in which the words seem (for a writer of Lincoln's great skill) weak or ill-chosen; for example, "portion," ("a portion of this field") and the unseemly emphasis on the weak prepositions, "of," "by" and "for."

These kinds of word usage almost always weaken the thought. They usually produce a dismal response.

The question is why, since any fool can see the Lincoln address is a masterpiece, something so obvious and indeed trite is suddenly not trite at all, but the most moving document in American annals.

Lincoln wrote many other famous short things, some of them more beautiful on the surface than the address at the battlefield

In all works of high art there are things that cannot be accounted for, even by careful and skillful analysis. Sometimes the words catch fire, for no clear reason. Often in Shakespeare they do, and usually it is clear why they produce such grand effects. But sometimes not. You can't say why some simple combination of ordinary words is magical, while other simple combinations that seem just as good, are not good at all.

It is possible the artist, Lincoln or anybody else, has no idea at all how to produce such a work, but merely understands when it is just right and leaves it alone and never mind the rules. The subconscious probably makes all manner of subterranean connections that we are not aware of between the words of Lincoln's address. Certainly words like "devotion," "portion," "dedicate" have elements in common, and at some unexplained and unreachable level they work together beautifully, though Lincoln wisely avoided Latinate words as a rule.

The dark magic is seen, or at least felt, most strongly in Shakespeare in such simple combinations as these:

"The bright day is done, and we are for the dark." Nothing as simple-minded as the repeated b's and d's accounts for the power of the line, neither does the weight of the individual words, though it is admittedly almost impossible to achieve so grand a rhythm. Rhythm in English is damnably hard, and has nothing to do with simple patterns. Any idiot can write in Shakespeare's meter but not many can make the words fit the meter so flawlessly that the meter fits the words, which is what happens in this line.

There must be a billion distant things in the back of the brain—all we ever thought of when we heard the word "bright" and the word "dark," and a billion other ghosts of experience we have all forgot, but which flesh out and begin to dazzle when the minor character of the play is given that line to say.

Not even Shakespeare could command those dark forgotten things, but when he let them flow through him and they appeared he knew when it was marvelous and when it was not.

Tonight you notice there is another performance of "Cosi fan tutte" at the Kennedy Center, an opera grossly neglected for decades by the Metropolitian Opera, it is worth pointing out in this season of Met fanfares for the Met. But then cosi fan tutti (which means they're all like that).

The first night I ever went to an opera it was this one and I had no idea what was going on. That was 40-odd years ago and I still don't know what's going on in it, although I know the plot now and I now know the words, too.

I went to it again a few nights ago and will say why I have great trouble with this opera still, after all these years.

The curtain rises and in a minute you behold four of the greatest jackasses ever produced by the Western world, which is saying something. Two male, two female. The ladies have sworn eternal fealty to their lovers who (on a bet) are testing their constancy. The men pretend to go off to war, then they sneak back in the costume of Albanians to woo the faithful ladies who needless to say are faithful for a good 10 minutes, no more. Then they change costumes again and the ladies are upset, not at their faithlessness but at their embarrassment.

Well, there the four of them are, the girls and the Albanian boys. They all start singing in good order. This is a comedy scene. It is dumb to begin with, and the words they sing do not help much.

It is arch, silly, fatuous, on the surface.

The question arises why everybody listening to these jackasses either starts to cry or feels like it.

At one level, as you behold this scene (and all the others in this opera) you are aware of two cretinous dames and two imbecile jerks in the most simpleminded of all farces. This is not the stuff of tears, usually.

The music, the voices, while paying some minor allegiance to the actual words and the story, not much, has taken off on its own and in a profound sense has nothing more to do with the stupid action of the humans than a phoenix has to do with a chicken-run.

Where does the glory come from? It is there, all right, and so powerfully present that the average listener is lost in wonder. It is one opera in which nobody rattles anything.

When I first heard it, not knowing the plot and not being able to make sense of the general waddling about (for in those days opera singers were not so beautiful or handsome as in this modern production) I assumed it was about gods and goddesses, or what happens to heroes when the wars are done and they see God. If you had told me when I was 13 that it was about two guys dressed up like Albanians to test the loyalty of their rather cretinous sweethearts, I'd have said you were crazy.

And would say so still.

It is an example—admittedly a dazzling one—of the mystery of art, in which there is the usual human mix of beans and sweat and haw-haw sex and guffaws and confusion and nonsense and lousy motives and barnyard morals. The thing is stirred together a few minutes and (as a good poet once said of such mixes) is immortal diamond. The Lord only knows where the beans and guffaws went.

This alchemy, this futzing about until everything turns diamond, was never comprehensible and probably, as long as the power stuns, doesn't have to be. (November 1983)

Religious Passions

You hesitate even to allude to religious passions, let alone discuss them with the probable result of being called bigot, rabble-rouser or sarcastic toad. All the same, the announcement of an embassy to the Vatican does raise the question anew of the position of a secular state toward great churches.

The American "wall of separation" between the two has foundations dating some centuries back, and while we are modern and trustful of good intentions, and have a certain respect for churches, it is a fact, not a fancy, that the agenda of churches will be implemented into law whenever possible. That is not because churches necessarily wish to seize political power, but because they cannot stand idly by while unspeakable crimes (as they believe) are committed.

The control that the Moral Majority would like to exert over all Americans is hardly a secret, on the Protestant side (joined by many Roman Catholics as well), while the Roman Catholic interest in contraception, divorce and abortion are familiar examples of sins they would like to see stopped. Some Protestants agree.

Jefferson among other earlier Americans was peculiarly sensitive on the issue of church and state and issued many warnings. But without further prelude, let us look into a courtroom relevant to religious enthusiasm. The defense witness is briefly silent and the judge speaks:

"Oh how hard the truth is, to come out of a lying Presbyterian knave."

The witness, alarmed, looks blank.

"Was there ever (the judge emits an oath at this point) such a villain on the face of the earth? Does thou believe there is a God? Does thou believe in hellfire? Of all the witnesses that I ever met with I never saw the like.

"I hope, gentlemen of the jury, that you take notice of the horrible carriage of this fellow. How can one help abhorring both these men and their religion? A Turk is a saint to such a fellow as this. A pagan would be ashamed of such villainy.

"Oh blessed Jesus. What a generation of vipers we live among," the judge goes on.

The witness, not overly encouraged by the judge, says:

"I cannot tell what to say, my lord."

The judge swears and reflects:

"Was there ever such an impudent rascal? Hold the candle to him that we may see his brazen face. See that an information for perjury be preferred against this fellow."

Having got rid of that witness the court got on with its business of ordering a woman, Alice Lisle, burned to death. She was a Presbyterian or something of that kind.

She told the court she had sheltered in her house two men after the battle of Sedgemoor, true, but she did not know they were rebels. One of them she knew was a clergyman and "a man of peace." She just gave them a place to sleep and some food, when they banged on her door.

"But I will tell you," said the judge. "There is not one of those lying snivelling canting Presbyterians but in one way or another had a hand in the rebellion. Presbytery has all manner of villainy in it. Show me a Presbyterian and I'll show thee a lying knave."

After he ordered her burnt alive, the clergy of Winchester Cathedral (who were not Presbyterian but Anglican) remonstrated, and the judge did not wish to tangle with such respectable folk. He reduced the penalty from burning to beheading, a sentence carried out at Winchester.

The judge in this case, which is famous enough but which is little remembered now, a mere 299 years later, was not some obscure temporary judge in the boondocks but the lord chief justice of England, George Jeffreys.

Jeffreys, who could "smell a Presbyterian 40 miles," did yeoman work for his king, James II, a Roman Catholic, who gave Jeffreys a peerage.

Two good-looking brothers named Hewling were brought before Jeffreys. There was sentiment to save them, since it is one thing to execute some old bag but another to execute teen-aged lads of good family.

"You have a grandfather who deserves to be hanged as richly as you," the judge observed. (The grandfather, a leading merchant of London and head of the London Baptists, was not on trial, but the chief justice thought he might as well mention him anyway.) The youths were killed.

In his history of England, from which these quotations are lifted for the interest of Baptists, Presbyterians, Catholics and nonestablishment types in general, Macaulay adds that Jeffreys (before going to work for the new Catholic king) delighted in the judicial slaughter of Catholics. "He always appeared to be in a higher state of exhilaration when he explained to Popish priests that they were to be cut down alive and were to see their own bowels burned, than when he passed ordinary sentences of death."

Nothing like burning a few Catholic guts to bring good color to the cheeks, except burning a few Presbyterians or Baptists. Or homosexuals or abortionists, or whatever else is seen to be evil.

Jeffreys did not get to butcher many Quakers. The king considered them harmless but this did not impede the campaign against assorted other Protestants.

It is now thought the chief justice was not a good man. O wind of fashion! Once his courtroom was full of sobs for a man being condemned. The chief justice called the spectators "snivelling calves." Once a young woman fell on her knees for the life of her sweetheart, but she was dismissed with an oath "so hideous" that Macaulay declined to print it.

Another woman who for all we know was not even a Presbyterian, Baptist or Catholic was ordered to be whipped through the streets, a disagreeable business, but the chief justice always tried to lighten things:

"Hangman, I charge you to pay particular attention to this lady. Scourge her soundly, man. Scourge her till the blood runs down. It is Christmas, a cold time for madam to strip in! See that you warm her shoulders thoroughly."

These excesses of zeal in the chief justice sprang from religious enthusiasm, of course. Extremism in the cause of virtue is sometimes thought to be no vice.

I hate to leave the Quakers out. Thomas Jefferson noted that in Virginia there had been no religious persecution to speak of since everybody who came in 1607 was Anglican. Puritans did not venture there. It's true, Jefferson said in his "Notes on Virginia" that it was once Virginia law that a Quaker could not live in the state. He'd be jailed until he was ready to leave, and if he came back three times he'd be killed. The main reason people were not executed in Virginia for religion was that there was only one faith.

Anglicans, however, became lax, since they ran everything, and eventually the other opinions crept in. By 1776 two-thirds of the people in Virginia were dissenters from the Episcopal Church, Jefferson said. Before anybody got round to tending to these dissenters, however, the church was disestablished.

Although things looked fine for freedom of religion in his day ("I doubt whether the people of this country would suffer an execution for heresy or a three-years' imprisonment for not comprehending the mysteries of the Trinity"), still the day could come when crimes were once again committed to help God, Jefferson feared:

"The spirit of the times may alter—will alter. Our rulers will become corrupt, our people careless. . . . They will be forgotten, therefore, and their rights disregarded."

We have come a way since Jefferson. You can hardly imagine him buddy-buddy with Billy Graham like some recent presidents or cozying up to Jerry Falwell; partly because he had a taste for brains and brilliance, and partly because he thought a nation had problems enough without the president scratching backs with sectarian heroes.

There is the argument that we do not send an ambassador to the Roman Catholic Church but to the Vatican state.

It's not a church, don't you see, but a force in world affairs. Before whom Hitler and Stalin trembled, you recall.

Besides, until we establish full diplomatic presence, our man at the Vatican gets no respect. Real ambassadors from other countries go ahead of him at receptions and gobble up all the cucumber sandwiches, while he's still arguing with the hall porter to get in.

Of course, in a non-Roman way, the institution of the prayer breakfast has become familiar to America. It is a grand forum for a president to pietate for the cameras and for the breakfasters to drool at their closeness to power. The breakfasts under Nixon and Carter were enough to curdle cream, some Christians thought, if I may testify to my own experiences at some of them.

We are well past Jefferson now. It may be quite a little jog back to him, too. Of course, there is the shortcut, via Jeffreys. Nothing beats a really lively chief justice for straightening a country out and clearing its thinking. Such a country shapes up quickly. England did after Jeffreys. Mind you, some of the spectacle of Olde England was lost. After 1685 they stopped burning ladies. (January 1984)

Bus Drivers

Nobody wants to read of my life and hard times with the bus system and I would not dream of boring you senseless with my recurring small agonies, no.

I think we could begin by saying the central question faced by this nation since the 18th century is whether a free republic can survive. Which brings us to the city bus system on Massachusetts Avenue.

Briefly—insanely briefly—the situation is this. If you show up at 45th and Massachusetts at 4:29 by your watch, which is two minutes fast, to catch the eastbound bus into town, you will have the joy of seeing 11 buses heading in the right direction, none of which stops to pick you or the other would-be passengers up.

The 12th bus does stop and you board it at 5:11 p.m. Mathematicians will perceive the wait has been 42 minutes. If this occurs on Friday, you do well to wait until Wednesday before inquiring of Metro what's going on. There is no point phoning anybody sooner, because your vocabulary will not have settled down.

You will then speak with several sensible, courteous, helpful people and wind up with the poor guy whose grim job it is to talk with the likes of you.

Three of the buses that sailed by were supposed to stop and pick up passengers, he figured out, even in rush hour. To pay the premium rush-hour fare after waiting nearly an hour for a bus is one of those indignities a human ought not have to endure.

"The problem is," I said, "that you have no way of knowing whether I am telling you the truth or not, because you have no way of knowing what buses ran where when, or whether they stopped or not. Bus drivers know this as well as you and I do, so for reasons of their own they simply do not stop."

Maybe it breaks the routine to drive all the way in without picking up anybody, or maybe there's time (if you speed by without passengers) to catch a beer on the way. Who knows.

Maybe the bus drivers are confused about which ones are supposed to be normal during rush hours, and think they should be Not In Service when in fact they should be?

"No," said the secluded authority at Metro, "they know."

Then—and this brings us to the future of the world as free men have known it—why don't they stop?

"Running a bus system," he said, "means you have to trust the drivers to follow the instructions about picking up passengers along their routes."

"Exactly," I said. "No business can afford (and I might have added that no nation can afford, if I had been in my cosmic mode, as now) to have hundreds of people along all the bus routes checking to see if the buses are running and are picking up passengers. All the same, it drives you bats when none of them are doing the job they're supposed to be doing."

Now the Supreme Court understands that if enough people are determined to break the law, the law is not enforceable, which is why a good bit of legal energy is devoted to enforcing the law even in minor ways, lest everyone get the idea that anything goes. You shortchange the tax collector $25 and the government is quite prepared to hound you through Asia, Africa and the South Pole to make you pay up. (Of course if you owe them a million or two, they may just let it ride.)

The bus drivers inbound on Massachusetts during rush hour know they are not likely to be held accountable for leaving passengers stranded, so if it is more convenient for them, or more fun, they coast right on by, much amused at the flailing arms and straining throats of people at the bus stop.

Theoretically, supervisors or finks could be secretly stationed along the routes to catch the drivers in their sins, and if a big enough deal were made of it, they could be chewed out or even fired.

But this brings us to a crisis of the free society: Is half the population to be conscripted as a sort of Gestapo to keep tabs on the other half?

Metro fares seem high enough as it is. Are they to hire a lot of additional snoops to make sure the drivers are straightening up and flying right?

Surely we have enough big brothers in America without fetching in more to make sure that every American is working his tail off at his job, as all good sturdy Americans are supposed to be doing. Like us grand folk who write columns.

It's said that the Germans and the Japanese are more conscientious than we are, when it comes to doing the jobs they are paid to do. A bunch of rural Tennesseans was actually shipped to Japan to see how factory work is done there, so when they returned to the Volunteer State they could do as well as the lads of Nara. (And my guess is that this was money down the drain, since as a Tennessean I feel we are largely unteachable, and the instant we get home again we start saying waal yass [well, yes] and resume our natal pace.)

And if one reviews the history of the German and Japanese empires in this century, one is not convinced they do everything right and we do everything wrong. There is more to be thought of, in a nation, than efficiency and obeying orders.

As a poet said, "There lives the dearest freshness deep down things." In common words we may say there is something glorious in many Americans who will die rather than take certain orders, and who will suffer beyond belief to defend liberty. I often notice this in myself.

The solution to the perils facing America, and to the bus schedules inbound on Massachusetts in particular, cannot consist merely of hiring more snoops, hiring more disciplinarians and establishing the death penalty for drivers who do not pick you up when they are supposed to. (I have given prayerful thought to this matter, and think it a close decision, but I believe execution is not the answer, however reasonable it seems on the surface.)

As the Metro executive said—and I suppose he careens about the capital in a limousine with driver—you have to trust drivers to do the job they're paid for.

In many centuries before our own, men have debated whether society can exist at all if men are free; if they are not coerced. The clear weight of authority has always been that such a society cannot exist, that fairly soon the humans composing that society will strike out for their own interests, their own convenience, and say to hell with the rest of the society.

There have been a few dissenting voices. Jefferson, for example, thought a free society could exist, and that we would so treasure its benefits that we would hold together in a sense of common and shared citizenship. Free men, he thought, would see for themselves the wisdom of not going off half-cocked to grab every dime, every hour, every short-term advantage. Free men, he thought, could master that compromise between pleasure and responsibility, between private advantage and public good, and they would do this because they would know how easily freedom may be lost if anarchy prevails.

But this has never been the majority view. It has always been more a dream than a history of mankind. In every generation the question is asked whether Americans are up to the job of a free society, and since the question is asked every generation, we begin to smile at it and say well, people are always asking that, yet the nation survives.

When the question was first asked whether America could survive in the 18th century, it was a good question, not a silly one, and it is a good question now.

Acids and rots are not far to seek. When the republic collapses, we need not hire scholars to find out why. It will be because people waiting 42 minutes at bus stops have had a bellyful of waiting and agitate for a new and more efficient management. And start looking for a man on a white horse (white bus?) to ensure the basic necessities of a complex society, such as transportation, police protection, ample information through the media, etc.

When the nation falls, when tyranny succeeds, when dictators replace presidents, when freedom is lost, I hope the bus drivers on Massachusetts inbound during rush hour will be proud of themselves. It will be they who did it. (June 1984)

Savagery and Science

Death and unalleviated suffering are perfectly acceptable in both humans and animals—even in your favorite hound—on occasion.

Not that those are desirable things, but when they are unavoidable they do not raise feelings of disgust. Thus an old bleeding heart like me has had no trouble at all being first on the scene when young men died in car accidents. It was not pleasant, but it was neither disgusting nor traumatic to pull one of them away from his truck where the gasoline was pouring down on him. He died a few minutes later, and anyone would feel a surge of grief at a life cut short, *senselessly*, as we would say.

But disgust and rage are absent.

Neither is there cause for rage when kids accidentally let your favorite hound out of his yard and he is hit by a car as you watch, and you pick him up and on the way to the vet's he struggles over on the seat to rest his head on your lap. No evil attaches to the kids or to the driver that hit him or the vet that tried to save him. The emptiness remains, but it is a condition of having been born in the first place that such events will happen not once or twice but many times and it is simple wisdom to accept them.

It is entirely different, though, if the same death or the same suffering is caused deliberately, for no sane purpose. Savagery is very much part of the nature of all humans I have ever known, and that is one reason civilized nations have gone to such efforts to restrain it or redirect it.

Most of us get through the world without murdering people or pulling wings off birds because we mutually support each other in civilized ways, but it must be a naive human indeed who has not noticed unattractive things in himself.

If we somehow miss that back-and-forth exchange with the civilized world, however, or if our laws, courts, government officials and so on slide back from civilized standards, then we or any other people allow our natural savagery to come forth, and this tension between what we think we believe and what we really are has always been the main crisis of civilization.

Almost every American, I think, would object strongly to a guy who for the sake of entertainment soaked small cats, or even large ones, in turpentine and set them afire. Civilization has insinuated itself so deeply into the national life that we may be startled to notice how civilized we really are cat-turpentinewise.

If, however, somebody tells us that animals are routinely tortured in laboratories, we do not for a second believe it, and we suppose the messenger is some sort of nut who perhaps is anti-science, or who is so hopelessly sentimental in the worst meaning of the word that we should avoid him in the future.

Most of us believe—though we concede there are various arguments to the contrary—that it is acceptable to conduct experiments on animals when the purpose is to advance medical knowledge, to develop new techniques (burn therapy comes to mind, for surely humans are now alive who even a few years ago would have died from burns before these sophisticated therapies were developed) and to add to serious knowledge generally.

We are convinced the government has set standards for humane treatment of laboratory animals. We believe it is the law that animals may not be tortured for frivolous reasons. We believe scientists are as humane as any other group of ordinary Americans and like the rest of us have known what it is to love a dog.

So we hear with considerable annoyance the repeated and now increasing volume of protest against practices in scientific laboratories with research animals.

At hearings this week by a congressional subcommittee chaired by Rep. George Edward Brown Jr. (D-Calif.) on the subject of legislation to regulate humane methods of research, one view was frequently expressed:

While there may have been one or two widely publicized incidents of heartless treatment in laboratories, by and large the animals are treated with tremendous concern for their sufferings. Especially in laboratories accredited by groups concerned with laboratory animals, it is virtually unheard of for animals to be mistreated, or housed badly, or otherwise made to suffer. And in those researches on animals that necessarily result in pain and death, every effort is made to insure that no animal suffers needlessly, but is given anesthetics or a humane death when recovery is not possible.

This is a highly civilized view. The only trouble with it is that it may be factually wrong.

"What evidence is there, after all, that mistreatment of laboratory animals is a problem in the first place?" This question was repeatedly asked in one form or other during the daylong session in the Longworth House Office Building.

It is a reasonable question. What evidence in fact exists?

There are reports of inspectors sent by the federal government to check routinely in laboratories. What do their reports say?

Well, I have read excerpts from many of them, and I think they say there is vast room for improvement in laboratory practices.

Unfortunately, it takes time and effort to read the reports. It takes some hours even to read the arguments submitted to the Brown hearings.

It takes time to read a report submitted to the regents of the University of California at Berkeley, a damning study of laboratory animals there, a report including interoffice confidential memoranda. It even takes time, and a stronger stomach than I possess, to view the tapes stolen from a laboratory at the University of Pennsylvania, showing primates in research on head injuries.

We by and large do not have the time to explore such questions, which do not concern us in our daily rounds. Since we do not want to hear details, we do not know details, and wind up saying there is no evidence beyond the shrill and perhaps paranoid cries of the few who protest so loudly. We turn our annoyance against the messengers, an easier thing than trying to weigh the facts, which can hardly be weighed without first hearing them.

We neither know nor wish to know the amount of money involved (detailed figures are available and suffice it to say many millions of tax dollars a year go into it) in scientific research involving animals. We do not wish to think of the extent to which researchers and universities rely on such money, and wish it to continue.

We have neither the time nor the expertise to evaluate the usefulness to science of prying a helmet off a baboon with a hammer and screwdriver after the animal, still alive, has been slammed (to use a laboratory world) to simulate the blows received by boxers or car accident victims.

I find myself unwilling to write about unsavory things, when what

I really want to do is relay some enchanting anecdote about the horse in London that was in a bomb explosion but recovered, etc.

If criticism is voiced about lack of anesthetics, or failures even worse, will this not be interpreted as sentimental anger against science and research altogether? And God knows nobody wants to read it any more than a writer wants to write it, so usually the thing is unsaid and unheard and we wind up saying there is no evidence.

There is evidence and it is sickening. Legislation is needed, and those who do not wish to concern themselves with what amounts to flamboyant sadism should at least have the grace not to obstruct the long hard thankless labors of those who have not shied from the evidence and who have at last come up with reasonable and moderate legislation. Which does not restrict any laboratory experiment, however painful or fatal, beyond requiring minimally humane methodology. It is inconceivable there can be objections.

It is also worth pointing out that the University of California and the University of Pennsylvania are not two-bit institutions. If laboratory abuses can occur there, they can occur anywhere, simply because humane care of animals takes time and money and careful administration—things always in short supply.

The tapes stolen (stealing is an important crime, needless to say) from the University of Pennsylvania lab were originally to have been shown in the Longworth Building, but governmental objections prevailed and they were shown at St. Mark's Church. I sat still for about five minutes of them, noticing the rather pretty windows over the altar full of angels making music. The tapes were shown a few feet in front of the altar, though the site is irrelevant. The language of the laboratory experimenters ("he's going to bite your . . . ," etc.) is excusable on the grounds that what was being done would naturally arouse anxiety and be reflected in words appropriate for uneasy men.

All the same, I left, thinking it probably an esthetic error to vomit in a sanctuary. (September 1984)

What Men Want for Christmas

You have noticed they never advertise on television anything you want. Unless you are a connoisseur of pills, toilet paper and soap that will make you irresistible in six easy washings.

The trouble with Christmas is not that there's too much stuff, or that it all costs too much. No sir, the trouble is that nobody wants it much.

I know you have to get undershorts and socks, but even if you put a big red bow on them (on the package) they are not going to make anybody squeal.

Female coresidents commonly say male coresidents are hard to buy for. It is true we can use only so many socks. Women think men adore mufflers, but they don't, and they don't like ties, either, at least not the ones women pick out. It would be interesting to know where they get their atrocious taste in ties.

This time of year you see all those shopping guides to tell you what to buy and where to buy it. They never suggest anything of the slightest interest. Usually they are all in a lather about some damned pot in Annandale that only costs $46. No wonder so many kooky little businesses go bankrupt.

Here is what to buy for a guy like me, and other men, I imagine, who are equally sensible:

Weathercocks. When properly mounted they turn in the least hint of wind. I have two, one an eagle and one a carp. They are copper. I need two because they point in different directions usually, because of lousy things like trees that deflect the wind. When they point the same way, as they do in a gale, it is very reassuring.

Sheet copper. An ideal gift. You can look at the sheet for some months before deciding just what to do with it. It is good to keep under the bed so from time to time you can pull it out and dream.

Sheet lead is grand. I once made a 20-foot fish pool out of it. It bends easily and is hammered to shape in no time. You can also hammer it around a wastebasket, put the wastebasket back, and strengthen your lead vessel with a lining of concrete, and then you can plant valerian in it for the garden.

Horse troughs. These are called stock tanks nowadays. They are galvanized steel. You paint them black outside and set them on the ground near where you sit outdoors. Goldfish or any carp do well in them if you put in enough seaweed, which you get at an aquarium or out of a stream.

Lath. Not lousy lath (though that is better than nothing) but one-by-two-inch clear pine. You can nail it together in squares and paint it black and it will last forever.

Dowels. I have never known anybody who used dowels and never known anybody who did not long for some. You can sometimes get a whole bag of them in different sizes and lengths. You never know when you will need one urgently.

Two-inch plank a foot wide and as long as you can afford. In my times I have had several such planks. Few things have given me more joy.

Telephone wire. This may not be the right name for one of the world's most desirable objects, but what I mean is copper wire covered with rubber, about a quarter-inch in diameter and usually gray. It is ideal for tying things outside. Once some linemen left about 30 feet of it in the alley and I parcel it out on various jobs like sapphires. I am now out. There must be some place you can buy it.

Tarred twine. The place I got mine was at Wisley, Ripley, Surrey, England. Not much is used but it has a smell rather as I suppose heaven smells. It could be kept in a bureau drawer to confine the fragrance.

Bale of hay. This stuff goes to pieces no matter how gently you handle it and should not be kept in the house. It is very good to have in a shed. On a dirt floor, it is lovely to walk on.

Rat poison. I asked the president of an internationally celebrated humane outfit the best way to kill rats. You can't shoot them in town, though I imagine that is the most humane way. He said he didn't really know but took my address, but never wrote. I am not going to put up with rats; on the other hand I don't want to dispatch them with agony. You are going to have rats if you have bird feeders or tomatoes or an empty garage. I get the kind that comes six boxes to a package and spend roughly $20,000 a year for it. A most useful gift.

Bricks. They used to cost two cents each, now more. I had a friend who once bought 10,000 to play with but his wife looked at them and hired a man to lay a new front walk and cover the floor of the front porch, with none left over. He was too embarrassed to buy any more. Except when one comes loose from the walk, he has none to carry around the yard on Saturdays.

Buckets. Few things raise the heart like a shiny new pail, but the ones I covet (they are not all that cheap) are black rubber. You can feed calves from them.

Dormant clematis vines. Sometimes in December you can find these at garden centers in gallon cans. Nothing in creation looks deader than a clematis resting for the winter, so sometimes you can get them for half price. December is the ideal month for planting them, much better than spring, when they charge an arm and a leg. Even at half price they cost too much but what doesn't. I like old Nelly Moser best. Never have enough of her.

Cedar shavings. You have to pay for this stuff now, a clear sign of collapse at the foundation of the state. If you get a small bale, you can take some out and stuff something with it for the dog and keep the rest in your clothes closet with church shoes. They cost too much but smell better than other shoes.

Four-by-four posts 10 feet long. Has anybody ever had enough of these? They are much better than those little Erector sets kids used to get. Be sure they are pressure treated.

Cut stone. I have rarely met a stone I didn't love, provided it's cut clean. How disgusting random paving is. My front walk is great hunks of slate in random sizes, but when I am rich I shall buy rectangular slabs of fieldstone. Sometimes I buy just a one-square-foot piece of particularly nice color and personality and mortar it atop a small brick pier (you see how valuable bricks are, they go with everything).

Lanterns. I go fairly to pieces for lanterns, as I do for hinges, rabbit wire and Persian tiles. They all make me feel God is up there. I have a Coleman that needs a new mantle. How wonderful a Dietz is. When I was a kid they had Aladdins at the farmhouse Aunt Marie spent the summer at. You can blow yourself up if you don't know what you're doing, but what else is new. Miners' lanterns of brass can sometimes be got for peanuts in England where, alas, many miners have been thrown out of work and mines closed down. I will not pay more than $16 for a good one. I already have one and need no more, but there is not a man alive who wouldn't steal for one.

I never knew anybody easier to please than myself or the guys I know. Somebody once gave us an old Meissen soup tureen that thrilled my wife witless for a month. It is lovely and was most generous and I like to see people happy, but my God, do you have any idea how much rabbit wire you could buy? (December 1984)

When a Little Girl Dies

I'm not sure silence is the best response to a brutal accident in which a little girl is suffocated when her clothes catch in the maw of a subway escalator.

The horror is reported, and in an effort to avoid the macabre, I guess, the account gives you only the most shapeless picture of the event. The point of the report was simply to say death came to a child in a bizarre way on an escalator, and that nobody seems to be at fault.

These things are easier to take if we can point to the subway system and growl that every safety feature known to man was skimped on. As it happens, however, those escalators are already the slowest in the entire world.

As far as anybody knows, no blame attaches to the subway system. And as far as we can tell, no blame goes to the grandmother, either, who was with the child. Nobody is to blame, evidently, but how can that be, when an innocent happy little kid is dead?

Usually by the age of 12 we arrange not to think of the question that keeps coming up, why is life so woven with horror?

Everybody knows about the little sea turtles that hatch off the coast of Queensland and race from the beach to the warm sea, decimated (torn apart, living) by hungry sea birds. This one dies and that one lives, and while at first we are horrified and do not understand it, we come by the age of 12, as a rule, to the conclusion the hungry birds have to eat and this is Nature's way of feeding them. As if that answered anything.

Any fool can see that "Nature's way" is hideous, but we cannot take ourselves out of nature, despite endless good tries. We say there is a balance, a kind of dance or a kind of round, by which it all comes full circle. Not that that explains anything, either, or answers what I assume is everybody's objection to the fate of the baby turtle.

But that happens to animals, so it need not be thought of, once the wretchedness of the arrangement is seen and dismissed.

Horror in the human world may be deflected a little if we concentrate on the tragedy by which a basketball team loses 50-52, or the allegedly frightful pain of some nitwit divorcing another or some tragic heroine who has broken a shoulder strap.

We focus on trifles because trifles are no trouble. I never knew a divorced person yet who didn't continue to eat like a horse and talk your ears off.

But then something really hard to deal with hits. Maybe a kid killed in a car crash, maybe an old woman raped by a punk. These cannot be brushed aside so easily as the tragedy of a heel coming off in the receiving line. Even so, there is usually somebody or something to blame fiercely, which makes it better.

If there is enough to be outraged about we can get things in balance by screaming for the criminal's head and avoid much of the horror of the event.

It never gets in balance again, does it, when a little girl dies horribly, without even the warning of a long illness (in which we could thank her deliverance from pain) and with nobody to blame at all.

Why a child is lost in a terrible way is a question wrangled over since time began, but Job never got an answer, or any better answer than the command to shut up, since his mind and heart were not up to comprehending ultimates. And one reason the Psalms have always been loved so much is for pointing out the pain of the just and the fat rewards of the wicked. Yet they offer no answer, either, beyond the assurance it will all be fixed at the last. To believe this you may need three martinis more than a reasonable faith.

Still, if you say there's nothing but random accident and blood, you haven't got any closer to an answer. You're not where you want to go.

If I ever find an answer, I hope to have enough brains to know it's the wrong one. If there were no answers for Job or the psalmists it's not likely I'll get the news that makes all things clear.

The real reason it hits us like a brick, when it's an escalator and a kid, is that we there see horror clean and pure, not veiled or clouded by the necessity of birds to eat or men to fight for ideals or drunks on the highway. The horror of those things we can push away by blaming somebody, but pure horror cannot be pushed and must be endured.

Ancient Egyptians thought righteousness was a talisman to carry you through fire and Socrates thought nothing bad can happen to a good man. But what chance have you got, when horror descends not only on good men like Job or Socrates but on a small girl?

The question is there, the answer is not, and we're supposed to be content knowing we are not going to get some thing we want. The question is no longer to find the answer—that was given up ages ago—but how to live without one. One of the good poets thought about it and got hot and told God off and grew more wild at every word, without feeling all that much better. And he thought he heard a voice say, "Child," and he said back, "My Lord." (February 1985)

French Studies

Take French. Say you have to "study" it two or three years to get out of college, and say you're an average kid at an average college. Here is the issue:

What is the difference, if any, between being ignorant of French formally (having studied it as a degree requirement) and being ignorant of French informally (having never studied it at all)?

Practical people and bottom-liners say there is no difference: If you can't speak French or read it easily and if you have never read Jean Rostand or even Montaigne, then you might as well not have bothered with French to begin with.

Everybody agrees you need a supersensitive Geiger counter to detect the slightest surge in a guy who has just finished college. When he entered he registered 6 on the scale, and when he finished he registered 6.04378.

Before he started French he knew how to say *mademoiselle* and could grin and grunt well enough to accomplish a little, and when he finished he knew Mérimée wrote the lousiest novels in any Indo-European language, and could say both *formidable* and *Eure et Loire* with a comprehensible accent. But this is a major gain?

Yes. It is a major gain.

It is very like shaving when you get up in the morning. You haven't made yourself gorgeous, you haven't even improved your appearance worth speaking of, but you have completed a tribal rite, you have saluted the herd, and if you doubt how valuable this is, you have only to observe a guy who has taken a train across India then a plane flight to Dulles. He is fit to be tied for no better reason than he has not shaved.

So is college a tribal ritual? Well, it beats spending five years in a long house, to absorb by osmosis the sacred values of the tribe. That is the custom in other primitive societies, and the main thing to be said for their way of doing things is it's not as cold in the winter as Yale. But in other ways, no better.

Nowadays, of course, there is this new notion that you should learn things in college, and at least begin the mastery of some subject.

Vigorously resisted, this notion has yet made headway in physics departments and football squads. Athletes are sometimes laughed at by eggheads, who think jocks are not much better than computer programmers or seminarians.

But jocks have an unarguable advantage over the typical liberal arts "student." The guy who plays football actually has firsthand experience of his subject and has spent enough hours at it to understand it in some depth. A man who has wound up playing right tackle for Sultry State has become a moderate authority on football even if nobody to speak of ever heard of his team.

He differs considerably from the guy who has glazed his way through economics and sociology without the least idea what is going on. Old die-hards complain of the lack of intellectual content in Home Repair 101 and History of Boiled Water (Neanderthal through Nader). But there is no greater intellectual content in Age of Jackson (Andrew) or Rise of the Carolingian Empire if the student declines to engage, as he usually does.

One would not wish to be sexist here. Take a woman who refuses to put rice in water and another who tries and makes the usual mess. No decent rice in either case. But the one who has at least been in the presence of rice, however hopeless in avoiding glue, has achieved even in failure what her sister has not.

Who doubts it is better to make a mess of rice than not to try? The wretched cook can look back at a life of stress and anguish, no more than that, but isn't it better than looking back at a complete blank?

So in the studies of college. The French student does not learn French, the geology kid can barely tell a brain coral from a gastropod, and you could argue college was a waste of time.

He did learn "gastropod." The rest of his life he can say, "You stinking gastropod," which is fresher than "Yeah? Well, up yours, buddy." The difference between 6 and 6.04378. It's not much of a difference but *Vive* It. And when our college product finishes school and get his job pumping gas or whatever (in my case it was chopping cotton for 40 cents an hour) he will have time to ruminate. Things will come back, like sun through a chink, distorted and dazzling. Since most American jobs do not require either thought or a sense of wonder (except how you wound up there) there is leisure at last (for there is none in youth) to pursue some subject in great depth. Some become little-known authorities on the Dandie Dinmont, neglected prince of

You need a supersensitive Geiger counter to detect the slightest surge in a guy who just finished college.

terriers, others on the marvelous variety in rose thorns or sow bugs (rather a little specialty of mine).

The whole point of college courses is that later the guy discovers much about the sow bug, so to speak, though he did not know this was to be his fate when he glassed his way through solid geometry.

Whether French should be required I am not competent to say, but I sense there is something there somewhere. I myself have enjoyed loathing Mérimée novels for some decades, and one night in France I won at bridge though the French do not know the proper names of the suits. *Zut,* sir, and *alors.* (February 1985)

Democracy in Ancient Greece

Naturally we stay in a fairly steady complaint or snarl mode about the American government, but I suppose it is taken for granted life is easier and in innumerable ways better in America than in any other state anybody can think of at any point in the history of the planet.

If we are Democrats we love to fling our arms heavenward and declare we have been delivered to the barbarians; if we are women or black or gay or Jewish or Arab or Catholic we like pointing out discrimination. Our farms are in perilous state, our streets are full of crime, our hospitals kill you, our lawyers and electricians gouge you and the price of cloves is hardly to be believed. Furthermore, it is colder than it should be in March and something should be done about the wind.

In my youth a neighbor, Aunt Frances, who strongly suspected the German Bund was infiltrating everywhere, used to say, and increasingly say as she grew older, that "it should not be permitted," though it was never clear which power in earth or heaven should emit thunderbolts on whatever outrage she was concerned with at the moment.

If she were alive today she'd be a virtual long-playing record.

Is there any American who fails to see things wrong, sometimes outrageously and unnecessarily wrong, with the country or who has failed to notice the American predilection for confusing American interests or even American policy (when it can be detected) with the will of the Almighty?

What annoys me, though it is probably nothing more than an incurable American romanticism (surely we are the only nation that ever existed that starts nostalgia fads for a past decade the instant a new decade begins), is the asinine claim that democracy now is very shaky indeed, compared with some presumed golden age.

It may be a coincidence but I have heard about 10 times in the last year some allusion to the golden age of democracy in 5th-century Greece. Then, you may hear some idiot say, democracy reached heights it never was able to maintain afterwards. Then people were truly free and moreover went to the theater to see plays by Aeschylus and all the men were gods and all the women wore gauze you could see through. Everywhere art and science flourished, zub, zub, zub.

As it happens I thank God I did not have to live in the Athenian democracy, which others seem to have confused with a South Seas fantasy or with paradise itself.

America for all her blunders succeeded early in holding together an empire far greater than the Greek, and in comprehending early what the Greeks never were able to conceive or effectuate—a union of states.

The history of Greece, at her greatest, is a history of continual war among brothers. Gaithersburg was continually marching against Falls Church, frequently slaughtering all vanquished males and selling the women and children into slavery.

The vaunted Athenian court, at the height of Greek democracy, executed Socrates, and was forever condemning to death or exiling some great hero of the immediate past. If you won an astounding victory at Marathon or Salamis it did you no particular good; you were soon fleeing for your life like Themistocles, or Alcibiades or Miltiades or any number of others.

The Greeks at their best did not hesitate to attempt unholy deals with their chief enemy, Persia, for some transient advantage over other Greeks, as if Charlottesville applied to Moscow for arms and troops to use against Warrenton.

And as for the vaunted theater, it was admittedly magnificent in a way ours is not; on the other hand the majority of theatergoers in Athens (the very crown of Greece at her best) had as much trouble with irony and satire as audiences today, and from a play like "The Clouds" they remembered nothing except Socrates was a fool. Not quite the intent of the author, but then it was as dangerous in Greece as any-where else to be overly sparkling.

When their history was far advanced, and when it was increasingly clear the only salvation of the empire lay in extending the rights of citizenship to other cities, the dunces of Athens went exactly back-wards and restricted those rights more than formerly. Slaves, of course, never had rights of freemen, no matter how learned, and of course women could not vote, nor residents of Athens who came from outside the city. But at the peak of her glory, Athens decided you could not vote unless both your parents were free Athenians. If your mother was a Thracian princess and your father an Athenian aristocrat, tough luck.

This common dream of a golden Greece has had the effect of obscuring some of the triumphs of Egypt and Persia, but worse than that has served as a never-never land, a veritable cloud-cuckoo-land in the modern imagination to the denigration of the startling glories of the American state.

It is not necessary to think an American president or an American court is the greatest thing since the invention of wheels to notice that even the worst presidents of recent times were a considerable advance over comparable Greek leaders of their greatest century.

They do not—granted—necessarily exceed Pericles in intellect, but they also do not steal all the funds of American allies throughout the world to build billion-dollar shrines to the Republican Party in the capital. For which, considering both official taste and the general level of architecture, we may be thankful.

It is worth remembering that when Adlai Stevenson lost the election neither he nor anybody else wondered if he would be executed on some pretext or other, and this is more than he could have counted on when Greece was at her democratic height.

Undoubtedly the natural wealth of the American empire has much to do with the ease and relative glory of American life today as our system of government, but an incalculable debt is owed to American institutions, too (those blasted bureaucrats are in some ways as precious as infuriating), and much is owed our schools and, for that matter (God save us all) some of our newspapers.

Freedom of speech is far easier here than in the golden age of Greece, so is protest easier and safer, and freedom to move around is greater than a Greek would dream of. The freedom to be let alone (though on bad days we whine pitiably about this) is at an all-time peak.

It's true we may all be blown to hell tomorrow, but that has always been the case, and in the meantime life has never been so easy for so many.

I know people sleep on heating grates and it is all too obvious that not everybody is rich. Things once thought luxuries—enough food to keep your kids from starving, artificial heating in the winter, freedom from arbitrary death at the whim of a governor, freedom to read—are now assumed as the most basic of necessities.

When someone says for a particular emphasis that it is worse for blacks to be ignored than to be lynched, we may see clearly enough the height the American civilization has reached. When the crime imputed to the state is not that one is hanged or denied a vote or denied a chance to compete, but is "ignored."

How fragile the singular state of freedom in America is we may judge from the course of events in our own time in other states; and how perilous a course we are following, trying to avoid anarchy while increasing freedom, anybody knows who has ever juggled seven balls across Niagara. It is breathtaking to see. (March 1985)

Life's Comedy of Errors

The editor in chief was madder than a terrier with a toad when he charged me with conspiracy at 7:30 one morning (in another city, and it was long ago).

"Mitchell, don't try to fool *me*. It's a damn conspiracy and I'm going to find out who's behind it. This is the third morning in two weeks we've published the date of Easter wrong."

I was the third, needless to say. We ran corrections all through Lent about the date of Easter that year. The reason was understandable and I won't go through the whole litany, except to say there was no conspiracy. Three reporters made the same intelligent (and wrong) inference from material sent by the editor himself.

Which taught me editors are not only occasionally the source of grievous error but also tend to believe reporters are plotting against them. Of course that is not true here, but in many places, and when I was an editor of a magazine in which the name of Clare Boothe Luce was spelled wrong twice by different writers in the same issue, I could only conclude it was a conspiracy to embarrass the editor and bring shame to the publication.

So one way or another I have been rather a connoisseur of errors, and their subsequent (often wrong) corrections for many years. Now a colleague, Sharon Isch, has returned from England with a very fine newspaper correction, as good as any I ever read. It's from a rural newspaper and purports to clarify certain "inaccuracies" in a story about a Mr. Harris:

"After returning from India, he (Mr. Harris) served in Ireland four years and not six months as stated; he never farmed at Heddington, particularly not at Coate Road Farm as stated; he has never counted cycling or walking among his hobbies; he is not a member of 54 hunts, and he did not have an eye removed at Chippenham Hospital after an air raid."

The story, I suspect, was essentially correct.

I once made an error—1949, if memory serves—and feel sympathy for those who write about the Mr. Harrises of the world, except when the correction is breathtakingly dumb, or more offensive than the original blunder. Thus a perfectly enchanting writer once referred to a secretary of state as living, some years after his death, and corrected it by saying she had learned he was "just a teensy bit dead." Which I thought a bit much.

A novelist friend of mine was once referred to as "cohabiting with a goat" in a letters to the editor column of a newspaper. He was on fire to sue everybody top to bottom, but I dissuaded him.

"What are you going to do in court?" I sensibly asked. "Swear on the Bible that you do not cohabit with a goat? And what do you want the correction to say, that you are respectably married and have a pet goat but do not cohabit with it?" This is typical of the outrageous error that can hardly be corrected.

But now for something completely different: I have in my hand a letter from a fellow in New York, John Mosedale, who I imagine is notably amiable and learned. He alludes to a recent comment of mine, that Shakespeare spoke so beautifully of the hound—that is, the basset—whose ears sweep away the morning dew and so forth.

The writer sensed something amiss. When I phoned to ask him to use some of the letter, he said sure, "but of course it's not a correction—you are perfectly right in the beautiful quotation from Shakespeare about the hound."

Yes. But the implication was that supreme types like Shakespeare adored the hound, a thing you might easily conclude from the quotation I used:

"I am the former owner of a truly dreadful dog, now deceased," he writes. "I once described him for a book I wrote as the world's worst animal and he was. So I came up short when I read your mention of Shakespeare's singing vividly of the beauty of the hound.

"That is perfectly true. But I blame part of my problems with Bounce, for such was his name, on my paying insufficient attention to Shakespeare, the patron of the world as you say; the name of one of our redeemers as Anthony Burgess says, and a man for whom no human epithet is enough, in the phrase of Edna O'Brien.

"Too little attention, for Shakespeare warned us. He hated dogs as he hated the stink and sweat of London. As Caroline Spurgeon notes in 'Shakespeare's Images,' it was the habit in Elizabethan times to have dogs which were chiefly of the spaniel and greyhound type, at table, licking the hands of the guests, fawning and begging for sweetmeats, which they were fed, and of which if they were like dogs today they ate

I have been rather a connoisseur of errors and their subsequent (often wrong) corrections for many years.

too many, dropping them in a semi-melting condition all over the place.

"So we have Caesar attack 'low-crooked court'sies and base spaniel fawning.' We have Hotspur speak of Bolingbroke as 'this fawning greyhound,' and Antony crying 'Villains . . . you fawn'd like hounds' and in 'Twelfth Night' we heard of 'fell and cruel hounds.'

"Indeed, in 39 hound images, Miss Spurgeon found Shakespeare on the side of hounds and hunters only once. . . .

"I figure if I had just paid more attention to Shakespeare I might have had better luck with Bounce."

Well, what the hell did Shakespeare know about hounds? Not much.

Even so, I concede that one nice pat does not a hound-worshiper make, and I apologize for unintentionally misleading anybody about Shakespeare's true (and revolting) distaste for those princes of the faunal kingdom.

It would be all right to go up one side of Shakespeare and down the other for his dislike of hounds. It is not all right to select a unique line of praise about hounds and imply that this was Shakespeare's view of the lovely dog.

This all resulted partly from lapse of memory and partly from my charity. When Shakespeare says snotty things about hounds, I ignore them for I am a kindly man and think anybody is entitled to be flat wrong in some passing comment.

This is not altogether, or precisely, the same as a writer's hearing what he wants to hear. But somewhat. And somewhat more than I am proud of.

When I think of mischief, I think it rarely comes from saying Mr. Harris was a member of 54 hunts. More often it is from implying unintentionally that Shakespeare loved hounds when in fact he hated them.

And yet you see what a project it is to correct even this simple misleading item. A writer really has to be virtually a supernatural genius to avoid error, and sometimes we, or at least I, slip slightly. Let's see, now, 1949, and now 1985. (May 1985)

Surviving English Food

"It's true," said all the folk of England about the time of Christ, "that for a long time the food of England was atrocious. Unimaginative. Overcooked, and desperately lacking in variety. But since the Romans came all that has changed, and now, sir, we fancy that nowhere in Europe does one eat better than in this island."

The English have always said this, and say it now.

"Ever since the Saxons came . . ."

"Ever since the Danes . . ."

"Ever since the Normans . . ."

"Ever since Waterloo . . ."

"Ever since the Common Market . . ."

The American traveler to England need have no fear that things are changed. It is still the only realm in Christendom in which the roast beef is still thin, still cooked to purple-brown and still inedible, though now it basks beneath vermilion lights until it is carved, and they give the illusion that once the stuff had blood in it. Once on the plate, however, it is the same soft mealy leather that once shod Queen Guinevere.

They have learned to eat avocados recently, and these come from Spain or Africa or some such place, and the English have not yet learned how to get inside them and ruin them before they reach the table. Their ingenuity is great, however, and already they have learned to mash the avocados up with sugar and run them through a baby-food machine to produce the familiar bright-green slime they call "pudding." You squeeze lime juice on top.

So vast have the dietary novelties become that they also now stuff the avocados with shrimps, taking normal care to see to it the shrimps are pale and utterly tasteless and the avocados are on the hard side, and the dish inundated with pink sauce.

The pink sauce is very like the yellow sauce except it is less tenacious. There is something they leave out of the pink, perhaps boiled hooves, so the pink is very like mayonnaise thinned with tap water, but the mayonnaise has no eggs, oil, or lemon juice in it.

The yellow, which goes on all fish and chicken dishes, illustrates what happens when the English get hold of a bechamel sauce and try to adapt it to the requirements of an island race. They take three pounds of flour, a quart of water (I approximate their formula but am not far off, since, man and boy, I have eaten for the better part of a century now and am not easily fooled about food) and boil it for an hour or so, then set it aside. When lukewarm they add two ounces of plain gelatin, four ounces of yellow food dye and put it back on the stove to simmer the balance of the day or until it is time to enshroud deeply whatever lies beneath.

They have a way of mounding this sauce up like a melon mold (the sauce will hold any shape if you slap it firmly with wooden paddles) and will hold its heat almost indefinitely. If properly aged in its cooking pot, it becomes almost as chewy as melted cheese, with the great advantage of having no flavor. The English think flavors are vulgar and primitive, maybe even French.

Inside their houses they eat well, in my experience, and I speak only of the ordinary English restaurant of genteel pretension. The only safe dessert, or pudding, in the entire kingdom is fresh fruit imported from sunny places and untouched by an English cook. Beware of anything native that includes gooseberries, currants or pastry. Smile firmly and say your religion requires you to eat only grapes and peaches straight out of the field. Otherwise they will think of something clever to do with them like stewing them in treacle and glopping them daintily with custard and cream.

Now their cream is far better than ours because we do not have cream in America. Instead of Jerseys and cows that produce cream, we have something else, and what comes out of our cows is the main reason sensible people never touch American milk or "cream" once they are weaned.

The English have real cream, and you get it not only in Cornwall and Devon (never make the mistake of calling Cornish cream Devonshire cream; the Cornish do not lightly forgive you if you confuse the two virtually identical creams) but throughout England.

A cream tea consists of two biscuits of gross size, such as they have for breakfast in Nebraska, with a pot of strawberry jam and a pot of tea and plenty of cream that has to be spooned out since it does not pour. This is a very good thing, and has sustained many Americans for weeks on end. They call these tasteles large biscuits scones. Fruit scones, which sound festive and cost a good bit more when acquired from the fashionable purveyor in London, are the same thing, only with dried currants in them, and are a dead loss.

Bacon is what we call Canadian bacon, and the English know how to find it with a wide slab of pure fat on the edge. They cook it limp. The usual breakfast sausage is the banger, and anybody used to Jones or Gwaltney sausage will go to some lengths to avoid bangers after a couple of trials.

They also have tomatoes for breakfast. Sometimes they are oval tomatoes that come in cans. When these appear at breakfast, you lift them to a butter plate and ask for them to be taken away somewhere. It takes about five days for the English to learn you are not going to eat tomatoes, then they stop bringing them.

They have excellent butter, much of it from Denmark I am told. English toast is like ours, only they serve it in toast racks to ensure it is stone-cold. In that kingdom I always put a dinner roll in my pocket at night and eat it with a glass of hot water in the morning before descending to breakfast. The hard dinner rolls are good and perhaps come from Paris.

They have better coffee in public places than we do. American coffee has not been fit to drink since the Depression, which was the period in which it was learned very few Americans will send the coffee back, no matter how dreadful. The result is that throughout America you can spend half a dollar to a dollar for undrinkable coffee, but it is better in England. This is partly because they have two or three good powdered instant coffees, but it will do you no good to write the manufacturer (we wrote Nestle, for example) since the drinkable instant coffees are not sold in the American market, but only the dismal product known to us all.

Food shops such as that at Harrods have excellent things in the way of cold meat pies. Ideally you rent an apartment in London and buy stuff at Harrods. If you are in a hotel of less than grand luxe you cannot very well feed yourself, and should shop carefully for a good Italian restaurant. The Indian restaurants of London are famous and if you like them, there they are.

They do not comprehend the salad in England. You should order a half-head of lettuce and a bowl, with a vial of olive oil and vinegar. Otherwise they will put a terrible sauce on it. You should carry a small shaker of powdered garlic in your pocket at all times. If you order chicken and they say "salad with it?" and you say yes, you will get two leaves of wilted lettuce, two slices of greenish-rose tomatoes, one radish, and two slices of cucumber with a strangely acidulous liquid over it. This is possibly the North Sea oil one hears of nowadays.

The best cheese in England is farm or country cheddar. They like Double Gloucester and Stilton, but if you should want a blue cheese you must ask for Roquefort and make sure it really is Roquefort. Stilton is only good if you pack it in a crock and fill it up with good port and eat it on winter nights with walnuts.

English potatoes are vastly better than ours, which is not saying much, since almost anything is better than the American potato. Since the sun never emerges in England, potato vines do not grow much, and tiny potatoes are always available. Always get them boiled. English french fries are much like our own, only more limp and slightly worse.

The fortunate traveler in England, with dinner roll and garlic powder in his pocket, some meat pies from Harrods, some cheese from France, some cherries from Italy and grapes from Spain, with plenty of olives in jars and an occasional roast of lamb (splendid throughout England), some French beans and plain boiled cauliflower, bread from a carefully chosen bakery—provisioned thus, the American traveler will survive admirably, hardly aware he is in the Land of the Yellow-Pink Sauce and the Loathsome Bottled Plum. (July 1985)

Dragonflies

There is a mystery in human endeavor. Digging daffodil bulbs is a mystery. You do this in July while frying eggs on the bricks. You cannot do it in June, which up here is cold and you have to wear a shirt. You cannot do it in September when fall is in the air and it's nice out there.

You have to do it in July when even the catfish sweat, because that is the time when the roots have died back and before the new ones have sprouted. But no matter how well you like daffodils, you think (crumbling the dirt and fanning through every cubic centimeter of it with your hands) it really is too hot to dig. And yet it must be done. The bulbs can sit there only so many years before they weaken and have to be separated and given a new chance.

After a long time digging I sat down by the fish pool to continue my valuable research of many years on Known Goldfishes. The small one with the white mouth and two rosy spots was all right. But why does he never attend the first sitting? You feed them raw oatmeal, of course, and it's a mystery why some of the fish rise instantly to feed, but others never come up. You wait a few minutes and put some more oatmeal in, and the second-sitting gang arises, and the white and rosy one partakes of the second feeding.

It's not that the biggest show up first or second. I cannot see any reason why some eat sooner and some later, but I have noticed the pattern. What a mystery. Which is why I continue my valuable research. Thus far this consists of feeding them oatmeal. It takes 50 years or so, like Jane Goodall and her wild chimpanzees, to get the feel of things; you don't just go barging in if you're working on Known Goldfishes, and in doing research you let the beasts get used to you. One of the disappointments of goldfish research is that the fish sometimes die after 10 years before your spectacular projects (the ratio of ginrin scales to missing scales in Big Pearly from 1971 to 1985) have got properly underway.

And then there's El Salvador and Lebanon and the First Colon; so many things going wrong in the world we are disheartened. And one's own research goes so slowly—the life so short, the craft so long to learn. And one's faith is so often shaken, as mine was this week when a hornet stung me on the eyebrow. I used to kill bugs until some potter friends of mine had a party once where some Indian potters were present with nose veils to keep from accidentally slaughtering some tiny bug accidentally breathed in.

At the time my wife questioned whether this was nonsense. Not while the Indians could hear, of course; that would have been unspeakably crude, but a few minutes later when she said religion can be carried too far by half. And precisely at that point (the drinks were in pottery mugs because potters do not have glasses to drink out of) she swallowed a cockroach. He had been hiding in the bottom of the pottery tumbler when the drink was poured in, in the kitchen, and probably thought he had hit land just in the nick. My wife, who does not go around screaming to the world, excused herself, got to the bathroom and one way and another got the animal out of her throat, but not before the bug had scratched her throat pretty bad.

This shows you should not say anybody's religious notions are absurd. If she had worn a mouth veil it would have been better. You can always learn from other cultures.

But to get on, I resolved not to slaughter God's creatures like bugs, and though more afraid of wasps than lions, I decline to kill them. The year the yellow jackets built a megacity at the base of a bush on the front walk, I never hurt a one and they never hurt me. So I figured my reputation with dirt daubers and hornets and so forth was pretty sound. One year I didn't even bother a hornet nest the size of a basketball that I walked under all the time at American University.

This hornet I speak of, however, came barreling out of a large viburnum while I was digging a hole nearby and stung me just below the eyebrow. This is international politics, this is man's place in the cosmos. You do good, you refrain from violence, and bam, the hornet gets you the same as if you never wished him well. Soda paste is best, by the way, just baking soda and water, spread on thick. The pain abates and you have time to think beautiful thoughts while awaiting death. It takes 10 days for the swelling to go all the way down.

So there you are, musing on the mystery of things, and how nothing is easy and the righteous suffer and wondering when the poor president will be able to eat Grape Nuts again and maybe the goldfish need some more oatmeal and you really ought to get back to digging the bulbs no matter how hot it is because it's not every day you have Time to Do It.

Clear out all the stuff in the head and just watch and not dig or sweat or do anything at all.

Is this all that life is about? One halfway effort after another, one minor anxiety after another, interrupted by an occasional hornet who has not even bothered to learn who his friends are.

Is this the world? Behind schedule on the bulbs, worrying about the president and running out of oatmeal. The mind is a cloud of anxiousness, the center is not firm nor the direction clear. You should head right in to one thing at a time and not let the cloud form. Do something about it or else dismiss it entirely.

This, I now think, was the glory of primitive man. I don't think he let the slow progress of his goldfish research bother him; and he probably encountered the usual ration of hornets without thinking one way or another what his relationship with them was, or how he should modify it.

Musing thus—and possibly I did doze for a second, or perhaps lost consciousness briefly from the burden of profound reflection—my eyes sprang open suddenly; and behold, a cloud of dragonflies was jerking about over the surface of the pool. They have not got grain one of brains. Some of them were laying eggs (despite what you may read, they can lay eggs just hovering over the water, not hanging on to a reed or anything) and others were coupling in flight, and others were zooming around reversing direction like a woman who is halfway to the car but only halfway and darts back because the stove may be on or the dog door may not be locked.

They don't make noise when they fly. They stop on a millimeter of air and they sparkle like pearls that have somehow caught the trick of diamonds. They are more ancient than almost anything and more beautiful than seems reasonable.

You can watch them for quite a spell. You could reach out and touch them. Unlike the chimpanzees and the goldfish you don't need half a century to get them used to you. They don't give a damn about you one way or another.

And I saw clearly, for a change, that this is the world. This is man's role, even more than to worry about everything, even more than to get some more oatmeal, even more than to complete the great work on Known Goldfishes.

Just to sit there and clear out all the stuff in the head and just watch and not dig or sweat or do anything at all except marvel.

Is this what seven millennia of civilization come to? All the wars, all the science, all the love and learning and lore so painfully collected— as chipmunks accumulate—over the centuries?

Sure. It comes to dragonflies on a summer's day. You watch them as they are flying. It's all there is and it comes to you in one second, it's all there's room for and all there ought to be. (July 1985)

What Love Is About

I've read that you "almost" wish they'd die, when you care for the desperately sick, and I've thought this is a pretty example of American baloney. We "almost" wish they'd die.

With a higher murder rate than the rest of the civilized world—probably because we are not very civilized—we might suspect that more Americans wish death on others than do the citizens of, say, Holland or Norway.

Given this national statistic of plain murder, it is unlikely that when faced with the inevitable and prolonged death of the grievously ill, we should suddenly reform and desire indefinite life for them. And we do not.

I know little of other countries but a good bit about America, and I suspect it is the worst place to be dying. Here people do not like to say they have cancer for the simple reason they have noticed (and taken part in) the American distaste for the weak, and they know they'll be written off long before they die in fact.

Americans are like that pope who could not motor through parts of an Indian metropolis because it pained him so to see the poor and the helpless. Of course sensitivity is increasingly prized in America and soon we shall all be like the princess who could feel the pea through six mattresses.

There are those who flame up when they see cruelty, but not many do, and those who fight when they see death, but in general in America we simply turn away from both, taking another route.

You would never have the slightest glimmering, reading a daily paper, that people are dying all around us, in pain and wretchedness. Friends of decades simply tune out; even sons and daughters do. Those who are dying usually have no great right to complain, since they never bothered with the sick, either, when they were healthy, any more than they bothered with the poor or the prisoners. They were all prelates in their time, routing their cars and their lives through agreeable neighborhoods, and most of them, in their own time of despair, know too much to expect other humans to give a damn.

Almost always, however, somebody cares for the sick in America. I don't mean hospitals, which is not my subject, and where care is usually quite brief and well paid for.

I mean those who care for the sick long-term. I knew a woman who cared for a paralyzed husband for 15 years—he was supposed to die the second night of his illness, according to great specialists flown in for the occasion—at what cost I do not care to think.

It is one thing to grieve and get it over with—an enriching and not entirely disagreeable experience, which accounts for our popular delight in other people's terminations of one kind or another, preferably sudden and preferably out of print and out of mind within two days.

It is something else again to hold the spoon, empty the pan, listen to the bitching for 15 years. Such a person, in my observation, does not "almost" wish the patient would die, but prays for it with active fervor.

In the care of the sick, as in virtually every other endeavor, those who know most about it, and who are most faithful and effective in their labor, are not usually those who have the prettiest thoughts and the prettiest sentiments.

In America, where the influence and effect of public glop must be greater than anywhere else, from the White House through the media through the marrow of our bones, we attach incredible importance to how we feel and what our consciousness is. We believe, either secretly or openly, that if we feel good we're on the right track—like those morons who used to think the smell of roses would cure everything.

The smell of roses cures nothing. Taking another route through Calcutta cures nothing. Feeling compassionate and loving to the unfortunate and the sick cures nothing and achieves nothing, beyond the commonly false glow of feeling just great.

What counts—and in this alone the Puritans were always right—is will and a fire that won't go out, and a remarkable capacity for boredom and unpleasantness. Naturally, it came easier for a Puritan, to whom luxurious modes were unfamiliar to begin with and whose aptitude for pleasure was surprisingly slight.

Still, in many cases they did the drudgery of caring for the sick better than the rest of us.

I have not said anything about love. It exists, even among the most luxurious. I suppose there is no less of it than there ever was, we just don't hear much about it. The woman with the paralyzed man was a case of love that came under my observation and, indeed, scrutiny.

My conclusion is as follows. Forget feeling. Forget whether or not you have a bright smile on your face, and forget whether you are fully conscious every day of the loveliness of life, and solidarity of mankind and all that zub, zub, zub.

Make up the mind what the work is, that is to be done, and do it in anger, in disgust, in whatever feeling arises, keeping as firm a control over the expression of these feelings in the presence of the sick as possible. But do it and keep on doing it until the end. That is not what good feelings are about, but it is what love is about, a god who cares almost less than any other what feelings come, and who requires, more than almost any other god, physical presence and the humblest of services, as well as the greatest.

If possible I guess one should feel loving at all times, cleaning up the john and all the rest of it. The sick man hates it more than his nurse, the loss of physical dignity; and everybody involved is diminished and affronted, probably like the prelate who could not endure the sight of Indian poverty.

When it is not possible to feel always loving, when a tension about the eye registers disgust, this is hurtful to the patient, who tries to understand, and hurtful to the one caring for him, who feels guilty at feelings he cannot suppress altogether. Imperfection is the human lot, and nowhere is it so brilliantly seen as in the care of a long-term invalid who is going to die.

I cannot boast I have ever given such care, but I have seen it and I also know important accounts of it. Plato used to say of men in battle that there's no doubt a guy could often save himself if he just split, and Xenophon pointed out there are some whose feet won't budge, thinking it shameful to run away.

The glory of the human animal is never so resplendent as when the fight cannot be decided in a day, or sustained by emergency chemicals released by almost superhuman glands for half an hour, but goes on indefinitely in the certain knowledge of ultimate defeat. Yet surrender's pure white flag is never raised.

Even in prolonged cases, even with boredom and disgust, there are rewards along the way of humor and delight. Good days. There may even be (for some say God is in the plan) Mozart on the day of death, and quiet breathing. Those who have given such care, with all their energy and will and such faltering grace as they can manage, have a reasonable and basalt pride, having given up so many concerts, as you might say, to play gin rummy with those whose minds are failing (down to gin rummy, actually) and whose bodies are a full offense. Except to love. Let's make that (lest it be confused with something else) except to Love. (September 1985)

Letting Every Dog Have
His Museum

The Museum of the Terrier has yet to be erected on the Mall. This may stand for all the glories of America that are not yet honored by buildings in our capital. To say nothing of endless groups of unsung heroes amongst us. Where, pray, is the National Museum of Pest-Control Artifacts or the Federal Collection of Clogged Drains?

You sneer. But wait till you get cockroaches, regrettably fetched in through a six-pack of 7-Up, or wait till 9 p.m. New Year's Day (bowl games) when the john fails and a plumber reels over to help you out. Then you know what heroes are.

Some will say yes, bug people and plumbers are important in our lives, but perhaps not of museum quality?

To that I say bull. What we honor and respect in our hour of need should not be forgot in our modes of public splendor, and I would gladly visit those two museums if they existed.

As for the national collection of important terriers, perhaps it should be the National Collection of Dogs, so we don't wind up with separate museums for hounds (who Lord knows deserve one), poodles, Turkish mountain dogs and so on.

There is a notion that science is the proper subject for museums, or painting. Attendance at the National Air and Space Museum exceeded 14 million visitors in 1984 and everybody thinks the world of it, there being no other place so suitable for dumping small boys visiting the capital, and then we all approve of Science.

When you get right down to it, however, you are really seeing a collection of giant Tinkertoys and you think of guys in Spitfires and the Lafayette Escadrille as you did when you were 8 and read comic books. All very well, but not really science, is it? A science museum would not be much to look at (while Air and Space is glorious to look at) since it would only contain a guy, labeled scientist, staring at a blank wall, making his brain work; a thing not terribly fine to peer at. What would docents do?

Whereas the Federal Canine Shrine would be the real thing. Around the marble rotunda would be carved (as at the Jefferson Memorial) some of the most profound things written about dogs. "Love Me, Love

My Dog"—Boethius; "Dogs Have Souls"—Luther; "If You Would Be Loved After Death, Be Like My Sealyhams"—Victoria; and "Down, Dammit"—Sophocles.

A circumferential complex of galleries would surround the central space, each devoted to succeeding exhibits, "The French Hound from Clovis to DeGaulle" and "Contributions of the Labrador to Bathysphere Theory." Like that. And outdoors, tactfully separated by tasteful landscaping, would be spacious runs for lively specimens of the 150 best-known breeds of dog today.

If done as well as Air and Space, I personally guarantee an annual attendance of 43 million. If attendance figures are all that big a deal.

There is no real reason such a museum should be built from scratch. The Hirshhorn already has roughly the right shape and could be adapted. The dog museum would not even have to be all in one place, since the Hirshhorn trustees, for example, would probably want to keep a few things already installed there. So there is the spectacular open space of the lobby of the new and wonderful National Building Museum and the rotunda of the National Gallery, now largely wasted with nothing in it but that figure of Mercury and the central fountain basin ideal for water spaniels.

The trouble is that science—Tinkertoys though science turns out to be—is thought to be dignified and worthy, while dogs are just thought useful or cute.

When King Edward VII died in 1910 his funeral began with his coffin on the gun carriage, followed by Queen Alexandra and the royal children, chief mourners, followed by nine reigning kings (the last time such a turnout was beheld). Immediately behind the kings of the nations came Caesar, who of course was Edward's favorite terrier (fox, but then the king did not always aim for the loftiest), attended by a good steady servant. Caesar acquitted himself with great dignity, I believe, for dogs understand when gravity is called for. After the mutt came lesser personages, the Privy Council, peers of the realm, the military, etc.

I cite King Edward's funeral merely to show that the dignity of the dog has always been recognized, when the chips are really down. The dog has often taken precedence, when there is no longer any need for pretense and the secret of all hearts is revealed, over figures (such as Privy Councils and Cabinets) who commonly wear more costly costumes than the humble fur of the fox terrier.

The central focus of the rotunda should be work of powerful esthetic value in bronze, displaying the Basic Dog. It might have to be antique, since sculptors nowadays are chiefly concerned with mowing machines and grain combines, but a determined search would produce something worthy.

Some modern sculpture at the Hirshhorn itself strikes me as heartbreakingly beautiful; the only trouble is it's not dogs. I think we want something comparable to The Calf-Bearer, that great archaic marble of the guy with the calf slung round his shoulders, only a dog. In a pinch there are superb Etruscan bronzes of mythical beasts and Chinese figures of animal spirits, all of which look as much like dogs as anything else. It is more important for the thing to be supremely beautiful than for it to look exactly like Max, in other words.

Some say we have enough museums already. Seventy at last count in this city. I say we have not nearly enough, and almost all of them free—let us never fall to the level of New York, say, where you pay upon entering. Our museum should be light and bright. I. M. Pei would suit, as architect, provided he did as well as the East Building of the National Gallery. Everything first-rate, everything flawless, full of dignity, but not ponderous. I do not think we want any Eternal Flame stuff in our Rotunda of the Faithful Paw, no. Nothing that might go out if Pepco fails, nothing of pipes and gewgaws and contrivances, but only what speaks at profoundest levels to the waiting heart of the visitor, who has come to do homage to the most ancient symbol of loyalty, faith and delight. Down, dammit, as the great poet says. Good boy, good boy, so say we all. We are talking catharsis here, to move a heart of stone. We are talking a museum that never abides updating, we are talking everlasting woofs, past any mutt's or any guy's short life. (October 1985)

E. B. White

Washington—E. B. White, who died Tuesday at 86, took pains not to be grand and all for naught; he wound up grand for all his avoidances of grandeur, and the more he avoided noble and elevated style the more convinced his readers were that he was noble—a word not always trotted out for writers of short and casual pieces.

He joined The New Yorker in 1926 (it was founded in 1925) and his work was often unsigned, as in his Talk of the Town sketches. His work was better than that of most others at the magazine, and readers soon started pawing through the pages for traces of E. B. White and were commonly rewarded.

But he did not assume superstar status and while there was, of course, a slight letdown when one passed from him to other writers equally full of comment, still his writing was a garland for the team, you might say, rather than a spotlight so blinding that the others looked poor.

He has been called the best American essayist of the century, though most of his readers possibly have wondered who the competition was supposed to be.

His work was civil and polite; he either had no gift of vitriol or else never felt any. He was commonly funny, never in the high breathtaking way of an Aristophanes and never in the sparkling knock-em-dead manner of the century's favorite one-line wits.

He gave the impression of getting through the day like an ordinary hard-pressed man trying to remember the hour of a meeting and the need to pick up dog food before the store closed, but then retiring for a time to think what the hell is this all about.

He achieved answers, and one of them was not to get carried away with words, to seem to feel more than he felt, and not to feel (in writing) in the first place without thinking it over a spell.

The trouble with many potentially nice writers is that once they think about things they either conclude (often correctly, no doubt) they have nothing to say and therefore write nothing, or they bull it through anyway to the temporary dazzlement of the easily dazzled, but not to the sustenance or delight of the civilized.

Nobody who only met and talked with White through a long and golden day at his house in Maine has any real idea of his life, however gratifying to see the deep courtesy and affection shown his wife of many years and his near-adoration of a rather grim and almost certainly brain-damaged terrier named Jonas who despised the world and everything in it except his master whom he had conveniently converted to slavery. To love an unlovable dog suggests depths of commitment worth remarking.

White was a lyrical man in the sense that if wonder is lacking it is impossible to write at all, but because he was polite and therefore restrained and because he descended from respectable people who had an iron vase on the lawn and doubtless thought well of Emerson, he distrusted a too-easy loveliness and much in general, first, because he wished to be honest all the way through and not to paint things sweeter than those things are, and second, because he had sufficient technical competence to notice that rhapsodies defeat the lofty effect aimed at.

He was not sentimental, or his work was not. He liked taking care of sheep partly because he simply loved animals, partly because he loved the bondage animals incur—lambs are invariably born at disgusting cold seasons and during prolonged and inconvenient hours—and partly, one may guess, because he liked to think of himself as a new Hesiod, bound through the night by the requirements of the beasts and through the day by the routine of the farmer's lot. He did not fool himself he was a plain farmer or did the hard work of a farmer, but he took extraordinary care to keep in touch with the cycling of the sun and the reality of growth and death.

Things must have welled up in him not just sometimes but most of the time. He had a powerful sense of life's sweetness and took the risk (a risk for a writer) of letting it show. He liked to set the stage by opening one of his pieces in a matter of fact way, forecasting in only the most tenuous way how the piece would end:

"To perceive Christmas through its wrapping becomes more difficult with every year."

He speaks of those ear-trumpets hunters can buy to hear the otherwise inaudible and distant music of the hounds, and says something of the kind would help us hear Christmas. But, alarmed this might seem a little too sweet, he follows it:

"We rode down on an escalator the other morning . . ." just to show you he does not avoid commonplace things or ugly words like escalators. Then he dares an emotional charge again, but damps it down at once, but goes on to prepare for the climax by orderly reasoning and useful but not blinding images. He remains conversational, casual, letting the effect of brooding build up very gradually, alluding to rabbit tracks, rocket travel, packages of energy and so on, to show you this is only ordinary thought and ordinary stuff. Then the thing he has with difficulty been holding back and is now ready to let fly:

"This week many will be reminded that no explosion of atoms generates so hopeful a light as the reflection of a star seen apprecia- tively in a pasture pond. It is there we perceive Christmas—and the sheep quiet and the world waiting."

Intellectually it may make no great sense; Christmas is not perceived by anything in any pond, but what he really wants to get to is "and the sheep quiet and the world waiting," and by the time he gets you to it there are few readers whose throats have not got tense.

One of his funny masterful wrenching sketches concerned a wimp's visit to a psychiatrist, during which he felt nervous, afraid, a general incompetent mess. He goes out on the street and something magical happens, he sees trees on the street and focuses on the second one from the corner. White wants to say what the Damascus Road is like, and how the soul can leap from a dingy cave to the high clear ether in a bound, but he will show it, not talk about it. He will show it funny, pathetic, stupid—he will sketch us as we are most of the time. He will also show the transcendent minute in which the wimp looks at the ordinary tree of a city street, and after the nonsense of his psychiatric session and its attendant confusion and garble about what he really wants, he looks at the tree:

"'I want the second tree from the corner, just as it stands,' he said, answering an imaginary question from an imaginary physician. And he felt a slow pride in realizing that what he wanted none could bestow, and that what he had, none could take away. He felt content to be sick, unembarrassed at being afraid; and in the jungle of his fear he glimpsed (as he had so often glimpsed them before) the flashy tail feathers of the bird courage."

Then he winds up with a paragraph of funny let-down. Only not before attempting and achieving in a mere handful of paragraphs a stunning salute to the soul of man in a way that makes nobody wince at the gush, and in a way that makes anybody proud to be a poor bifurcated simian and immortal diamond.

Never mind the "classic" children's books so lavishly praised, and rightly praised. Turn to "The Second Tree from the Corner," a good start and a good finish to the man or to any man.

Virgil reported on the kingdom of the dead and Socrates, too modest to claim any knowledge of it, yet looked forward to speaking there with the heroes, arguing the sweet day long. They wrestle (Virgil assures us) on the yellow sands in sport. And there are the sons of Teucros, they are not without beauty.

White's sad and grateful readers may in their own vision see that wrestling on that yellow sand today. Dear Lord, if it isn't E. B. White and his dachshund Fred, the one so interested in the farm pigs, the one so full of mischief (White used to go visit his grave) and with whom White could not romp for all these recent years. Look at them going at it. They are not without beauty. (October 1985)

The World's Horrors

Twenty-five thousand dead in Colombian mud flows sounds like the end of the world in a horror movie but the news of it hits like a blow.

The truth is the world is always coming to an end, it's just that the world does not know it. The mind draws back from immensity, the endless massacres and acts of God through the ages, and I have tried to think why a mass death numbs us and a single one does not.

Some people think that if the quantity is increased enough, then the quality itself will change, as some say the Hiroshima bomb was new and different from the mere sum of 100,000 deaths.

I have never quite seen it that way. No doubt the horror is easier to see when it comes to so many at once, but was horror ever so hard to see?

I've heard it said that mass death is what turned cavemen to discover or invent their gods. Though others say this is why so many say the gods do not exist and never did.

The old question, what is man, attracts new interest today. The size of the jaw, the ridge of the brow, the volume of the brainpan, the bones suggesting bipedality, all are examined by seers to see when beast became man.

But at the other end of time there is still some doubt how long a man will live. We are not fully sure even when he is dead.

There is also curiosity, renewed after every disaster, how the gods were discovered or dreamed up in ancient times. Some say they were invented to ensure good harvests or luck in hunting, but I think they were discovered to ease human pain. It would not surprise me if they were born the day a woman, having lost a kid, first comprehended the magnitude of it as no animal ever did, and knew a grief more terrible than theirs.

There is no way to know, for all the fossils of this world, just when a vivid consciousness of suffering first occurred, but the day it did is the day we first were us.

It is thought some people hurt more than others, though we do not know that, either. Everybody hurts sometimes, we can guess, and it makes a difference, we usually think, whether life amounts to more than an odd arrangement of molecules somewhat different from rocks—and whether human suffering means anything to speak of, or is worth enduring.

And those who believe in God, as surveys report so many Americans do, have the thorny fact to deal with, that innocents may be smothered while those who seem less innocent live comfy lives, dying full of years and honors in their beds.

Some work this out to their satisfaction, but I no longer expect to understand it, not in Colombia and not in a hospital and not in a country road where some kid is wailing over a dead pup.

But I think it may work like this, that man first dreams the dream, then the dream dreams the man. So that he invents or discovers symbols, but they then have a life of their own and shape him anew. Not that he ever knows how close they are to reality, only that he will not live without them.

In troubled sleep one may dream of a flood without foothold, and wake up with a body trembling. Or see in a dream a pit of human cries, stifled in a trice and level with seething mud. And moving across that surface with dry hoof a sheep, of all creatures; maybe one once fetched home by a shepherd who now lies lost with the rest. How poorly designed the beast is, to carry a banner, yet it carries one, and the shepherd's sign is on it. The shepherd once cared for him, but now the sheep alone still lives to bear his standard.

These are strange dreams and we all have them. But then we are the stuff of dreams, bizarre and surreal distortions, but human for all that and well worth knowing.

So I saw in my dream the thousands vile in death, and didn't know why they died or why I had to see them. Then in the way of dreams they were changed. These are they that are washed and clean and before a throne.

And I wondered how old and ragged this dream was, screening for me in my sleep, like film from some flickering archive. And again I saw the pit and again the dumb unsullied sheep. And he entered the dreadful field, to bring his shepherd home. (November 1985)

A Few Words about Syllables

As you know, there is a comedy program on television called "Monty Python's Flying Circus," and each program begins with that title spoken, so you can hear it in the kitchen or the hall or the john and come dashing in.

But the hearty local announcer, who is terrified we will not know how to spell python if he calls in PIE-thun, bursts forth just before the show begins to tell us the Monty PIE-thahn show comes next. He hears, no doubt, that he pronounces python differently from the sound track of the show itself, but that does not bother him, because he wants us to know the word is spelled with an O.

I have always liked pythons. Sacred to Apollo and all that. Pythons to me are like cats, dogs and wows. I already know how to spell all those and do not need an announcer or any other speaker to hammer it home.

I go along just fine with "pylon" pronounced pie-lahn, but am much discouraged at what is happening to most words ending in "on."

Everybody knows Oregon is pronounced AHR-uh-gun, but I increasingly hear Oar-e-GAHN, with a heavy beat on the last syllable.

So far, Solomon is still SAHL-uh-mun but any day now I expect Sahl-uh-MAHN, and of course I am already braced for LEB-uh-nahn.

Already the dumb dictionary I find on my desk authorizes PIE-thahn for python, though until recently I never heard anybody say anything but PIE-thun.

Some will argue that English words should be pronounced the way they are spelled, but that stupid argument overlooks the fact that even such a syllable as "on" may be pronounced a number of ways (as in lone, wagon, micron) and nobody says Leb-a-NOAN to rhyme with telephone. Yet.

These strange half-accented "on's" come about, I suspect, through an increasing illiteracy among us. If we don't read, we don't know many words, and when we come to a real blockbuster such as Lebanon we naturally take it slow on the curves, sounding out each letter cautiously, and by the time we get to the last syllable we lay down our burden with relief and a heavy accent. Whew.

But you never hear anybody mispronounce cat, dog or wow. Of course some people say dog with the same o sound you find in otter or ocelot. The word is pronounced dawg, not dahg, but the people who say dahg for dawg are few and tend to come from places where there are no dogs. And cat, at least, is secure for the foreseeable future. Nobody says caht or cawt or cate yet.

Why? Because these words (cat, dog, wow) are known to all.

You might ask why anybody uses a word unfamiliar to him, the pronunciation of which is therefore chancy, and sure enough, the steady American sticks pretty much to gee, wow, my God, damn and Friday. The only trouble is that these words do not fit every situation of life or discourse (though God, damn and wow are making considerable progress here) and when Cousin Will acquires a python for a pet you have to learn this exotic new word. It's not as long as Lebanon, thank God, but it's still pretty strange, so you go slow and come up with PIE-thahn.

I used to blame this on Bulgarians, Basques and Albanians, whose languages are said to be difficult, which means they will find English difficult. But the more I think of it, the more I see there cannot really be 200 million Albanians among us, still speaking their native tongue.

In general, words of the English language should be pronounced just sufficiently to make the word clear in its context, and the accent should be pushed as far backward, to the beginning of the word, as possible. As Monday, Tuesday, Wednesday, Thursday, Friday, Saturday, Sunday.

There are different notions in Greek, where any number of short words end in a long vowel or diphthong and bear an accent. Translated into English, the accent moves back toward the beginning and the long vowels become short and are commonly dismissed.

The theory, in English, is that you don't have to know how to spell it. If you need to know, ask somebody. But spoken English does not exist in order to give spelling lessons to people.

The primmer, prissier and more ignorant people are, the more they are determined to accent syllables that are not properly accented, and the more determined they become to distinguish every unaccented vowel from other vowels.

My own name is pronounced MITCH'l. You either know how to spell it or you don't (Webster's Collegiate Dictionary lists it as one of the commonest names of the language) and there is no need to pronounce it Mitch-ELL just to show off the fact that you know it has an

E in it. Showing off your knowledge of spelling commonly results in showing off one's ignorance of, and full indifference to, the way things are spoken.

I have never heard anybody mispronounce the names of my dogs over the years—Jack, Teddy, Fritz, Dinah, Inky, Spot, Luke, Bass, Max and Lucy. But I am braced, mind you, so that my face will not register amazement when I hear somebody—probably a television person—sooner or later say Mawks, Makes, Mahks or Lewchey. I resolve for the New Year to give no ground whatever on these. Or python, either, dammit. (December 1985)

Snapshots

A day in the life of this city—well, much luck to the photographers in town who are trying to capture us (as you might say) for the enlightenment of the world.

They might start with a woman I shall call Mrs. S., who is 96 and is worried about some roses she ordered from California. They haven't got here yet.

"I can't get out so much now. But I have a rail thing that when I hang on to it I can pull dandelions."

She also has a new iris about to bloom, she thinks.

"Paid good money for it," she went on. "I can stand at the front door and see it and I have some good purple irises that ought to be divided, they're too thick."

Well, if you ask me a chapter on the life of this capital could well begin with Mrs. S. peering out the door to see how her new iris was coming along. The Vision of the Future. This capital is much interested in the future.

And then—I am doing all the work for these photographers as you see—for something completely different there could be a street person.

There was one on K Street, almost certainly still is, who had a way of catching your eye half a block off. One balmy night I noticed him in an overcoat and deliberately avoided his eyes as I passed him. Then I thought, why am I in so big a hurry? That guy clearly wanted to speak and I pretended I was unaware of it. So I went back and said, "Sorry, were you about to say something?" and reached for a couple of quarters, assuming he hoped for a handout.

"Yes, I was. I have been over to the White House to warn President Reagan. There is an invasion from Mars heading right for the White House. They wouldn't let me in. Somebody should tell him."

He got this warning through his teeth. The overcoat man, not the president. I thought once of phoning the White House about the Mars invasion and then thought the hell with it. If it comes the president will probably be surfing or visiting the Annenbergs or something and won't get hurt.

And then a sharp change—you know how cameras leap about to

something completely different. Suddenly we turn the page to a shot of David Acheson (about to wind up his task looking into the NASA problems) toward midnight, walking his fine black poodle, Gus.

He has moved—and the Achesons also—to a posh apartment and Gus has to use the back elevator. He is, however, a happy dog.

This little set of pictures would show, at one blow, a bit of Washington high life and a bit of wild nature. Or if Gus is not wild enough, they could get S. Dillon Ripley, former secretary of the Smithsonian Institution, in town with his wife Mary for supper with the Achesons. They were in Texas earlier in the day where they saw billions of birds in a short time including the perhaps uncommon yellow-something chat. Ripley also has some new wild Javanese peacocks. Wild kingdom, indeed.

Such a picture would show that people here are strongly into birds and wildlife and also can fly up from the Texas coast to dine with friends. High life and wild life in one swoop, you see.

Then to a Bethesda grooming place to see the world's most beautiful Welsh terrier getting trimmed for the summer.

The photographer would get there in time for the preliminaries:

"You got that good girl who makes terriers look sharp?" demands a dog person. "Because once she wasn't around and you made him look like a scalded badger."

"Yeah. She's here. He'll get a good trim."

And then—the climax of the volume, I suppose—a shot of the terrier emerging later, looking sharp indeed. Power cut. For this is a capital of appearances as well as substance. On the march. Feisty. Often breathtaking in beauty.

Then a switch to a gang of people. Say the Billy Graham Crusade with more people than you can shake a stick at. Don't know what his topic is. Probably equally fine on any topic at all. Last time I heard him on television was during the Profumo scandal in London. Fancy girl, you remember. Graham was letting Profumo have it. Valuable to the folk of Knoxville (I think he was preaching there on this occasion) who might otherwise have gone nuts and flung a lot of money at big-buck call girls, dropping 100,000 here, 100,000 there on riotous living.

Besides, the most attractive preaching consists of sharp warnings against sins that are sadly impossible to fall into. This would illustrate the deep spiritual aspect of the capital and you'd get a lot of great faces; careworn, perky, baffled, innocent, a whole range.

A chapter on the life of this capital could well begin with Mrs. S. peering out to see how her new iris was coming along.

Then a rough tough biker type, clomping into a suburban tavern. Heavy metal and lots of hair. Naw, he can't have another beer because he promised Mom to put the cat out before midnight. This shows, well, that somebody has to put the cat out.

Then the Lincoln Memorial by moonlight. Reflecting Pool. No mosquitoes in it. Full of gambusia. Underwater light shows the little fishes darting about keeping things pure. And the camera captures the statue of Lincoln. (The loftiest dreams of the republic are tied to little fish who keep the algae down, get it?)

Then sunrise. We see the waves of dogwood. We can almost hear the slow movement of the G Minor. We once again see Mrs. S. She is holding on the railing and pulling out the damned dandelions.

Life in the seat of power. (May 1986)

Advice

Look, stop trying to help people.

You don't just walk on by when you see a child getting its hair pulled out by an orangutan escaped from the zoo. In such a case you must interfere, no ifs, ands or buts.

But when I warn against helping people, I mean in your own trade or your own milieu. On several occasions I have broken my back, once working till 3 in the morning, to help out some editor or other who wanted a story instantly because something they had counted on fell through.

Once I got a note saying thanks. But if they get something, they assume it can't possibly be any good. It's only when they don't get it that they start thinking how wonderful it would have been.

Now when I was young there was nobody in 15 counties round that was such a little old helper. I recall a time at another newspaper when the two music critics fell ill from too much caviar and champagne, evidently, and a young reporter interested in music was sent to review a symphony orchestra in their stead.

"God, I don't have the knack, you know," he said. "I can judge the music but I don't know how you sound like a critic."

To the rescue in a flash, I gave him a 15-minute course, which is all any critic needs, and I could tell he caught on, as he spoke strangely the rest of the day. But then he asked me to sort of bat out a review of a symphony on the typewriter so he could see something on paper.

Sure.

"This reading of the fourth was notable chiefly for the clarity of the brass, always difficult to achieve in a scherzo, especially in the tuba motif. It should never suggest the Salvation Armpah. Equally restrained and accurate was the line of the second violins, a pleasure throughout the work, neither obtrusive nor muted—not lost in the general lushness of sound. The Pomponia Divertimento, far less ambitious of course, had a swirling country freshness, albeit the bassoons were unduly timid. Turning to the Mozart, one must object to the failure of the legato, which in Mozart does not mean a dreamy mindlessness like a cat purring over eggnog, but an all-encompassing serenity into which no sudden assaults

By and large I decline to give advice. Sometimes the young actually think their way is better.

may intrude. Here the musical director seemed almost to be thinking of Smetana rather than Mozart, and yet blah blah blah."

Mike got the idea perfectly and said he spent intermission getting somebody to identify the various instruments for him—oboes and English horns and all those vague things that don't look at all like a bass viol.

Next morning his review read well, I thought. He noted the "reading," which in those days was much smarter than "playing," though it has probably gone out of favor now. His comments made sense until I read with horror that "the bassoons were unduly timid."

Imagine my despair. Here these bassoonists, highly professional, were being roughly criticized by a fellow who barely knew the difference between a viola d'amore and an organ grinder's monkey.

"Great grief, Mike," I cried, "I gave you the sample just to show how you want the review to flow right along. I didn't mean copy the line about the bassoons. There probably weren't *any* bassoons in that particular piece."

"Oh, yeah, there were two bassoons and they were unduly timid," he said.

Well, I felt very bad about it. A few days later Mike got a letter from the conductor, welcoming Mike to the circle of music reviewers, and adding that he especially appreciated the obervation on the bassoons' being timid. Exactly what he thought. Told the bassoonists so himself.

Maybe they were timid. But my own fear was that once a reviewer said they were timid, the conductor got to rumbling about in his head and concluded they were. Conductors can be quite hypnotized sometimes by the comments of outsiders.

So I stopped helping out newcomers to the newspaper trade. Oh, once I did suggest to a cub (a word quite useful for infuriating new reporters) that perhaps the tirade of the archbishop was more important (and thus should be higher up in the story) than the fact that orange juice was served in the lobby instead of the rose garden.

But by and large I decline to give advice.

It is not wanted, even when needed. It is not appreciated, even when tactfully given. It is not rewarded, even when most valuable. Listen, we live in a cold world, in which our good works are barely tolerated and never applauded. Sometimes the young—in an age of collapsing standards and the republic gone to the dogs—actually think their way is better. Good grief. Good almighty grief. (May 1986)

Of Destiny and Departure

There are people who want to be buried with their dog or cat, and who think they have it all worked out by having old Rover buried at Aspen Hill (a pet graveyard established in 1920 by Silver Spring) with space for their own cremated remains.

But what if the land, now commercially valuable, is rezoned for office buildings or some such use—what then? The business is before the Montgomery County government, which will decide.

One proposal has been to leave the present burials alone but allow no new ones. Fine, unless Rover is already there and you are not, and will not be admitted when your time comes. Or suppose Pompey, Rover's pup, dies two years from now and cannot be buried with old Rover.

As world problems go, I see no dilemma, no matter what the zoning decision is. Even if eventually the land is zoned for gas stations, Rover could be moved to a new site and you could still be buried with him, and nothing should be simpler (as legal problems go) than establishing the rights of those who bought grave sites.

Most of us do not wish to be buried with our animals, but surely it is understandable that some do, and all we have here is a relatively simple task of sorting out, which any court can manage.

But I have been thinking of the long haul, not 50 years but 50,000. There have been billions of people who have died, and the grave sites of extremely few are now known. You can visit the grave site of St. Swithin and King Canute, but not of Achilles or Homer.

It does not bother most of us if we are unsure where the bones of our great-grandfather's grandfather now rest. Or the poor remains of some forebear of the 8th century.

Occasionally somebody digs up bones of the Bronze Age, and it is hard to look on them without reflecting the guy was probably much like us, and people have always marveled that the bones of an obscure peasant may be preserved intact for eons while those of great emperors are lost—there is something quite satisfactory in this.

Time, which antiquates antiquities and hath an art to make dust of all things, hath yet spared these minor monuments, as Sir Thomas

Browne observed of some urn burials dug up, having lain many centuries undisturbed.

I do not, myself, mourn when I get a haircut or trim my nails. They were part of me, but hardly the essence. Hoof and horn make fine fertilizer, and Christopher Lloyd, a celebrated gardener of England, says he always leans out the window when cutting his nails so they will enrich his garden below. I think that a delicate sentiment.

In times, all graveyards will disappear, even the most august repositories of kings, because even stone and bronze at last decay. There will be battles and floods and earthquakes, sooner or later, and if no trace remains of great ancient capitals, who supposes the grave of Adam's hound will be eternally marked, or Charlemagne's terrier?

As for religious views of a bodily resurrection, it seems likely that if God can raise the dead, He can equally well collect whatever molecules are necessary, if any, no matter how widely dispersed. It strikes me odd that a religious person would worry about divine competence.

Respect is due a dead body not because it is still the person or animal that was loved, but because its physical appearance necessarily reminds us of the life that is no longer in it, and that was cherished. Because of that association, a certain dignity, propriety, cleanliness, all seems right, but once the thing is done with decency—I would not dream of flushing a pet goldfish down the john, for that matter—then the rest can be left to God or, if one has no religious faith, to nature or fate or what you will.

But we all know that customs differ, according to the person. There are some who feel the bones, even when they are dust, still deserve respect, and that they should ensure, as well as they can, a perpetual preservation of graves.

Surely they are laying up sorrow for themselves, since perpetuity is hardly within their power, and it is more sensible to come to terms with reality. Dr. Donne, who was second to no man in respect for the dead, used to say they were like a library that was not destroyed, but the scattered leaves all gathered up again; and not lost, in some forgotten language, but translated into a new and better one.

Socrates had the opinion that nothing bad could happen to a good man, and if you say well, something bad happened to him (he was executed for his virtue, which was called a crime by the state) he would say that was not bad, no matter what we think, since it did not cause him to do evil. He was, of course, a better man than any we

As for love, I entrust that not to marble but to the universe even beyond all measurements of stars.

know now, but if we could attain to his level, we would fidget less and be happier.

I cannot imagine my old Luke—now there was a dog for you—gave a fried damn what happened to his great ears, once they were dust, or worked himself into unnecessary sorrows about either life or death, being concerned almost entirely with love, marrow bones, and the glories of this city such as steel utility poles into which he frequently hurtled during his investigations. We never knew why he ran into things. He was not, by Madison Avenue standards, a superachiever, but was none the worse for it that I can see. As for love, I entrust that not to marble but to the universe even beyond all measurements of stars, being more remarkable than a batch of suns.

So the disposition of old bones can be worked out satisfactorily to everybody, beyond doubt, and there is nothing here that cannot be resolved. Now in picking out a new pup, you want to . . . (June 1986)

Commencement Primer

Nobody knows why schools have commencement speakers, and I, at least, have no idea why people agree to speak to the Youth of America on these occasions.

Having returned this week, however, from addressing the graduating class of Millbrook School, N.Y., a high school, I shall print here my all-purpose baccalaureate effort in the chapel:

Distinguished headmaster, distinguished guests, ladies and gentlemen (in case these categories do not overlap), and worthy graduates: Greetings.

Our daughter graduated from college a few days ago and I noticed the speaker was an imbecile so I said to my wife, don't you think it's asking a good bit for people to sit and listen to him?

She said, Oh, they're all the same, aren't they, no matter who they are. Of course nowadays they ask just anybody.

How true this is. But I take comfort now, in this hour of despair, foisted off on you as a speaker, from an incident at Henry VII's chapel at Westminster Abbey.

Because of crowds there, they have separate stairs for coming and going. I was on the downward path, as usual, when to my surprise an impressive tweed-bearing matron was ascending with a breadloaf-sized parcel, which she dropped a few feet in front of me.

Ever the gentleman, I accelerated to pick it up. The lady looked up terrified. They know when you're an American. But before she was murdered (as she doubtless expected) she faced me with courage and said:

"I know I'm on the wrong stairway. I know you are right and I am wrong. Nevertheless, here I am."

Is this not a guide to life? Not that we should block traffic by going the wrong way, no. But when we botch it, we are still human, with human rights and dignities. Like the tweedy lady, we are nevertheless here.

Now it is customary to remind you that you are going into the world. This is supposed to inspire you with awe. Where you are supposed to have been the past 18 years, God only knows. Mars, maybe.

But I think the world you are entering is very like the world you are leaving. That is, dreadful people, weak coffee and injustice all about. How do you deal with it?

I have often wondered, but of course never known.

The trouble with people, you will see, is that they are not exactly like yourself. Naturally, then, they will have unsound views on Milton. But then I questioned myself: Would the world be better with 4 billion H. Mitchells in it?

Not necessarily. Thus it is not really a crime for others to be a trifle different. Within reason, mind you.

Obvious, perhaps. But much of the misery we suffer results from nothing more than assuming or demanding that others conform to our clonal ideal.

Further, I see I bond well with dogs. They neither offend nor disappoint me. They may slurp as they like—I love to hear them eat. I do not call them pigs. They are dogs and eat like dogs, and I would not wish them different.

I apply this insight to people. At our office—and by the way you should prefer to die rather than say "work place"—we have bulldogs, poodles, German short-hairs and numerous ridgebacks. I take them as they are, or as they seem to me, and as long as I imagine a fine dog for each, it works well.

There is no need, if you should bump into my boss, to tell him you hear he's an Irish terrier. Bosses are often touchy. Often they lack insights that we have, who are mere cogs beneath the chariot wheel.

Possibly something should be said about truth—it is the custom on these occasions. Well, truth is hard. I have no great experience of it. But do not too easily trust those who think they are masters of it.

Because truth is seated on a high mountain, and anybody who would reach her will do considerable zigzagging. If truth is easy and obvious—and to your advantage—it is probably not Truth with a capital T at all, but only expedience in its commonest mask.

My admirable grandfather—I shall give you an easy example of truth's difficulty even at a low level here—went to Denver about the day after the railroad was built, to address some surgeons meeting there. My grandmother, who fancied herself a pioneer woman since she would be in Colorado two weeks, took along provisions including some China tea and plenty of jelly.

On the long hot trip the jelly melted over her husband's suits in the luggage car. Dry cleaning was not perfected then, as it is not now, and my grandfather drew flies in Denver.

In later years sometimes a person would say Denver was so high up that there were no bugs there.

"I hear people say that," my grandfather would say, "but it is a myth. I never saw such a bug-infested place. Flies settle all over you when you walk down the street."

Does truth require a grandson to set him straight? Betraying his grandmother, who took care he should never know? Sometimes truth is not only hard; sometimes it is also wrong.

Now let's see. What do I know at 61 that I didn't know at 17? That is worth passing on?

I should reassure you this is going to be a short speech. But what experience has taught me, well, I think it dangerous to move suddenly. When I do, I bump into things. It is not necessary to react on the instant. When aroused, sometimes a slight postponement serves well. So does counting to 10,000.

This is not much wisdom to give you. But then wisdom does not rain from the skies, you know, at least not on me.

On the other hand, disassociate yourself promptly from anyone who deems you a liar. Even if they try to patch it up, you may smile agreeably in the same room, but never have anything further to do with them.

Sometimes as citizens you must act quickly. In spite of what I have said. If you see a man murdering his wife, phone the police without thinking twice. Of course he may have reasons.

If you see a man kicking a dog, stop him. Don't wait. Even if he is bigger than you. This is one of the few absolutes. You have no choice in this.

You may some day marry. There are good rules for a lasting marriage:

First, do not have money enough for a divorce. Then, let the good wife learn to cook rice. No marriage will last if she does not learn this. Our terrier, Max, likes slimy rice and chicken stock on top of his bowl of Mighty Dog. It was a near thing the day I got Max's rice, but in general my wife cooks fine fluffy dry rice, a thing she learned in 1949, though it was a near thing then, too.

Third, agree with your partner (before you leap) on the few basics—religion, money, opening and closing windows at night. Finally, be certain before you take the fateful step that the partner has a good, even a divine, disposition.

I imagine I have covered the main points. Except the injustice in the world. A kid hungry. There is only so much one can do. One never does even that little, perfectly. You have to come to terms with this. It is harder to deal justly than to sing piously. There is incredible sorrow in the world, but I shall not ruin your day dwelling on it. You will do better, alleviating it, than I and mine have done. You can hardly do worse.

Concern yourself with your motives. You will often be vain, deceitful and so forth. Try not to be. But at least learn not to fool yourself.

Others, oddly enough, will often praise you. Do not believe everything you hear. Try to think straight on this.

Force yourself, if at first it is strange to you, to become ecstatically interested in something apart from—that is, in addition to—sex. Learn some subject at least well enough to absorb you to an O altitudino, as Thomas Browne said. It is necessary to have grand excitements that you can control all yourself.

Oh, and don't waste your life making money for the sake of having power. What is the point of that?

As I near the end of this, I remind you fashions change, in literature, political thought, religion, science and everything else. Here, for example, is the wisdom of Mrs. C. W. Earle, writing in 1896 (she was an educated, compassionate, rather wise, and generally gifted woman, probably well in advance of the thought of the day, and her book is dedicated to her sister the countess of Lytton, so you know it is reliable):

"Every girl can do something." (The word something is in italics.)

Finally, one more trifling thing: Happiness. Sometimes people your age are not happy. Older people insist you should be; you have everything in the world, health, bright eyes, physical beauty, zub, zub, zub.

At your age, you are not supposed to be happy. That comes later. With men, happiness usually starts increasing at age 35, and for women I am not sure, perhaps a bit later, but then with them it lasts the rest of life, and with men it tapers off about 70.

So if you should not be happy, do not feel guilty about it. Happiness will come. Get up every day and throw some water on yourself and start the day. It is better than not. Sometimes young people are fully miserable without knowing why. Keep going. Ask God for luck, and whatever else you do, keep hanging in there. It will work out. (June 1986)

The Normandy Cemetery

Most of the men who died at Omaha Beach in the 1944 invasion of France are buried in the towns of America, but about a third of them, say 9,000 to 10,000, lie in the graveyard of the coast of Normandy.

The French gave these few acres to America, somewhat as these men gave France back to France, and a good many visitors come here every day. Most of them are French.

The parking lot is quintessentially American, modeled on that curious desert which is the prototype of all American parking lots—a blasted sort of place with a few wild poppies and some wild mustard at the fringes, but generally open to every blast of heaven, and a scene of considerable babble as people get out of their cars and buses and prepare to enter the field of the graves.

"*Pardon, monsieur,*" said a French boy about 10, one of a full-throated bounding knot of French boys spinning through the lot. He had seen this solemn-looking old crock of an American, and thought maybe an American would be offended at the high spirits of the kids who had come to visit.

I thought, not for the first time, how delicate the feelings of the French often are. I grinned back, to indicate Americans take no offense at kids full of ginger on a summer excursion.

One would not presume to speak for the dead; still, since those dead are the very sort of guy one grew up with, it is quite certain the last thing to trouble their souls is the fresh animal rowdiness of kids in a parking lot.

They died, after all, not to bring on tears but to bring on freedom.

As you enter the graveyard you are pleased, all the same, to see it is a place of dignity. Most of these men, I reflected, probably never lay down before in a setting of such geometrical formality.

The walks are very wide, of concrete subdued by the addition of red oxide of iron, as I guessed, to prevent the glare of the sun. The grass is very green. There is a great reflecting pool, a black crystal broken with clumps of red and white water lilies in full bloom.

Along the walk are substantial live oaks, clipped regularly to a formal shape, like those thin high-crowned mushrooms you see in American woodlands in October. There are two flagpoles for the American flag.

At one end of the great walk is a somewhat heroic statue of what I guess is a soldier, flanked by stone wings, as in a theater, with various lofty things inscribed. It was fitting, no doubt, but I would have preferred something more piercingly beautiful, but then what difference does it make. One does not come to view the sculpture.

At the other end of the walk is a circular temple of stone. Inside there is a sort of altar, and a few chairs on which you can usually see an old woman or two sitting with expressionless face, just thinking, or just emptying her mind.

From both sides of the walk the graves fan out in precisely straight rows with white marble crosses. After a time you notice some of them are not crosses but marble stars. The first grave I walked to had the name Basinstoke carved on it. He was from Massachusetts.

The sky was blue and the sun brilliant. Not a cloud.

A walk to one side takes you to a parapet with an iron grill through which you look down on the beach. We have been up on higher ground, but from here you look down to the water and the remains of the improvised harbor shelters that were brought in to protect the landings.

You could go down to the beach, but it was completely empty; nobody was down there walking. It was very clean. It was not white, like the great American beaches (as at Destin, the most beautiful one) but yellow. No doubt a beach as Virgil had in mind when he said they wrestled on the yellow sand in sport. Here there was no such wrestling in sport, except possibly, as the guys advanced, each one with some invisible angel to demand a blessing.

The country around here is small fields, some of them very small, bounded with rough high stone walls and hedgerows tight as stone. Moving supplies, moving tanks, and moving on foot are all clearly impossible. Inland the fighting was as bad or worse. At Caen the whole town virtually lived in the great church of St. Etienne which stands untouched since it was finished by William the Conqueror. But the town itself was much damaged.

But back in the cemetery all was spacious and ordered and serene. You did not hear even talking there. At the sides, beyond the clipped oaks, are little groves you can walk through.

There it is common to see a man with his back turned, peering intently at a leaf. He does not want you to see his eyes, not because he

They died, after all, not to bring on tears but to bring on freedom.

is afraid of a few tears, but because he does not want anyone to think he is more sensitive than anybody else. Least of all does he want anybody to think he suffered more or lost more in the war than anybody else. American delicacy is of a high order, too.

Looking from the grove to the fields of graves, you see our system is better than the English. They plant lots of flowers. We have none. They would not look right to me. We have the clipped oaks. We have the white stone. We have the blue American sky that here extends so far as the Norman coast. (July 1986)

Survival, and What It Doesn't Mean

Endless mischief has been done to our understanding of the cosmos and our place in it by the unhappy phrase, "survival of the fittest."

As everybody knows, who ever read "The Origin of Species," Charles Darwin did not coin the phrase, using instead the words "struggle for existence." He specifically credited Herbert Spencer with thinking up "this survival of the fittest," which appeared in Spencer's "Principles of Biology."

But in any case, "survival of the fittest" was harmless enough when the concept was Darwin's or Spencer's. All it meant was that some species adapt to new conditions, or exploit them, and survive, while others cannot (or did not) adapt to a change of climate, competition from new challengers, etc., and die out.

It is not too gross an exaggeration to say cockroaches and rats are therefore more fit than dinosaurs, since the former have proved marvelously able to adapt to, say, Georgetown in Washington, D.C.

The trouble came from the Anglo-Saxon passion for fitness, or at least the widespread admiration of it. To this very day if I wish to say a certain man is extremely handsome, lively and personable, I say he is "a very fit guy," because it is not our custom to say men are handsome, charming (a strictly taboo word for males) and so on. "Fit," however, suggests not only the ability to walk five miles for a Camel, but also trails visions of good musculature, clean living (that is, only the most approved vices), the ability to cope and to grin in a healthy way at life's trifling annoyances, zub, zub, zub.

No man would ever complain of being called fit. People have said President Reagan is fit.

It is a slight step indeed from our general admiration of fitness to the following totally unwarranted and semi-insane interpretation of "survival of the fittest."

We ourselves survive because we and our ancestors were fitter than others. I am richer than most people because I am fitter to have money. The fact that I am rich and healthy is not a matter of luck, but a judgment of nature herself, and (if you are of religious bent) is obviously the specific wish of God.

But Darwin never meant to imply there was anything inherently wonderful about the survival of a species, or anything necessarily pejorative about the extinction of a species. He certainly never meant there was any grave defect in the dinosaurs that brought about some deserved extermination.

What he meant, and it is inescapably clear in his book, is that all creatures have to eat and propagate and so forth, despite competition from other living creatures, and that in the eons of life on earth, some creatures have died out and some have not. Cockroaches are a classic example of heroically ancient insects that have survived, but that does not mean they are inherently more glorious, more courageous, more intellectually gifted, more prudent, than the endless forms of life that no longer exist.

What it boils down to is a self-evident fact, that what has survived has survived, and what has died out has died out. Darwin's contribution, on this point, was not this obvious fact, but the elaboration of a theory that birds, beetles and all other living things change, to take advantage of new food supplies, new levels of survival, in the (often unconscious) struggle to keep eating and breathing in the presence of other forms of life that are doing the same.

If put in terms of a single human, Darwin's understanding of "fittest" is more easily understood. A man sitting on the edge of Mount St. Helens on eruption day was not fit, in the sense he did not survive. But it is perfectly possible he was in better health, possessed of a better mind and had higher standards of morality and altruism, etc., than Joseph Blow who did survive, having had the fitness to be drinking beer in his undershorts at home during a telecast of the Redskins game.

Nobody supposes an individual who rises to the pinnacle of renown in some field or other is therefore the best. All that can be said ultimately of a corporation chairman, a king, a president of a learned academy, a champion bowler or a celebrated poet is that he occupies that position. He may, in fact, be fairly mediocre within his field. This is less obvious in the case of sports (which is why sports are justly admired—there is less chance of flimflamming the truth in athletics) but very easily seen in politics, religion, painting and so forth.

Unless you wish to say the chief administrator of the largest religion of the world is the holiest man alive, or the chairman of the largest corporation is the most gifted example of free enterprise, or the best-

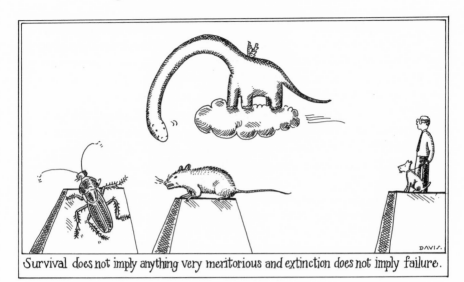

Survival does not imply anything very meritorious and extinction does not imply failure.

selling novelist is our finest writer, you have to acknowledge that there is a good bit of slack in things.

There is a good bit of slack in nature, too. If you like you can say a rat or a sea slug or a jellyfish is endlessly admirable because it has survived eons, but that does not mean there was something inherently discreditable in the Carolina parakeet. Many creatures survive simply because their requirements are so minimal they can get along anywhere.

Often I suspect I am rather like that myself. If I'm hungry I'd as soon eat a hot dog or a cold potato as a purée of lark's eyebrows or the other elegant fodder of this capital, and somewhat to my annoyance (for we all give ourselves airs) I see I have been equally happy and unhappy in cotton fields, London, Paris, the South Seas and Washington. If push comes to shove, I propose to be equally happy and unhappy in (God save us all, but it can be done) Hickory Bush, Tysons Corner and other fabled dead ends of the world. It is a question of making up your mind.

If I am a survivor, up to this point, I credit it largely to having avoided killer doctors, trucks, cliffs, defective brakes and undiagnosable dips at parties. And yet this is mainly a matter of luck. Once in the Yucatán I was so hungry that in a remote village I said the hell with it and gorged on delicious chunks of fruit sitting in glass basins with flies buzzing in and out. Not a twinge. Whereas my poor traveling companion fell gravely ill of a salad in a fancy (waiters in formal dress) French restaurant in Mexico City. Heh-heh-heh.

Cleopatra died young, Bess Truman died old. Both remarkable women, to my mind, but without belaboring the point, I hope a moment's meditation will assure anybody that survival does not imply anything very meritorious and extinction does not imply failure, except in terms of some statistician's book.

Queens, as a poet observed, have died young and fair. So have small dinosaurs. A fact, of course, and a fact of almost utter irrelevance. (December 1986)

All the King's Men

Good buddies are forever helping each other out, often making things worse, of course, but then friends commonly blunder in their love. Hence the expression, "with friends like these, who needs enemies?"

Who can forget the outstanding loyal activism of King Henry II's loving knights and drinking companions? Henry was having ferocious difficulties with Thomas Becket—no more than Henry deserved since he alone had raised Becket from lowly deacon to archbishop in a flash.

Terrible mistake, but by the time the king realized the archbishop was actually going to oppose him on such a key matter as the authority of the king's courts versus ecclesiastical courts, Becket was securely enthroned with no way to get a better man.

In our own sentimental generation, in which heroes are readily created overnight by proclamation to a citizenry sitting about with a Lite, receptive to the hero of the week and rather expecting one, Becket's reputation has soared, partly because of Eliot's endorsement in "Murder in the Cathedral."

Becket may have been a holy man—it depends on how holiness is defined—but he of course presided over the devastation of French towns, was an admirable combat soldier, and somewhat given to pettiness on matters of less consequence to the English church than to Becket.

Henry, who was not a saint either—or not a saint, since Becket was promptly proclaimed one—had a few faults including violence, favoritism (how else would Becket ever have got the ring of Canterbury?), a number of irregular loves, and an unattractive series of forceful struggles with his four sons.

But Henry, unlike Becket, created what is probably the chief gift of England to the world, the system of the Common Law, which was more or less in place by the end of his reign in 1189.

Henry also understood, as Becket perhaps did not, that the authority of Rome was not quite as unchallenged or secure in England as in continental nations. Medieval popes traveled to various countries but never to England, and the English crown had greater authority in the

English church than was customary in other countries. A lowly deacon in France might not so easily be converted into primate there.

The king was far more interested in good government and law than your average king. The shameless abuses of the ecclesiastical courts offended him, and he pursued the establishment of authority in his own courts with uncommon zeal.

The common and probably correct view is that one day Henry, exasperated with the troubles Becket was causing him, roared out the inquiry whether no man could deliver him from this pestilential priest.

A group of the king's "friends" therefore promptly hied to Canterbury and murdered the archbishop in the north transept—not that it would have been any better or worse if the murder were done in the choir, the retrochoir, the south transept or the crypt.

To the surprise of these good friends, the king was aghast. He could have used the support of Becket, but murdering a man does not generally sway him to your side. The whole kingdom might have been immediately excommunicated by the pope, except the pope was not keen to alienate England, having substantial political problems of his own without stirring up optional hornets.

Henry II was a man of excellent intelligence—it is no accident that every year of his long reign he became progressively popular with his subjects. Almost certainly the last thing he desired was an archbishop's murder, but presented with the fact, he announced far and wide it was a heinous mistake. He made a great show of contrition, probably sincere, as he understood immediately that even if the murder was directly contrary to his wishes, he would be stuck with it. If his friends thought stabbing Becket was what the king wanted, everybody else would think the same. He did not go about claiming innocence and incomplete information on the crime.

He would have committed himself to a madhouse before saying Becket's murder was a good thing—high time we stood tall for a change, etc., etc.

He is said to have gone through the church of Canterbury on his knees, making all manner of public penance.

He was one of the great kings of England. He managed through intelligence and comprehension of his realm and the political realities of his position to negate the otherwise catastrophic effects of the crime at Canterbury. And he got on with his great project of enlarging the authority of the civil courts. Any kid poking into precedents in the law of English-speaking nations will often be astonished at the influence of Henry II.

Despite a life that must strike anyone as full of misery, and a regrettable tendency to stretch the truth (he got into a convent to see the fair Rosamond by saying he wished to view the roses in the garden), he nevertheless bequeathed a legacy, the law, greater than that of most kings.

He had, moreover, the unfair advantage of possessing a brilliant mind. (December 1986)

The Eternal Rigors of Democracy

The question is whether we can govern ourselves; it was the question in 1787 when the new republic began, and the question will remain always.

Americans often like to dream back to Greece of the 5th century, as if that were a time of unflawed light when democracy was born, the arts flourished, etc.

And you must admit that public life was lived then on a fairly high plane. But even Athens (which modestly thought of itself as the school for all Greece) survived only for a brief time, before the temptation of empire seized her. And the Greeks, for all their gifts, never even managed to unite their small peninsula. Or establish their economy for the long run. Or devise effective arms against invaders.

Themistocles, whose skill saved Greece at Salamis, when it seemed certain the Persians would win, was exiled. The brilliant Alcibiades, also exiled, seemed at first to have every golden gift of man, yet it was on his motion that every male in conquered Milos was massacred. Even Socrates, commonly called the wisest of the Greeks, was executed by majority vote in the much-vaunted assembly of free citizens.

So democracy frequently did not work even in Greece at the height of her grandeur. If there were 420,000 people in the city-state of Athens, only 41,000 had the vote. The rest were 208,000 slaves, 70,000 foreign residents, plus women and children. With only a tenth of the population entitled to fix policy, and that tenth the best educated, richest, and most experienced in public affairs, you might think "democracy" would have its best chance, free from the thoughtless enthusiasms of an illiterate rabble, etc., but even this elite of free men did not govern very well for very long.

In America the vote is held not only by an elite of free males of a particular race or station, but by all men and women. Not only that, we have a republic of people from every society under the sun. Some cannot read. Some never heard of the Constitution, some know and care nothing of the long struggle to bring full rights to all inhabitants— an extension of democracy that would have seemed insane to the Greeks, and which seems perilous even now to most of mankind.

At every stage—when slaves were freed, when women were granted the vote—the chorus arose that democracy could not survive if its blessings were to be scattered at random, without regard to the "qualifications" of those holding the right to vote.

And yet, for all the perceived dangers of giving power to women (who were thought ill-equipped by nature to govern or even to think rationally) and ethnic minorities (who were once regarded as a kind of helpless children needing control and guidance), the American republic still offers a greater degree of personal freedom than any other nation in history.

If it is said that we tend to elect incompetents and loons to office, the same could be said of Greece even in her most exalted centuries. You can (for all our faults as a nation) still speak and read free, and move about as you please from one state to another, and apply to courts that on balance are as little corrupt as any that ever existed.

And in no other country is it so easy for those of humble origin to rise.

These are triumphant accomplishments, even if this freedom has dangerous seeds in its flower—rapacious wealth on one hand and poverty on the other, with a widening gulf between rich and poor.

Thanks to a land rich beyond comparison with any other (it is surprising how many Americans attribute our riches and power solely to our brains, virtue, etc.), we have prevailed when, if the land were poor as Greece, we would have failed almost before we began.

But the triumphs of the republic, great as they are, should not lead to a gloating complacency of cockcrowing in this bicentennial year of the Constitution. There should be a thanksgiving, but also a concern that even riches can run out when mismanaged.

There is a good bit of discussion about the economy, even if the average American pays no attention. Certainly the size of the debt is troublesome. Do we intend to service it forever merely by devaluing the dollar to the point that a trillion is no more than a billion and a billion is no more than a million? It is one way, but hard on the poor.

And much remains to draw the races together. If a man is black, that is the most significant fact about him as far as most white Americans are concerned. The goal must be to reach the point at which it makes no more difference than the color of his eyes.

There is also the overwhelming question of how to deal with Russia. This can never be far from any American's thoughts, yet, like incest, it is not much discussed in polite society. You get the impression that we are all agreed it is an evil empire and no more need be thought on the matter, except to invade Grenada or bomb Libya from time to time to show how tall we stand.

And yet these are three awful problems of the republic, which we treat with the concern appropriate to lesser problems such as parking on Massachusetts Avenue. We behave, nationally, as if great problems were annoyances, yes, but where shall we have lunch?

It may be, at the last, impossible to hold together a huge nation of free men, as it was impossible in Greece to hold together a small nation, but we owe it to the freedom we have known to head in, more seriously than we have done, to those weak places of the republic.

A free republic may work, even with many who care nothing for national policies, but it cannot work if the great questions are at last debated only in ivory towers while the rest of the country gets on with its personal luxuries. In the country's 200th year we might argue more and spend less, to a national advantage. (January 1987)

Individual Rights

The president's notes, his private diary or personal doodlings are thought likely to shed light on the sale of arms to Iran, and there have been mutterings in Congress that these notes should be demanded.

The president, for his part, seems willing to turn over the relevant notes. That is a mistake. Surely it is obvious a president's personal notes are no business of any Congress.

There might be interesting things in them, especially if they contain reflections on Ted Kennedy, Sam Nunn and other luminaries. And if the notes happened to get Iran and Iraq mixed up, or showed the president thought Basra was the capital of Uganda, they would be fun to read.

But whether a president is your hero or not, he is still human and still protected to some extent by the Constitution and the civilized behavior implicit in its various articles.

In the case of Richard Nixon's tapes, there was some question whether these could be demanded by Congress. The Supreme Court ruled unanimously the tapes should be surrendered, but that case concerned high crimes in high places.

Reagan's notes are something else. Presumably they are his own words (not veritable recordings of what, say, the attorney general said) summing up his understanding, his impression, his interpretation of events.

They are in no way public documents. My own guess is that the president's notes might obfuscate rather than clarify any issue touched on, but they are his own in the way his innermost thoughts are his own, and it is an outrage even to consider a demand that he produce them.

Suppose he does produce them (a poor precedent for future administrations) and suppose they do not contain the information a congressional committee hopes for. What then?

Well, we could try torture. Despite its bad press, torture is one of the most effective means of producing information that the victim does not wish to give.

Torture is unconstitutional, yes, but any competent sophist could argue his way over that trifling hurdle. Indeed, the administration itself, in its apparent distrust of the Miranda doctrine ("read him his rights"), seems a bit soft on the rights of accused people. Torturing a president might be a dandy prod to the debate.

No man, not even a Republican president, can be compelled to incriminate himself. Not even a president (servant though he is) can be probed, milked or dragooned by a panel of cops or a panel of Congress against his will and without lawyers on his side. And the evidence may not be forced out of him. If there is not independent evidence then there is no evidence.

It is shocking to hear the criticism of Lt. Col. Oliver North for appealing to the Fifth Amendment before a congressional committee. If I were North's lawyer, I would insist on his using that amendment before the committee, and if I were North I would use it myself. That's what it's there for.

My chief interest in protecting the president and his men like North is not that I love them unduly, but that I know the power of the state against a lone individual. If North can be hounded for using the Fifth and if a president can be forced to surrender a diary, then what happens to Tim Jones, 34, rounded up (God knows how and on God knows what evidence) and charged with rape. A few discreet beatings, a little deprivation of sleep, some grand strong lights, etc., and no telling how quickly the rape case can be solved. Which is fine unless you are Tim and are innocent.

It is not the protection of a president or a lieutenant colonel that should primarily concern an ordinary man—presidents and colonels often have resources to protect themselves—but the protection of an American who may lack wealth, prominence or the concern of powerful friends.

It was for such a man that the Bill of Rights was voted into the Constitution, and the least erosion of those rights should be a cardinal concern in America.

Through luck, possibly, I have never been inside a jail, or ever been questioned by a cop, but I know as well as you do that investigatory zeal can easily shade off into torture once we adopt the idea that "sometimes" and "for important national reasons" an American can be made to testify against himself. Truth serums, polygraphs, prolonged "consultations" with shrinks in jail or in locked wards can follow easily once the constitutional prohibitions are blurred.

Americans seem to think they live in a benign nation in which the state could never play the role of tyrant. The founders of the republic had no such illusion. A government of certified Boy Scouts will be a government of tyrants if power is not bounded, checked and watched with great suspicion, as the nation's founders well knew. They would agree, I am certain, that erosion of rights can start at the top as easily as anywhere else. (February 1987)

Giving Donkeys Their Due

Fat men should not ride donkeys. A 10-hand donkey should not be ridden by anyone over 112 pounds, a fact perfectly well known to anyone who has studied "The Professional Book of the Donkey" or the admirable paperback "Down Among the Donkeys."

Some troublemaker will probably argue that Christ weighed more than 112 pounds yet rode a donkey on Palm Sunday into the Holy City. The answer to that is that maybe it was a Nubian ass, not a small donkey. Besides, it is despicable to use a religious celebration to justify cruelty to living creatures.

Undoubtedly everyone read The Washington Post story from London about a donkey, Blackie, who was about to be subjected to some religious parade in a Spanish town, an event that a Spanish animal welfare organization thought should be abandoned.

After much hullabaloo the donkey was spared and sent to "a home for sick and aging donkeys" in England.

Now this donkey sanctuary in Devonshire is more remarkable than any isolated case of barbarism, and thanks to some recent correspondence I can tell you about it. A certain Elisabeth Knowles grew up a respectable, wholesome Yorkshire girl, fond of donkeys since she got to know them at English beach resorts—those rocky, gray shores to which families resort with the kids. They all have donkey rides, much as Americans have merry-go-rounds and pony rides.

She married Niels Svendsen, and they operated a small rural hotel, somewhat like Fawlty Towers at first (they closed the bar early the first night, as their customers, who were mainly bikers, got into fights all over the place), and they worked like dogs to make a go of it. Before that, they invented a device for drying babies' diapers and made and sold these, winning an industrial award. Mrs. Svendsen made many sales in her last month of pregnancy because (she said) people were afraid if she didn't get out of their offices instantly she would have the baby right there.

From the beginning one could guess this marriage would march to a different drummer. Few newlyweds invent and manufacture diaper-drying machines or enter the hotel business knowing nothing about it.

Indeed, Elisabeth met her husband when her car caught fire on a country road and Svendsen stopped to help, then went on about his business unaware that within five minutes he had smitten Ms. Knowles permanently. She spent several days roaming about to find him. At last she did find him and pretended this second meeting was an accident. In no time she married him.

Well, no sooner were they into the hotel business than Elisabeth started taking in donkeys. She would hear on Tuesday of an abused old donkey in one town and go fetch him. On Friday she would hear of another. In this way she accumulated 38 donkeys, which took endless care and ate up any profits from the hotel. This all started in 1969, and in 1973 her amateur donkey sanctuary became a registered charity, able to appeal for money and subject to inspection by charity commissioners.

The work was incredible, but the young couple seemed not to notice. Elisabeth's donkeys were chomping steadily along when a lawyer came to announce "a legacy."

Thank God. How much and from whom?

Well, no cash, actually. But Miss Violet Philpin died and willed Elisabeth 204 donkeys.

Here the Svendsens were, struggling along, when 204 more donkeys were either to be cared for by Elisabeth or be shot. Killing the lovable beasts was unthinkable. She didn't know how she'd manage, but she accepted the legacy, got the donkeys moved from Miss Philpin's farm a million miles off and flung herself, as you might say, on the grace of God.

It all worked. New land was bought, new stables built. People pitched in. Over the years the Donkey Sanctuary has become the greatest refuge for these beasts in the world—the sort of place a threatened donkey in Spain would naturally turn to.

It's not just for the sick and disabled. Sometimes a donkey arrives in foal, and the colt is raised. Males are gelded, but no donkey old or newborn, sick or hale, is turned away. In cases of grievous illness or old age in which the donkey can no longer stand up, eat, or enjoy life, it is shot in its own stall. This requires consent of one of the sanctuary's vets and a member of the governing board. There is nothing casual about it, and it is not done merely because the donkey has become a nuisance.

On endless nights Elisabeth, and now the staff, have been up all night trying to save a donkey brought in near death. One donkey arrived unable to eat because his teeth were broken and the jaw full of clotted blood. His skin was full of sores in which bits of blanket were embedded. And he lived.

Another donkey had both his ears almost completely severed. Another had been castrated with a broken glass bottle just for fun. In these and many other cases the beasts were nursed back to life. There are now 740 of them on the hundreds of acres of the sanctuary. They all have names. (Sometimes they eat their names off their stalls.)

Once a lady could no longer keep her old pet donkey and the sanctuary went to pick it up. Fat as a tub. There were crates of food to go with it. These were all ginger biscuits, little cakes like Twinkies, and all unsuitable for donkeys. The owner had read you feed hoofed animals "cake" (made of soybean residues, etc.) and for years had been feeding him cakes from a bakery. In time this donkey lost weight and became beautiful on a good diet.

If a donkey is in good health it (or preferably a pair) will be entrusted to someone who promises to care for it, but the animal belongs permanently to the sanctuary, and twice a year the new "owners" are called on to inspect the animal.

Once three ancient ladies applied for three donkeys. They had superb facilities and when inspected one June the donkeys were flourishing and the ladies delighted. But in December a call came that Ben and Bill "have got to be such naughty boys" and the old ladies could no longer manage.

"They have got so disobedient. Boots goes straight up the stairs when we tell him, but no matter how we push and pull, Bill and Ben refuse to go up. You know we are elderly ladies; we can't be expected to do such heavy work."

Ms. Svendsen was puzzled about those "stairs," but the ladies, nettled at such obtuseness, said:

"You don't think we can lie upstairs in our warm beds at night and leave those three little pets in the stables do you? It gets cold, you know. They use the guest bedroom."

So, regretfully, Ben and Bill came back to the sanctuary, soon followed by Boots, who didn't like it once his friends were gone.

In other cases, however, where people have not tried to make the donkeys go upstairs to bed, both man and beast have been happy.

Once television crews showed up for a documentary. One of the cameramen had an Afghan coat, shaggy and brown. In the middle of

Where people have not tried to make the donkeys go upstairs to the bedroom both man and beast have been happy.

things, a donkey thought he was a mare and came bounding across the pasture to mount him. He was only moderately injured, photographers being tough and used to groupies.

I wrote the sanctuary after reading about it in a magazine, This England, and got considerable information from Elisabeth Svendsen, including the two books. People can visit the sanctuary at Sidmouth, Devon, EX10 0NU, England. For the record, the registered charity number is 264818.

"We have many critics," Ms. Svendsen has written, "those who feel the money we spend on donkeys could be better spent on old people, young people, on battered babies, the list is endless. All worthy causes, but my love is donkeys and it is to them I wish my efforts to go. And as long as they need my help they shall have it."

It is common, of course, for people of easy circumstances who have never sat up all night for anything to criticize Elisabeth Svendsen, who for decades has been tough enough to get her beasts in and out of casts and braces, to scrape off the gore and to feed starving donkeys scientifically and sparingly to get them back on their feet. She cries like hell when a bad case comes in, but gets on with the messy task of care.

It has been argued over the centuries, especially by those who do nothing much for anybody, that such money should go to the poor. The answer is, nobody's stopping you from helping the poor, so get on with it. Donkeys are animals bred for human use, and it's a human responsibility to give them good care and at the last a painless death. That's Elisabeth Svendsen's task. She has also founded a center for grievously handicapped children, and has pioneered in work where these kids pat and cuddle and ride the donkeys, sometimes with startling therapeutic effects.

It would be better if she ran the whole world and took care of every injustice and cruelty in it, instead of just a few donkeys and pitiable children. But something is wrong when a good deed is sneered at for no better reason than there are a thousand other good deeds still to be done. (March 1987)

Dreams of Summer at Home

Great weather. Day by day we are steaming out the impurities of the blood and night after night we are building up a heat reservoir to get us through next winter.

Now you know some people who complain about our glorious July here in Washington. They have much to mutter about blast furnaces, hell and air-conditioning repairmen. This only shows, once again, how ungrateful the human animal is in the face of blessings.

Recently I returned from a tour of Wales and England, where summer is utterly unknown. In London the press alerted us to a heat wave and sure enough the next day it was 71 Fahrenheit. The English got all exercised and more or less dropped on the street the day it went to 79.

Most of the time it dipped into the 40s at night, and much of the time skies were gray, enlivened by drizzles and a daytime temperature in the 50s. There were "sunny intervals," which means that the sky turned paler gray, sometimes with a patch of milky blue to excite the Americans. If you looked intently at a tree trunk or lamp post you could debate whether it was casting a shadow. Some say yes and some say no. Occasionally there was a definite shadow, however faint, and then you could say for sure the sun was out.

This means there are no edible tomatoes, corn, squash or honeydews within the realm, but I do not propose to take up the immemorial dirge about English food, especially as I have solved the problem. You get a house or a flat or someplace with a stove in it. You go to the grocery or the vegetable markets (which are fine, now that stuff is imported from the Continent) and do your own cooking.

Anchovy paste and curry powder are cheaper and better than ours. Lamb is vastly better and cheaper, even with an unfavorable dollar exchange. So the main thing is no tomatoes or corn or honeydews or cantaloupes. Their cream is infinitely better, which is a bad thing because you return fatter than when you went, and it is awkward to remark on poor food when you have gained seven pounds on it.

But as I say this is just the cream. Their single cream (as they call it) glugs after the first day and can be spooned after the second. Their double cream, which they get from new improved atomic cows I imagine, has to be spooned to begin with. You take two small meringues and glue them together with cream and let them sit in the icebox awhile. This is why the English have bad teeth and why Americans come home fat.

They grow tomatoes in plastic bags in greenhouses and get rosy ping-pong balls which they eat to achieve their daily minimum requirement of acid. They also have corn but I had sense enough not to buy any. They do not, for all American purposes, have corn. They do have nubile potatoes of celestial origin and often serve you two kinds at the same supper. The best ones are roasted.

Wales may be even colder. You never set forth without a sweater and raincoat, except I do not believe much in raincoats and just got wet. We stopped once on a mountainside to view the lovely Vale of Clwd, or maybe it was the next one over, maybe Cwdnxrll. The Welsh are friendly, wholesome folk—very like Richard Burton on the whole—and nowadays all speak Welsh. The signs are in English also, but sometimes you can tell they just want to be mean, and then they put up a road sign at a critical intersection: Brwllnwlld, followed by a big arrow. No English subtitle and you do not realize that means Welshpool or Swansea or Ruthin or some other place you have heard of.

Ruthin is pronounced Rithin. We stayed at Ruthin Castle. The castle was rebuilt in Victorian times and has vintage elevators and gorgeous views out the window. The former owner was a woman said (in a historical folder you can get) to have had 200 lovers, not counting any stray stable boys. They have a special supper at which you sit on benches and people throw food, which is historically accurate. I once saw a well-researched movie in which Henry III threw hunks of bread at his father.

At this Ruthin supper they pass basins of lambs' necks in a kind of stew you eat with your fingers. There are bowls of water on the table and a bib round your neck. It does not do to wash in the water first. You wipe the goo on the bib first, then wash. Otherwise your bib gets sopping wet and quite uncomfortable. A lady plays the harp. Thus one experiences the 12th century, which like other centuries had the merit that it only came around once.

The sheep of Wales like Americans. If you stop to admire the view on a road, the sheep come barreling down by the dozen, bleating as if their little hearts would break. You feed them bread. The lambs eat bread then run to their dams to nurse. They welcome pats on the head and they all are fat.

In the Cotswolds the sheep do not expect Americans to feed them. They are more reserved. I was told that when a Cotswold shepherd died, his buddies went out to collect tufts of wool from bushes in the pastures, and this was stuffed in the coffin. When the shepherd arrived at heaven, surrounded by bits of fleece, the guardians saw at a glance he was a shepherd and let him right in. Feed my sheep.

I sat down once when I was cold and damp at some picturesque Cotswold inn and wept when I remembered sunshine. Of course the whole point of travel is to shake you up and make you quite unhappy for tomatoes, and in Wales and England you see marvelous things and broaden considerably; indeed, the whole island is somewhat of a paradise to see.

Still, I kept thinking of the great river I knew as a boy with the cypresses steaming in their excellent swamp and the sun white and the egrets deigning to shift a plume once every half-hour, waiting for the sun to go down. The mounds of cornbread and bowls of butter beans and big tin coolers with a block of ice in each that sat in the pantry. The house dark, the blinds closed, the furniture all covered with a kind of white burlap and the dogs asleep on the bathroom tiles. The fans droning, the dirt-daubers still working on their nests in the garage, adding mud from beneath the faucet out the back-porch door, though somewhat impeded by the thick growth of the ginger lilies that also like soppy clay.

And now at home again and no more cream, no more sheep, no more sleek cattle or anchovy paste or Norman naves, the wonders of Britain. But to land safe by the Potomac in the evening, the temperature still above 90, and to get home to the mutts asleep on the bathroom tiles, and in the icebox real tomatoes and real melons. And at last the fans droning and the sky held high by the heat and the blue waterlilies nudged by the red fish and the bugs all singing in the oaks.

If I had any sense at all I'd drop everything and organize a tour of this capital in July for the Welsh and the English. Let 'em live a little. (July 1987)

Conservation

All great causes make strange bedfellows, and as a general rule you should not kick too hard merely because you are getting squeezed out.

So when I hear that the chief point of the conservation movement is to preserve flea beetles, lichens and hippopotamuses for the sake of scientific study, I never call those who say it half-witted jobbernowls. We're on the same team.

But there is room for amplification and clarification, and I shall now explain what conservation is all about.

First, it really is true that science and study are monumental undertakings of urgent importance. We have all heard, ad boredom, that tremendous numbers of species will die out before they have been catalogued and their unique status identified. It is right to insist that this kind of study is needed more than it ever was before.

Second, it is also true that plants and animals, including noncuddly types like toads, may have uses in the treatment of disease, the manufacture of lemon sherbet, etc., not yet discovered. What if it were true (as I have so ardently prayed) that some humble organism of the Suriname forest, lightly sprayed in the studio, would transform the fundraisers of public TV stations into semi-literate, semi-civilized people? It is not beyond the bounds of hope or miracle.

Third, the gee-whiz factor of beauty is worth reckoning. I know a fellow of Carolina whose life was changed the day he saw wild jungle fowl scratching about, and it struck him that without committees, without budgetary allocations, without research and without thought he was seeing a natural gorgeousness that surpassed Solomon's.

We are not all so moved by the sight of wild chickens as the Carolinian, or that superb Frenchman who said after long reflection that he never expected to see anything so beautiful as a blue tree toad. But some people are changed and changed for the better, which is why hope is practical.

But when all these good things have been said there remains another thing and the most important thing. Wild things should live because life itself is an overwhelming value. I am not arguing vegetarianism here, though arguments exist for it. And I am not so young as to be unaware lions eat gazelles. I even know that with the best will in the world a dog will die and some of the grandest—hounds, say—die even sooner than many lesser breeds. There are days I think even we shall die, outrageous as the possibility may be.

But if one dog dies it is a comfort that other mutts are coming along, lest future men should miss the road of love. And it is the same with flea beetles, termites, hornets, crocodiles, and the rest of the glorious host that has waddled, buzzed, swum and otherwise burst forth from the beginning of the world.

People say our early forebears began to worship gods to ward off bad luck and avoid disasters of many kinds. But it is possible, surely, that awe came before fear and that the first source of awe was the panoply of life.

Most people would say it is sad if a criminal dies through touching a live wire; sad because the ending of life is sad, and this is true even if the life were inconvenient or threatening. You could wish the life had been different, but that it has ended is something else.

If there is a divine order, as most Americans are said to believe (though I have always doubted any such general belief exists among us), then to exterminate it willy-nilly must be a wrong interference in a divine setup.

If there is no divinity, on the other hand, it is still the case that the richness of animal and plant life is complex beyond comprehension. At the least, this life exists in accordance with natural forces more awesome than anything in human life, and to blunder about ignorant of what we are doing, like a young setter romping through the garden, or like a madman hacking works of high art, is stupid or worse.

I am not all-wise. No, really, please. But I have come to the conclusion that when a hornet gets in the house (and I yield to nobody in my terror of hornets) it is as easy to open the screen and let him out as it is to dash around for the hornet spray. And I feel better about it (in this age of trying to feel good) afterward. I do not get stung any more or any less than when I thought slaughter was the first order of business, hornetwise.

Is it conceivable that the better we think of lichens and flea beetles the better we behave toward humans? Maybe, maybe not.

But visualize an animal that has no usefulness at all (such a creature does not exist, but the mind can invent one for purposes of the argument) and no beauty at all and no value to science at all. Even so, it was born, it was "meant" to live, and if it has enough neurons in the brain to live it has enough to suffer. If it is killed, there should be a "good reason" for the killing, and the extermination of that whole species at human hands is something to give thought to.

Those electrical wire lures that zap bugs on the terrace at night are an abomination, and while the gung-ho types consider them a dandy fruit of technology, such devices are nothing more (and nothing less) than an expression of a mini-brain and an ill-developed conscience. Fly swatters have one advantage—the ordinary man of sense soon notices they are not worth the effort.

The purpose of conservation, then, is not the perpetuation of gorgeous form and color, nor the preservation of useful creatures, nor the advancement of our knowledge of the world, however good all those things may be.

The purpose of conservation is to celebrate life, which in itself is good. Good may fight against good, of course. If a dog races toward you with open fangs it may be right to kill the dog. But that hardly means you exterminate dogs in general.

Life, for God's sake, is supposed to be on the side of life. (August 1987)

The Nature of Greatness

You're pretty good at analysis, so take a look at these clues about a youth and tell me how you think he'll turn out:

He takes some thread and sews shut the eyelids of a pack of hogs, effectively blinding them. He does this because the farmer thinks the beasts will be more tractable if they can't see, and our bright lad helps him out.

Again, he is inconvenienced by a little yellow mongrel, that yaps and alerts the household when our boy wants to sneak out at night. So he kills a coon, skins it and ties the fur around the mutt. Terrified, the dog dashes home where other dogs tear it to pieces.

This paragon of the frontier was no other than Abraham Lincoln, the greatest of American heroes and, with Washington, the greatest of American presidents.

As he matured, Lincoln grew fond of animals and refused to kill them, or to hunt anything except possibly small creatures like squirrels.

But I think you might guess that any kid who sewed an animal's eyes shut, or deliberately sent a small dog to its death would probably turn into an ax murderer. He was, in fact, a lawyer, but that is not quite the same.

If you predicted such a kid would wind up a monster it would be an understandable error. We naturally judge the whole by the part. We see a particular action of a person and assume it is typical.

But if we knew a great deal more about the young Lincoln, far more than the two actions cited above, we might have predicted success or even grandeur for him. His remarkable memory, his taste for great literature and his determination to raise himself by his bootstraps might all suggest a future better than killing a dog or blinding some pigs.

Ever since reading "Lincoln's Quest for Union" by Prof. Charles Strozier, now at the City University of New York's John Jay College of Criminal Justice, I have been thinking of some curious behavior of Lincoln's before his (somewhat strange) marriage to Mary Todd. And throughout his life, no doubt, he sailed over darkness, as you might say, and I always had the feeling he was barely held together by a little baling wire.

Still, we can boast no other president of equal depth and grandeur, and I wonder if his early education had something to do with it. Few presidents have had a sense of humor, as Lincoln did. Certainly a lack of humor is one of the major defects of Jefferson. Lincoln as a youth had only a few books (he knew the Bible and "Pilgrim's Progress" and some of Shakespeare), but these seemed to have shaped his mind. Jefferson had endless books and endless interests—if he was not trying to tell the Carolinians what kind of rice to eat (one of his numerous failures) he was urging Lewis and Clark to keep an eye out for any stray mastodons out West as he wanted one the worst way for his park at Monticello. But I don't think he ever saw anything funny about himself.

But not to wander off to Jefferson, always a temptation for an American, and sticking to Lincoln, the point of the pigs and the dog is that any human has a central mass, maybe, but also an extraordinary number of oblique angles, tangents, storms in the nebulae, that do not fit the central character.

Mussolini, who has no great reputation as a merciful St. Francis sort of man, nevertheless did much to preserve songbirds that before him were killed on their long flights from Africa to northern Europe.

National leaders are undoubtedly shaped by circumstances over which they have no say, and by luck, as well as by character. Even as a boy or a youth, if Lincoln had grown up in Philadelphia in a settled respectable family, instead of in the middle of nowhere in a shack, he probably would not have bothered the luckless pigs. The kind of people you grow up with has a lot to do with how you behave. Americans watch stupid TV shows because that's what Americans do. Americans do not read Herodotus because that's not what Americans do. It has nothing to do with brains (Herodotus has more violence and horror in 50 pages than has ever yet appeared on the goriest American TV show, virtually all of it gratuitous and included for its sheer entertainment value to the reader) and everything to do with custom.

Custom is king. Art, ethics, morals are all closely related to custom or, as people like to say now, peer pressure. A great deal that passes for art, or that passes for morality, has nothing much to do with esthetics or with virtue, and a lot to do with what the guys in the office, or the Army, or the street happen to think. A lot of people who adored Elvis

Presley did not care so much about the music as about the fact that he spoke for them in the sense that he made it big though he was not educated. You found many who liked him chiefly because he was not white-collar. I never heard Elvis make grammatical errors in his speech. Do you suppose he would have been an even greater success if he got his verbs and prepositions all screwed up?

Enough. I have concluded not to judge Mussolini for his kindness to little birds or Lincoln for his barbarism with the little dog. Men can change and continually do. A nice cause for despair. A dandy cause for hope. (August 1987)

Ties and Things

Ties with diagonal stripes never struck me as mysterious until one day outside a church where I was pallbearer at a funeral a guy walked up and said:

"Excuse me, did you buy that necktie in England?"

I asked how he could tell.

"In England all diagonal stripes point to the left shoulder. In American they all point to the right."

Since then, of course, I watch ties on television, a thing I never did before, and from time to time I feel like crying out, "Hey, look, he's got a lefty tie."

If anybody knows why English and American stripes take off in opposite directions, I'd like to know.

Men pay great attention to their own ties, and not many men feel their wives are competent to pick them out at a store. I don't know why it is, since any number of ties at any store will do fine, but women seem to have the knack of picking out a tie you would not be caught dead in.

Once I slopped gravy or something on a tie as I was heading somewhere and stopped in Lord & Taylor to buy a clean one. Found just what I wanted and roamed about for 20 minutes trying to find somebody to sell it to me. Never did. (The poor woman who apparently spent a week in Lord & Taylor before being found and returned to her family made me think of this.)

I see you are wondering why I wore a striped tie at the funeral. The truth is, I have two or three black ties, but discovered if I wore them at a funeral people assumed I was the undertaker, so now I wear dark stripes. (Women have no idea the trouble men have getting dressed.)

My ties, about 150 of them, came largely from two sources, the ones I bought in college and the ones that used to be my father's. His ties were strange. His all came from Sulka's, a clothes store that ran to swirls in ties. They all looked as if they were made from somebody's brocade-covered sofa, and several of them were lavender. Never could wear any, except on the rarest occasions, but one thing you don't do is throw away ties.

The ones from college days all seemed to be from a store called

Steven-Shepherd. You could go in blindfolded and reach for the first tie and it would be fine. But possibly as the decades went on my old ties were not in the new fashion and besides they were wearing out. One day I rounded up a bale of these oldies and gave them to a charity which I guess put them in the furnace.

A sad day occurred not long after when my bow ties, all dating from the early 1950s and therefore the right size and shape, somehow attracted the attention of my personal hound. The rack fell on the floor and the hound, who hates lying on the bare floor except in summer, made her bed on them. In her old age she has not had full command of her bladder, and most of the bow ties had to go to the trash.

You have no idea what ties cost nowadays. Wool challis ties are rare. You could drop scrambled eggs on them, wait a few hours and brush them into pristine neatness. So the incentive to stop making them was great.

Silk ties were standard, and stores still adore them (and in some places will probably actually sell them to you) because one spot and that's that. And I felt polyester or linen or cotton ties were beyond the pale.

And then one day I saw a guy at the office with a glorious tie. I admired it, a thing I don't go around doing, and he took it off and gave it to me. It was made by a store called Lilly Pulitzer and it was all polyester. This changed my view of chemical ties. I had, by this time, the few ties from college that survived the giveaway, and Lilly, and three or four bow ties the hound missed, and a sparse assortment of other ties that were more or less wearable, mostly regimental stripes.

And then I found myself in London where I discovered all-chemical regimental stripes. They cost about two bucks. I bought a dozen and have worn them ever since. When ice cream falls on them, you put them in the washing machine. Some people say they can send silk ties to the cleaners and get them back looking great, but this has never happened to me. They always look limp, and do not tie properly.

Lilly Pulitzer's tie finally wore out and I only wear bow ties twice a year. But the dozen cheapos from England did me fine until the fellow asked me if they were English because the stripes pointed the wrong way.

Since then I cringe whenever I see Bob Hope flashing his Made In America labels on his clothes. Am I disloyal around the neck? American companies, when they make polyester ties, take pride in designs that shout, "Look what I got for two bits."

I read a piece by a good columnist who said he believed his readers

On days when I feel defiant I wear khakis and a blazer from London.

should know where the writer was coming from. So I thought I'd just tell you. I also wear wing-tip shoes, white or blue shirts, none of them short-sleeved, boxer shorts and black socks or white sweat socks. All others give me the creeps. I have two tan raincoats, without shoulder straps, grenade hooks or other warnings, and a white rain hat that wads up in the pocket.

On days when I feel defiant I wear khakis and a blazer from London, and if I feel persecuted and to hell with everything, I wear a safari jacket from L. L. Bean. That'll show 'em. If it's not a working day but I have to be in the office for a time on the weekend, I wear blue jeans and an orange T-shirt. Those are, needless to say, the days I bump into the chairman of the company. I guess life hits us all pretty much on the same butt.

Some people do not know anxiety, do not know pain. It has been said women take thought for their underwear in case a bus squashes them, but they do not have orange T-shirts. They do not have old hounds that pee on bow ties. They do not find mud on their shoes when dressing for dinner. The sorrows of life just pass them by. (January 1987)

On Jimmy Swaggart

It would be easy to attack poor old Jimmy Swaggart, wouldn't it? But it would be wrong.

Instead, what candle can we light today, for a wretched sinner (as he has insisted at some length and volume) hung up on pornography?

How can we help him get over it? Well, you've got me there, not being a therapist, you know, or a Grade A Christian either. But if it might help, I suggest he take off for Paris and enroll in a course of live sex shows, three a day for as long as strength lasts. It is possible that if he adheres faithfully to this regimen he will at last lose interest.

I always say your passion for anchovies diminishes with the fourth can. And once, at an eating house when I was in school, the proprietor found a sensational buy on guinea hens and stacked their crates up to the sky in the back yard, and we had to eat guinea hen day after day. Not one of those guys still has a taste for guinea hens today.

I also cured myself of an obsession with chocolate cherries by eating a two-pound box at the age of 8. Today I do not like them. In a Whitman's Sampler I usually give them to my wife, along with the coconut stuff, and at present she is not eating candy so I don't know what I'll do. I mean it's wrong to throw the chocolate cherry away, what with kids starving, but never mind my own struggles. I just wrestle with them with the strength God gives me and let it go at that.

In any case, there are some obsessions fairly easily cured by going whole hog, and Swaggart might want to give that a thought.

Then support groups are a great thing today. If there is not a Drooling Anonymous in Swaggart's neighborhood, where guys sit around and tell how they got over Hustler and Penthouse, he could start one.

In addition he could read through the Bible and mark in red all the passages warning against pornography. It is not, as far as I recall, the great preoccupation of the Gospels. That might give him some comfort.

And might not. The American Constitution, after all, guarantees freedom to bewail any sin at all. Many people get mad as hell if told to

It was Playboy and magazines that he hated. I never heard him preach against hiring a whore to do shows.

come off it, buddy, it's not worth going on and on and on and on about. Your average guy doesn't like it when his soul-shattering confession is received with a yawn.

I know of a man who worked in a newspaper wire service and he thought the word "rat" was the most disgusting thing in the language. Never in his life would he say the word, though possibly late at night in the privacy of his bed he may have said it for chills.

Well, everything went along all right until some city—I think it was Atlanta—had a campaign to get rid of rats. The cat was out of the bag. This man could not say "rat" and could not allow anybody in his presence to say it, either, and when the great anti-rat program began it was more than his sensitive nerves could stand. Don't know what happened to him, maybe he confessed and found peace.

My dear mother served on a civic beautification committee once and they decided to clean up around billboards. They cut down a mini-field of marijuana at the base of one sign and there was some kind of stink raised. I was just a wee tad, but the committee ladies took some jeers from those who said they ought to be smarter than harvesting mari-juana and hauling it away. I grew up understanding that marijuana was something dreadful, perhaps a code word for incest.

Something of my mother's billboard-marijuana trauma may have affected Swaggart at an impressionable age, so that he never got over it. There are experts now who deal with phobias and compulsions and obsessions, probably well worth their fees.

I used to go to pieces over wasps. My wife used to say I could never be secretary of state because if a wasp landed on the podium at Geneva or somewhere I'd bolt and be in the next county instead of finishing my speech. I just got some books on wasps and knowledge cured me of my irrational fears. Didn't cost a dime. Same with spiders, which didn't bother me so much, but still some. So I believe in reading up on things that scare you terribly. Study less and read more is a good prescription for many.

Now Swaggart would be in less trouble if he hadn't spent so much energy thundering in public against pornography. To hear him, you'd think it was like breaking a dog's ribs or snapping at an ugly woman.

Naturally people wondered why he was such a hypocrite, roaring against it then doing it. But in fairness I think it was Playboy that he hated, and I never heard him preach against hiring a whore to do shows.

I just hope this latest commotion among TV preachers will not rouse the nation into some unthinking reaction like burning Playboy. If it didn't cost too much I'd buy it myself, but even if you don't like it, you can see it does no good to burn it. Guys who don't read could still hire somebody to jiggle about in person. Frankly, there is just no end of sin in this world, and frankly I have flat given up trying to sanctify the heathen.

Sometimes I get snotty letters about my virtuous work in this very space, but as we know sometimes seed falls in weedy ground and what can you do? Tares overwhelm us, indeed they do. So I just go on and hope I get through the world alive. And then all this misery and grief business—sometimes it's a nervous stomach, a bad digestion. All preachers should check that out first, before deciding it's God or something dreadful. And if the day's work brings only grief and jeers, that may be nature's way of saying simmer down, good buddy. Take five. (February 1988)

Drop Me Down in Mississippi

I knew a dowager of Clarksdale, Miss., who in her eighties told her nephew that integration was a good thing—"we called ourselves Christian, but we weren't being Christian dealing with them. So it's high time and a good thing for whites to have integration. There's just one thing I don't understand, where did they all come from?"

Her own Sunflower County was thick with blacks, but she never saw them or thought about them much. They didn't walk on the sidewalks or go in the drugstores, and when integration came it amazed the old lady that all of a sudden they were everywhere.

The South is one thing—definable by climate, history, and institutions—but southerners are something else. Black or white—a tenant farmer or a field laborer or a professor of Greek—will see the region differently, though all were southerners.

One of the shocks to the white South was the discovery that blacks do not like the mansions of Natchez, say, as much as a white architecture buff fond of going on pilgrimages.

I grew up on the Tennessee-Mississippi border but had strange notions that blacks should vote. Since I wrote for a newspaper, my views in the early years of the civil rights movement were well known in Mississippi, where such views were anathema and a betrayal of what was called "the southern way of life."

All the same, when I was in Mississippi I never heard a single rude remark. Some good folk there may have thought it would be a grand idea to shoot me, but personal face-to-face rudeness was something I never encountered.

Because the South had been poor, because people could not rely on money to make things easy, hospitality was greater in the South than elsewhere.

If I were to be plopped down somewhere without a dime and not knowing a soul, I had rather be dropped down in Mississippi, whether black or white, than any place I can think of. I would be fed and given a place to sleep. I have seen their courtesy time and again. Which does not change the fact that racial pressure—pressure to change old ways—could result in bald murder.

It is also hard now to believe the power of such institutions as the Baptist Church, whose clergy were a bulwark of segregation, and who did their damnedest to prevent it.

But that, of course, is merely to say that none of us likes startling change.

It was not entirely easy to be a "moderate" let alone a "knee-jerk liberal" in the South.

Often I sense strongly in southerners I know a kind of exile mentality, a kind of living apart from the mainstream. Partly for this reason I think southerners are more likely to muse over their navels, as it were, than Yankees. More likely to see life in terms of great issues, less likely to devote major energy to making another buck. Less likely, I would say, to manage business or banking well, and less impressed with wealth and fame.

More hostile, on the whole, to hustlers (unless they are in the religion business) and more keenly fascinated with land, whether it produces money or not.

All people love their home country, surely. Maybe southerners are no different at all in this. Probably we are no different from other people, apart from being more polite. It is obvious that the incredible complexity of life, the interaction of people, is as rich in Nebraska or Wisconsin as in Tennessee.

But anybody who grows up along the southern Mississippi, along that River (which is always thought of as upper case) never gets over it. A great mind could probably explain what the influence of the River is, psychologically, with its quiet horseshoe lakes and meanders, its frightful power in flood, its rebelliousness and terror. Nobody thinks of it with the loving tenderness given the Potomac, the French Broad, and other pretty rivers. The majesty of the great River has a more complex effect which I am not bright enough to define but perceptive enough to know.

For me, at least, the South is the River, the bluffs of Vicksburg and Memphis, the bald cypresses with egrets dangling their great plumes in the heat of a July noon, the warm lakes full of leeches and covered with cottonwood fluff.

The rest is just life, and could be anywhere. You would not, of course, want to be buried in the North or the West, unless it cost too much to be shipped back home. (March 1988)

Our Republic for a Horse

My thinking has run in a different direction, so I am annoyed to hear the acrimonious talk about Jesse Jackson—whether he could win the nomination, whether America is ready for a black president, etc.

I have given much thought, on the contrary, to whether America is ready for a horse. As you recall, the emperor Caligula named his horse consul of Rome, and one thinks how asinine that was. And then one thinks again.

Underlying my meditations is the fact that everyone agrees on, that our present system of getting a president is absurd, costly, inefficient and likely to present us with a circus clown who does not drink, swear or ride on boats, and who has never said or written anything that anybody can discover, and who is therefore unobjectionable to all.

The true problem, needless to say, is that democracy is still evolving, and its limits are uncertain. You find some who profess to believe in democracy all the way, but when you pin them down they don't really favor popular elections every four years for, say, the Mississippi Supreme Court. They also do not favor referring free speech to the opinion of a majority of voters.

In other words, a number of aspects of American life are carefully hedged off from majority rule, but why is that, if we have such profound trust in ordinary good folk?

The answer is utterly clear: We do not in the least trust the majority in questions of justice or many civil liberties.

But we do increasingly believe the president should be chosen by a majority of all qualified voters, and almost every adult is now qualified.

Washington, Adams, Jefferson and the early presidents were of course chosen by a minority of adult Americans. So was Lincoln. But we now all agree that everybody should have the right to vote, and I would not change that.

But surely we might have better presidents if greater weight were given to experience? Or does it work all right as it is, with a president who keeps getting mixed up about whether he saw a movie about something or whether he did something?

There is no question of limiting the vote. There is little chance of turning to a parliamentary system, which clearly would work better. So what can be devised to improve our present system?

Which brings up the horse. It is ironic that the two most stable democracies in the world are England and Holland, both of which have queens at the moment. Royal families, and don't forget Sweden and Denmark, are said to be a stabilizing influence. They are utterly bound by the legislature and courts, but they bring people together, as the saying goes, even better than the Redskins and with less anxiety about game scores every year.

At the time of George Washington, an American monarchy was considered and abandoned. Even then it was obviously too late to establish a monarchy. You really should start that kind of thing about the time of Alfred the Great, and certainly no later than William the Conqueror—a monarchy has to be ancient enough to be beyond petty nitpickings on whether the monarch is playing with a full deck or can speak the national language. (The English in particular have rarely liked English rulers, and usually have turned to the French, Germans or Dutch to establish the royal house, and the system has worked fine for them, especially as they have played somewhat arbitrarily with the succession over the centuries.) So a unifying royal house is out, totally out, for us.

Instead of a royal house, how about a national animal? The eagle might have done, except our American eagle is extremely likely to become extinct in a century or so, and we want to build for the ages. The wild turkey would do, as Benjamin Franklin so eloquently urged, except that grocery stores keep having undignified sales.

Possibly a horse, a descendant of Traveller or Trigger or Flicka. Or the current winner of the Derby—the details are not important, really. But perhaps a dog would be better, as more Americans have dogs than horses or anything else. A cat for second in command, in deference to the feelings of many.

Such an animal would not govern, needless to say, though reasonable attention would be paid to the activity of the paw, eye, tail and so forth. I have noticed Max, Luke and other personal dogs I have had have all been right on target about the general wisdom of any course of action in our house, through many changing circumstances.

We would elect a National Guardian of the horse, eagle, turkey, dog or buffalo, whatever we decide on as the national beast. This guardian could make of the office what his brains, skill and heart permitted.

Our present system of getting a president is likely to present us with a circus clown.

Some guardians (like some presidents) would be brilliant, others mediocre, but his first duty would be to care for the national animal.

Neither he nor the dog would have the title of commander in chief, however, and his duty of daily walkies would probably prevent his getting too big for his britches. On the other hand, if the Congress started seizing too much power, National Guardian would be a flexible post that could rally sentiment to limit it.

The major business of the nation would be in the hands of the legislature, but tempered always by the tremendous national affection for the national dog and, by extension, his guardian chosen by popular election.

There are other routes, mind you, if the national beast is not thought good. I would even go for a national empress, who would have roughly the same duties as the guardian of the national dog, and her grand title, Empress of the States, might please females. We would not want an emperor, who might be tempted to meddle.

The great Justinian, the Byzantine emperor, chose wisely when he made Theodora his empress. She had great influence, as some presidents' wives have had, but was always under the restriction that she was empress only because Justinian chose her.

Of course there were always nervous nellies, the kind who are never satisfied with anything no matter how practical or wise. Even Theodora was complained of, because she was fond of getting on the stage naked and had hearty appetites. But even Gibbon, the historian from whom most of us get our understanding of that lady, said some good things about her. He did point out she kept hopping in and out of beds, and that some who thought they had her favor for a night were ousted in the middle of things for a replacement who paid more or offered more. People say that was shocking, but you see how wise Justinian was to select her. No doubt he hoped to keep the intrigue and bribes and scandals limited to the empress, who did not have ultimate power.

She also had high qualifications for her office, apart from her fabulous beauty:

"Her skill was confined to the pantomime arts; she excelled in buffoon characters . . . the whole theatre of Constantinople resounded with laughter and applause."

In other words, much that we love in Ronald Reagan and some other presidents could be taken care of by an Empress of the States, who would be a friend to all. Without access to the red telephone or the Army. She would fulfill many, perhaps most, of the things we value in a president.

Either way, a national dog or an empress, we could set up some unifying symbol we could all share, whether Republican or Democrat, and then the government itself could get along in a methodical way without our customary hysteria. Horse, eagle, Welsh terrier, empress, I am fully flexible in the matter. Any of them would be an improvement over present ways. (April 1988)

Spiritual Revival

I guess I've been in another world and missed getting the word, but ever since I left Salem I keep hearing about "the great American spiritual revival" and it turns out—you won't believe this—they mean the 1980s.

Salem is one of those pleasant Massachusetts towns lucky enough to have saved some of its 17th-century houses, and on a Smithsonian Associates tour up the coast from New Orleans to Canada I think Salem was the highlight. There you can see clearly the merits of the religious life.

That's where they hanged about 20 witches in the late 1600s, and I was lost in admiration at the house of the judge who questioned the evil ladies. Considering that New England was the end of the world, they built extremely well. The beams were magnificent, and heroic (if slightly pathetic) efforts had been made to give the house details of refinement in the chamfering and general woodwork. The leaded windows were generously sized for the period, suggesting a civilized concern for sunlight and air, and in general I was more favorably impressed than I expected to be.

The guides, apart from some whining stridency of the voice, which of course they cannot help, were informative, gracious and blessed with humor and good sense. They apologized for hanging the witches, as if modern Salem had any responsibility for it. You cannot hold Dallas, Memphis or London in contempt merely because Kennedy, King and Charles were barbarously slaughtered in those towns.

Besides, at Salem they hanged the witches instead of burning them, which is a refinement in itself. So for several days I assumed all this "American spiritual revival" business referred to the delicacy with which our Colonial fathers dealt with horrible people like witches.

It may be true, as they say now, that the women were not witches at all, and were thus unjustly executed, but anybody can make a mistake, any court can, and besides it was long ago.

But then it has turned out—and I suppose it's partly because I have been watching television for a change that I have finally noticed it— this spiritual revival is going on right now. More Americans go to more churches than is general in Europe. That's all they really mean.

Except I would call it a church attendance revival, to be accurate. It need have nothing at all to do with anything spiritual.

There are many reasons, all of them adequate, why people might go to churches, especially the ones that have increased their membership notably in this decade.

First, people get tired of television after a bit, and tickets to the theater are too costly for most people. Also, the proceedings at churches are live, and as I discovered years ago (when I found myself much moved by a freshman college production of "King Lear," in which Gloucester was played by a champion basketball player in blooming seven-foot health) there is nothing like a live human in front of an audience, when he has mastered his lines and stage business reasonably well. You don't need Judith Anderson for the theater to be magical.

Not only that, it is therapeutic (they say now) for all of us to be stroked a good bit. We need to hear each other say, "I love you" and to hear I'm OK, you're OK, and pardon's the word for all.

Our current spiritual revival has taken it a step further: We're OK and the rest are headed for Hell. That gets the juices going and gives one a sense of stature. The elect. What a dandy surprise.

Another aspect of the revival is the message that God wants us to be happy and especially He wants us to be rich. Get yourself saved and see your income rise. This is an enchanting message likely to be favorably received by those who have never tried it, which is always a majority.

Classically, just as a point of information, a spiritual life has meant humility, compassion, perhaps poverty, certainly self-denial and other similar things that rarely sell very well and almost never draw crowds.

But if today the spiritual life means superiority to street people, a goal of upward mobility and a general sense of having made it, thank God, then you see that this spirituality is no different at all from what used to be called the world, the flesh and the Devil. Of course it is popular. Always has been.

The clever thing is to take worldliness, ambition, greed, class hatred and all the other things we are a bit embarrassed about, and simply call them religion and salvation. In this way we can be (thanks to redefining a few things) virtuous, rich, superior, in solidarity with most Americans and free of burdensome welfare taxes all at once.

That was the good thing about Salem. They lacked resources that we have today, but they had the basic knack of hanging a batch of

Get yourself saved and see your income rise. This is an enchanting message.

women with a clear conscience and a ring of alleluias. They came to America to be free to worship God as they chose, and for some time they enjoyed their blessed spiritual life without criticism.

And then came some heathen bastard—Jefferson with his Statute of Virginia for Religious Freedom is as good an example as any—to say in effect that Salem spirituality was imperfect.

The same techniques, of flattering the faithful, pointing out the enemy, providing communal emotional outlet, and achieving as high a level as possible of material wealth, are in use today and attract support as solidly as in Salem. The only difference is that now we have a much greater population and much more effective ways of selling an eminently salable message.

So of course we have once more a great American spiritual (is it the third or the fifth or the hundredth?) revival. Which is fine with me, as long as I've figured out what is meant by "spiritual." It means be a slob as usual and let God rain the dollars down. (June 1988)

To Hell in a Hand Basin

I've been a housewife for a whole week now and do not like it.

The person with whom I live decided to have some bones drilled in a minor operation, since when she has not scrubbed a floor, pulled a weed or done anything else.

I yield to nobody in my respect for and pampering of women. I am a man of the '80s and therefore assumed all kinds of extra labors. Tonight, if strength holds, I shall scrub the kitchen floor, which is beginning to go bad.

It is said that clothes-washing machines are not difficult to run, and I have examined the one in the basement. I do not understand it.

"It's a good thing you bought some shirts," I was told. I have 16, counting the ones that have terminal collars. So I have a few more days left. Same with socks.

But the terrier has to be walked, you know. Besides that, he has two water bowls, upstairs and downstairs, and these must not only be filled but also scrubbed daily. He also needs periodic dipping in the lily pool, an exercise that causes all the fleas to go to his head where he can scratch them off into rugs and chairs. He also has developed a fondness for a bowl of ice late in the day. He licks it and in due time drinks it. He howls if neglected.

A gentleman from western Tennessee recently gave us a five-foot orchid, which is blooming steadily but has to be soaked and syringed daily.

In the icebox there is a roast beef, cooked the day before this hospital nonsense began. We are nearing its end. Eight days old and still smells all right. Last Saturday I stopped in a strange grocery and acquired spring rolls, dried black mushrooms, pickled red ginger and curious things in cans, which I made into a nourishing soup for the invalid. Just yesterday it turned out there was still a toddy glass of these things all mixed together. I have added them to some spaghetti sauce I found in the freezer.

Fortunately the invalid eats nothing to speak of. I have made a million pots of tea and I do both toast and English muffins. Found some cooked chicken in the freezer, just boiled, and if you get hungry enough you run a hunk of it under the hot water and chew it with musings on mortality.

I have always said it is absurb to make beds, when all you have is two sheets. I sleep on the top one. It has not been necessary to do anything, thank God, but the hand basin is something else. It has to be scrubbed twice a day. Toilet paper has to be fetched from its inaccessible lodging back of bath mats, croup kettles, foot baths and flea dips.

It's not that I am a helpless person. In two different periods when I was a bachelor I managed quite well. In one case I cooked a cornmeal sludge on a coal-oil burner, following the excellent directions of M. F. K. Fisher, who is right when she says never add beets to it. It turns carrion purple.

The other time I cooked in a fireplace. One pan, which is good for making a soup of parsley, onions and milk. Very good with semistale bread. There was no problem in those days with "running a house." Life was simple. I spent no more than five minutes a day, or perhaps a week, on general maintenance. The only awful occurrence in those days was when the cat had kittens on top of a pile of 12 shirts.

How different it all is, once you are snared into buying a house. I cannot recall from bachelor days any of this business about hand basins. I believe I did nothing but wash the soup pan in it every few days. There was no garbage; I only bought what I ate and I ate it all. The onion skins I threw out the window on Mr. Hoxton's Japanese anemones.

There was no such thing as vacuum cleaners or washing machines or brooms or any of those other newfangled engines that do nothing except make more work. The main trouble with America, I have always known, is too many moving parts, all of which are bound to get out of order or need oil or new bags or washers or some other damned thing.

But with somebody upstairs in bed—it will be weeks before that person can drive me to the subway or do the kitchen floor or cook properly or work the endless machines—you cannot live sensibly as you once did.

In the middle of it all the car stopped dead in the middle of Massachusetts Avenue. The prestidigitator or some such thing refused to fire, the man said. It was towed here and there, winding up in Silver Spring, where I picked it up on a blazing afternoon. They are building something and have usurped the public sidewalks, so you walk down the highway with a billion cars all operated by maniacs. In London they tear down huge buildings without so much as one day's inconvenience

"Nothing is so engaging as the little domestic cares into which you appear to be entering."

to pedestrians, but in Washington any tin-pot half-baked blank-faced developer freely closes a whole block so he doesn't have to look for a parking place for his Rolls when he occasionally visits the site.

The time comes very quickly when there isn't any more ice in the icebox. Something has to be done about dish towels. They smell if you just run water over them, which I think is all I used to do. I want to go to Magruder's for melons but am afraid to. The customers there are mean.

The only respite from this drudgery has been Elizabeth Langhorne's "Monticello, A Family Story," though it has shaken my faith in Thomas Jefferson.

His daughter, Martha, is trying to run Monticello by herself with a batch of servants and has gone almost mad, she writes to her father in Washington. No time for reading or anything else, and "our beautiful cups are all broke but one."

Jefferson replies: "Nothing is so engaging as the little domestic cares into which you appear to be entering."

An imbecile like that wrote the Declaration? (July 1988)

Seer Suckers

You have heard the Russians are going to mind-read all our national secrets with a team of seers in Vladivostok or somewhere, and the question is whether we should fight back with our own committee of psychics.

To hear some people talk—the ones that buy a shower curtain only on the day the astrology column recommends for financial dealings—we should have a good kennel of extrasensory perception folk to zero in on Moscow. And why not? It would keep them off the streets and do no harm, as long as we know it's all balderdash, as so many government operations are.

I once knew a spectacular Persian lady who laid her wedding plans in strict accordance with advice from an astrologer, but she said it was just one of those things brides do over there, like putting a dime in the shoe. Still, it seemed to me the astrologer was inconvenient and made a real difference, because in her case all the tentative plans had to be changed.

And just this week at a morning coffee break a woman of excellent sense told me she had lost an Accounts Receivable file from her office and had been utter-utter about it until she thought of some wonderful psychic in San Francisco. She phoned him and he said look in the bottom drawer right at the back.

Well, she said, that was nonsense, since she had not only gone through all the files with care but had torn up the whole building searching for days. But you know what? There the missing file was, right where the psychic said.

You can't say baloney; it's the same as saying you're a nut, a fabricator of facts, and gullible as well. But I did point out the psychic knew her from the past and doubtless had a good idea where she would stick a file. Besides, I went on, anybody can be a seer, and to demonstrate this I turned to another woman who had just filled her cup and was coming over to be agreeable:

"What ever happened," I asked her, "to that fellow in Italy, the one with bright yellow hair and brown eyes, that you thought the world of?"

"How in the world did you know about him? Did I tell you?" she replied, casting an eye about like a fox hearing the hounds crossing the stream after all.

"Why would you have told me?" I said. "Of course you didn't. It's just that anybody who ever knew any woman knows she once knew a guy with bright hair years ago." (And he gets more wonderful in retrospect and he was neat and thoughtful and didn't read the paper at breakfast, and once on a ski slope he etc. etc. etc.)

The question is not whether all this psychic stuff is baloney, for it unarguably is, but why people love to believe it, and I can guess why that is, too.

Here's an example:

When we cut for deal in a card game I announce the card I am going to draw from the deck. Four of diamonds, say. When it's the nine of clubs nobody notices, but when (once in 52 times, roughly) the card I draw is the one I have announced, we are all rather pleased and feel deeply in touch with the cosmos.

But once it was different. I announced the queen of spades, and as my finger touched the card to pull it out, I *knew* it was the queen of spades, and if it had been any other card I would have been astounded.

Why was that? Well, one explanation is I am a psychic. Another is that God wanted me to be right for a change. But the most likely explanation is this:

The queen of spades is sometimes called the "death card," so if you know that, you are likely to feel a little differently about it from the four of diamonds. And as you touch it you may have a strong feeling about it, and since everybody is concerned about his own death and thinks what a calamity that would be for the whole world and civilization as we know it, it's not surprising you should have an emotional charge, as you would if you touched a device that sets off atom bombs.

Another thing happens, too. When I say I was "certain" when I touched it that the card would be the queen of spades as predicted, how do you measure that "certainty"? A human, looking back, is easily able to think he was "certain" when in fact he was only moderately hopeful. But suppose my feeling of certainty was as strong as I say it was.

Even so, that means nothing. Some people, including me, are always having vivid hunches, which are usually wrong and they forget it. But when a strong hunch proves right, they cannot get over it.

The trouble here is that the feeling may be sincere, yet have nothing to do with the seemingly miraculous event. To say psychic events are nonsense does not mean the feelings themselves are imaginary.

If I see my entire experience with the queen of spades as an ordinary event explained without recourse to the occult, I may even feel a bit deprived. Something that was magical and wonderful has turned into something understandable.

So what is really curious is why I was disappointed to see the reasonable and ordinary explanation for all that occurred. Why should I have been disappointed that nothing amazing happened? Did I really want something magical to intervene?

Well, in a word, yes.

A lot of sensible people are like that. We know magic is baloney, but down in the primitive brain somewhere we still believe in magic, and are still quite sure (never mind the paltry "evidence") we have occult powers, or at least that somebody does. We still believe, at depths undisturbed by reason, that our words or our feelings can change physics or geology or anything else. And when our rational mind examines and informs us there is no magic, we are disappointed or even resentful or even defiant. The dark brain thinks rational proof is a killjoy.

These amazing certainties we may have from time to time about psychic events are not usually so certain we would bet much cash on them. A scientist (if a betting man) would not hesitate to wager a fortune on his prediction that an apple dropped from the roof would fall. A psychic does not hold that kind of certainty, preferring (when sincere) a cloud of fuzz.

All seers and psychics have one thing going for them that no reasonable man does, and that is an audience predisposed to believe him. You discover the wonders of penicillin and you have to scrap like a tiger to convince people. You proclaim (as I now shall) that President Reagan will startle the world with an announcement this Aug. 17 and half the town will say gee, wonder what it is this time.

Don't ask. (July 1988)

American Summer

The American core was shaped by the American summer. As you know, there are some who complain of it, partly because they have never interested themselves in any aspect of nature and partly because they were born with squinty eyes and mean spirits. But for steady and bright folk there is nothing better than an American summer, such as we find from Canada to the Gulf, and from the Atlantic to the Pacific, not counting the upper fringes of the Pacific Coast, which has a quite different and rather dreadful climate in which you cannot grow watermelons or corn.

What a joy to the American traveler to discover that Minnesota, the Dakotas and Montana yield nothing to Tennessee or Mississippi in restorative heats. But of all summers, the best is the August from Washington south to the Gulf and up the great river to southern Illinois.

We could have slightly cooler nights, perhaps, without ruining the summer's glory, but the discomfort of Washington nights is largely the fault of incompetent designers of buildings. Outdoors even the hottest night is agreeable.

Nobody likes to sweat at night, and in a properly run nation there is no need to. Fans are best.

Before getting back to our American core, I should say the price of leeks came down this week, inviting their use in vichyssoise soup. When leeks cost too much, you use onions, but they are not as good. This soup has cooling properties like iced tea but you get excellent calories as a bonus.

On "unbearable" nights, the right thing is a tub of tepid water. Read a book and soak half an hour and let the water out and continue reading till dry. Pajamas are un-American before October. American openness began with a tendency to throw off clothes, a thing we would not know how to do except for summer. American optimism springs from day after day of sun followed by melting nights. Nobody believes in death when the corn is growing.

Corn and tomatoes, melons and cucumbers, rightly did the Israelites weep for their loss in the desert. Who would not feel abandoned if these things failed? They do not fail in the American summer.

Soak half an hour and let the water out and continue reading till dry.

What this town needs is more stores with wooden porches and red hounds asleep on them. The sound of footfalls on such porches is near the center of the American soul, and is lost only at a great price. Equally central is the choir of bugs, cicadas and singers of the American night, while in the dark trees the lunas and lesser moths lose all restraint.

London and Paris have no such music. Unconsciously, American travelers there wonder what's the matter. No bugs, that's what's the matter.

American ingenuity began with protection from mosquitoes and American armies were the first to rig up showers out of nothing. A perpetual outdoor spray for water buffaloes in my old town displays American sympathy with animals, brothers of August. They never shower their buffaloes in Geneva because they don't understand summer, which is what's wrong with them.

All that is good about us comes from our summer, magnanimous and freewheeling and lusty and free. Some countries have no summer, which leads them to creep about in raincoats, suspicious of strangers, terrified of novelty, hoarding soup and locking up the flour.

The American core is more expansive, more trusting. We learn trust in our summers. Day after day without snow and lye soap.

My last hound has died—what a connoisseur of summer she was. Her great sorrow was never to catch bumblebees, which she chomped her jaws at, missing considerably and a good thing, too, but like all animals she never understood the blessing of disappointment. The young terrier lacks gravitas, dozing spread-eagle with every paw out at 45 degrees but precisely calibrated to sleep (as summer progresses) on a bedroom bench, a bedroom floor, the bathroom tiles, behind the shower curtain inside the stall, or out the dog door to the stone stoop with iron railing for chin-rest. Plants and animals, except humans, have exquisite adaptations to summer, but we have surrendered too much to the illusion of efficiency, by which we mean hot asphalt and many appointments.

Considering the innumerable benefits of our summers, the intense light and the purifying heat that gets rid of our poisons and strengthens us for one more winter, I hope we shall hear an end to complaints about dog days. The days of Orion's old dog, Sirius, prince of hounds and brightest of all the stars. Is there no end to insolence, to complaints?

Up at 6 and the paper's there and the day promises fair and the birds bustling with matters of avian moment and the dog patrolling his empire and the waterlilies swelling to greet the sun and the sow bugs back under their bricks. There's a jar of cold water and the fans are working. Joy is what life is for. (August 1988)

Olympic Torch

Greg Louganis, the big diver, has been such an inspiration to me painting the porch floor.

There he was, superb in strength and grace, and he was some points behind the fine Chinese diver. He might lose. Unthinkable. But everything depended on his final dive.

He dived, got out and began to cry.

Oh, my word, I felt like crying also. The last dive was not so hot. Poor guy had lost and no wonder he was overcome.

Then it turned out his final dive was better than I thought. He had won. These were tears of triumph.

And I thought how instructive the Olympics are. So much like daily life with its defeats and victories and confusion which is which. All week I have been painting the porch floor, and even now I don't know if I've won or not.

Would you agree with me, I have always said a nation's recreations and amusements are charged with moral significance. I sought my gold in porch-floor painting. Now I know that some will say that is a trifling amusement, unworthy to be compared to Olympic events. And I freely confess not quite as much strength is required for my endeavor as the Olympian.

But what makes the two things identical is the moral significance with which both these activities are charged.

Like Louganis, I have trained for years. Like him I am patient. I bought the brush a year ago, I bought the paint two months ago. Time after time I was ready, but then it rained. Or there was some onerous task I had to do. And then the day came, high noon at last.

I painted most of the floor, leaving a path of newspapers to the door. Forty-eight hours later I moved the path and painted what was not painted in the earlier round.

When the second part was painted and dried, I raced down in the morning to admire it all. Dear God, there were two footprints on the beautiful pewter gray surface.

Would you blame me if I threw in the towel. All that preparation (and words cannot say the boredom of scrubbing and preparing the floor for paint) and all that strain, the agony in the back and knees, the tension of avoiding gobs of paint on my khakis—and for what? Two ugly footprints on the uncured paint. Wash away, O wash away the stain. But it will never wash out.

This is what separates men from boys, champions from also-rans. I thought of Louganis. I thought of other heroes, Prometheus and Sisyphus and great Achilles who saw the body of his friend violated. He did battle. But his mother (and she was a goddess) said no, he must desist, for he himself would die. And he said (despising death and danger) then he would die, but only after he had done justice on the unjust.

I knew what lay ahead. It meant another 48 hours. It meant making a new Wet Paint sign, and waiting two days for it all to dry. And maybe there would be a stripe where the old and new paint joined, maybe it would look amateurish and not elegant.

A good man lives with anxiety. With uncertainty. I repainted.

I waited two days, came racing down to see the grand effect of this long labor. Good God, there were three dreadful footprints. Adidas I believe. Surely this was too much to endure? Two sessions of painting, then a third session of repainting. And now this, a fourth session to paint once again?

I watched Louganis on TV. He, too, was behind. All his skill was set at naught by some kid from China without even any body hair. He, like me, was humiliated, to go through the same agonizing exercise yet once more. With no certainty of triumph. The gods never grant us certainty, they merely command us to do what a brave man must.

And now I face perhaps the final test. The fourth session of painting.

I am not the first to ask if it will ever end. Now some will say Oh, shut up, all that's at stake is your simple-minded amusement of painting the porch floor.

They do not comprehend that American recreations are charged with moral meaning. I could no more refrain from correcting this last injustice, these dreadful footprints on the paint, than Achilles could. Than Louganis could.

Augur me better chance, good friends, as I now set out once more, a mere mortal with my can of paint. It is getting low. My paintbrush (which I thoughtfully soaked in paint remover and wrapped) is getting a bit stiff and may leave marks but if so they will be marks of struggle, marks of character, marks of morality.

I sought my gold in porch-floor painting.

Louganis old man, thanks. I would have met the challenge anyway, I think. But you made it easier to do the right thing. Thanks.

(Oh, yes, Happy Birthday, Saar. Another hero it would take too long to tell you about.) (September 1988)

More Advice

Ann Landers gives great advice generally, but she's a real trouble-maker for the lady in Oregon who wrote to ask what to do when her husband's first wife comes back from overseas for a visit with her old mother-in-law.

The husband's mother is going to have the former wife for some days and is planning lots of events at which the second wife is expected to be present, so the second wife asked Landers what to do.

Good grief. I fell out of bed at 5:30 (I read the paper early) when Ann said just go to everything and be real nice. The whole family will think the second wife is just great, going to all the teas and dinners and things. "Trust me," said Landers.

I hope I'm in time. Trust her, my eye. This is the correct advice:
Dear Second Wife:

No need for you even to meet the first wife, but if you're curious about her, I suggest you go once to meet her for 17 minutes. One cup of tea. Period. This way you can get a pretty good idea why your husband dumped her.

If your mother-in-law is stupid enough to invite you to further meetings with the first wife, simply say you have a previous engagement with a can of soup. As for your husband, who may not be much brighter than his mother, tell him to meet her once, if he must, but he is not to go to any cocktail parties, teas, suppers, beds or anything else with his first wife. Get a rolling pin. Use it.
Dear Sir:

(Actually, these are fictitious letters, but once you start giving advice it's hard to stop, especially when you see how poor the advice is nowadays.)

"I am just a dumb jock, but I grieve for the hockey player killed when his car ran into concrete. They say he was drunk and going 80 miles an hour, but I feel terrible all the same about this tragedy. He was a hero of mine."

There is no reason a jock should not grieve like anyone else. We are all programmed for it. You have to work through your grief over some time, yourself; it's not something others can do for you. It is always sad when a human dies. It is the nature of men to do dumb and reckless things. This quality is what got us out of the sea and down from the trees. This recklessness has a dark side, too, and the chance of getting through a car ride at fantastic speed while drunk is 1 in 87. So this is a case of statistical folly rather than a tragedy. It should be some comfort he killed only himself. But which of us would be alive today if we paid the full and probable price for all our blunders and stupidities? I share your sorrow, and only wish a large friend had said, look, dammit, and driven him home.

Dear Sir:

"I am a writer myself and I must protest the praise that has been heaped on the late E. B. White, of The New Yorker. He can hardly be deemed a great writer, for he rarely involved himself in the grave problems of the day. You yourself wrote a glowing tribute, as if he were much more important than he really was. No good writer can live above the fray and struggle."

Gee. I just didn't know any better when I praised him. But hold on, I'm working on a 26-part study of the shoe industry in Nicaragua, with a chapter on incestuous rape, and I mean it to be a regular feast of grave problems.

Dear Sir:

"I must beg to remain anonymous as I am a future king of England and cannot afford to be quoted in the daily press, but as I recently visited Washington I would like your opinion of the whole event."

Good show. Admired the red watchband, by the way, but suggest a man not wear identical shirts two days in a row—people think it's yesterday's shirt. And of course nobody knows when the camera snappeth, resulting in two pictures the same day of a prince pointing to something with his finger. Not good form here, to point. On the ultraplus side, the visit to the Library of Congress suggested a desire to learn more about the Constitution, and a wish to pay respect to learning in general.

Dear Sir:

"I live in Lula, Miss., and wonder if it's worth a detour to see the country house show at the National Gallery."

Yes. Worth a detour on your way to Memphis. Almost anything is, you might say, but the show is unique. When they let the press in on three days, I spent some hours there and saw the thing five times. Study the catalogue and go back.

Dear Sir:

"I saw a guy kick a yellow mongrel or yellow Labrador, not sure which, on Western Avenue, and think I should have done something. The thing is, I'm not very muscular, but this was several days ago and it still bugs me."

You should have decked him, or gone down trying. Or cussed him out and then ducked quickly into the nearest large building with multiple elevators. You are not expected to right all the wrongs of the world, but some things may not be ignored and this is one of them. Same if it had been a little girl or an old lady that got kicked. Regular woman, maybe and maybe not. But a dog—and of course it is very hard to tell a yellow mongrel from a yellow Lab and it makes no difference—you have no choice but go into action. Now an Irish terrier, heh-heh-heh, and it would have been the last dog he ever kicked.

Dear Sir:

"We are proud parents of an infant son. My first name is deMontmorency and it's hard for people to get, first time they hear it. What do you think are good first names for a boy?"

In the following order, Henry, Michael, Jim, Tom, Jeff, Bob, Clay, John, deMontmorency and Larry. Ben, in a pinch. But do not try to be clever as the boy will have to live with it. Luke is a splendid name, but then you won't have a name for the dog. I had a great-great-grandfather named Zion-Zebulon and a great-uncle named Joab (Joe-abb) and fear both suffered somewhat. Samuel-Minton proved an awkward Christian name also. All things considered, Henry is about as good as you will find. Trust me. (November 1988)

Silencing the Neigh-Sayers

You have known guys like Sunday Silence, the thoroughbred that recently won the Kentucky Derby and the Preakness and who is entered in tomorrow's Belmont stakes.

A wit said Sunday Silence runs like a loose grocery cart, possibly because he's knock-kneed, possibly because his sense of balance is off. There are swimmers who cannot stay in their lane and no matter how they concentrate they veer to the left. It's one of the bonds between man and animal.

Sunday Silence was never a favorite as a colt; others may have sold for more than a million, but Silence did well to fetch $17,000. And his new owner, somewhat like the horse, was no golden boy either, but had the reputation of drinking a lot and playing the guitar. The Wall Street Journal, which is (as it confesses in its ads) the daily diary of the American dream, would not have given you good odds on either horse or master. Or, for that matter, trainer—a gentleman past 70 who is not on anybody's fast track and who says he's lucky just to be alive.

The triumvirate of horse, owner and trainer has surprised most and annoyed many by winning the first two legs of racing's Triple Crown.

You can read what connoisseurs of horseflesh say: Sunday Silence is not much of a horse. They don't say it in those words, but that's the gist of it. The competition this year is poor and you gather Old Paint pulling a plow could have won. And what if Silence wins the Belmont, and becomes that rare beast, a Triple Crown champion? Well, he may win (it's said) but he still won't be a great horse.

The thing about sports that has always been admired is that performance is all. A great ballplayer may be less than an optimal example of responsibility, judgment, learning and so forth, but if he performs superbly on the field he rightly gets the praise due a winner.

The lovers of spectator sports should be timid at playing the field six ways for Sunday, because either there is something great about winning or there is not. If you can win the highest honors on the field or the track but still be judged a not very good athlete, then the foundation of sports is undermined.

I knew in school a cross-country runner who made us smile when he came out for the team. He was stocky and looked like a swimmer who had become a football player. His calves were beefy, and while he was not knock-kneed he had the build of a duck instead of a heron. He could, however, surpass all the rest in speed and endurance. We came to like him very much, as people always like preeminent success, and while we thought it a miracle he could run at all, we admired him the more for becoming a dandy runner in spite of not looking like one.

That is the way I feel toward Sunday Silence. Coming round the bend he looks as if he has too many legs and he seems to want to wander over to say hi to the horse next to him. In the finish, however, you can almost see his heart—he means to win.

He may not be a "great horse," but sports lovers have nothing to gain by saying so. If he wins the highest honors on the track but still is not much of a horse, it makes you think twice. Maybe marathon winners are not much in the way of winners? Maybe the spectacular pitcher and hitter are not much as ballplayers? Maybe winning doesn't matter much?

In life, as everybody quickly sees, the race sometimes goes to the fast talker, the one who is too clever by half, the one endowed with more than normal avarice, the one who can fool or deceive people most easily.

Sports and the law have one intimate bond. Both institutions settle things. You win a race, you win a case, and that's that.

Since the law is staffed by humans, human values apply. A lawyer or a judge who doesn't win cases or legal arguments among his peers may yet be a superb jurist and may be revered long after his death for his wisdom and clarity.

This is not true, as a rule, of racehorses. It is clear to everybody that the ordinary or nonprofessional horse ranks only with the dog as an animal likely to go to Heaven. There are horses who never won anything, never tried to win anything, who are remembered with love many years after their death, simply because they had ingratiating ways, stepped on some great bastard's foot and otherwise showed such decent character that no human could fail to love them. There are horses who love you first. And mules too.

But a thoroughbred, while he may have lovable qualities, is there to win races. Such a horse need not hope for love, being bred for victory, which is a different thing.

I hope to hell he wins the Belmont. There's nothing better than a horse who isn't much of a horse peering about and neighing with three crowns sprouting between his ears, of which he has (and here I stand up for that horse's classic build) only two. (June 1989)

American in Paris

Today is the national holiday of France, which I salute without any illusions but with objective clarity.

A couple of years after the big war, I seized my life savings of $700 and spent four months in France, over my father's objection. He himself (I discovered later) once had to be dragged home from Paris by my grandfather after he had spent two years there after World War I.

He pretended his presence in France was necessary. He had been a colonel in that war and kept on presiding over some bailiwick. As he was young and his French was flawless (he often said) and he was good at polo, and as he said Berlin should be razed and salted, these attainments and sentiments made him more popular than is good for an American. I do not speculate on my grandfather's techniques to fetch him home.

So when I took off in 1947, my father was sure I would never come back, or come back half-French, or otherwise be ruined for the somewhat restrictive horizons of our dear home in the Tennessee-Mississippi border country.

He was right, of course, but after four months my $700 ran out and I had no choice. Some Americans, veterans of World War II as I was, pretended they were going to school at the Sorbonne and got government money to support them, but I was too proud for that.

Now it may be that when one is 23 any foreign travel will tear down the prison. It is conceivable a French youth might find America liberating, in an extreme case.

The train pulled into Paris and I began to breathe. My landlady understood this and always said she did not breathe (*Je vous assure que je ne souffle pas*) outside Paris. She left the next day for Brussels, and in later years when I called on her she was always abroad, having become expert at not breathing.

In Paris, one can eat cherries right on the street, spitting seeds left and right. I had never heard of such a thing, let alone done it.

One night a guy and I went to the Lido, where they bring you a bottle of champagne whether you want it or not. And—get this—they charge you for it. You can't just get coffee and a roll. Later it seemed proper to take our clothes off and swim across the Seine, and this was

It is hard to say how freedom comes or why, when it does come, the world is new.

refreshing, never mind what was or was not in the river or in us. I cannot think how we got our clothes once we were on the other side, but I don't recall riding home naked on the subway.

I was forced by the charwoman where I lived to attend cultural events, such as a huge show of Maillol sculpture. She would go to such things then badger me. She banged on the door in the morning with coffee and before my eyes were open she would start in on some new scheme to turn a boorish country boy into a civilized man.

One night I went to a bar where Sartre was in full throat with some friends and I was asked to join them, but I had never heard of Sartre and furthermore knew I was too ignorant to take part. Thus I missed a chance to say today, "I remember Sartre once said to me, etc."

Everywhere in France I blundered about like an ox. From one faux pas I moved blissfully to another. I was invited to French houses at St.-Germain-en-Laye where I ate better peaches than we get in America, not that that's saying much, and in Fontvieille, where garlic is only a penny a bushel.

When I hitchhiked, the French picked me up. When I discovered on my own the Palais Royal and pronounced it suitable for living in (not realizing it was a major monument) the French took it in stride.

Once, hiking down the road, I bumped into a little inn at Les Baux.

I ate cantaloupes filled with Muscat de Frontignan and said I had discovered a dandy place in the middle of nowhere, not knowing it was famous even in Albania.

Hiking into Lyon one night I flung down my backpack, as ragged as my shorts, at a little bistro where I told them I had a certain sum to spend and was starved. How was I to know it was one of the great restaurants of France? I can still recall the crawfish bisque.

I went to the tomb of the Chevalier Bayard at Grenoble and the French did not blanch when I observed he was certainly a very short fellow like Napoleon.

I pulled a French infant out of the water one day. Saved that baby's life, but that was the only thing I ever did for France (and it ruined my flannels and my passport) in exchange for all France did for me.

It's not the food or the wandering; they are just shorthand symbols for awakening, and no telling how many Americans first smelled the coffee in Paris. It is hard to say how freedom comes or why, when it does come, the world is new.

Needless to say the French are as vicious as anybody else. They can produce a rabble as inflamed as that of any nation. They are as boastful as we are and (for they are not as puritanical as we) even more inclined to forget shameful episodes of their history.

My old father sighed with relief when I was dragged home by hunger. It was an outrage, he said, for a young guy to spend every dime of capital like that.

Yep. And how fortunate I had 700 bucks and the instinct (implanted by God, obviously) to see the city of light. (July 1989)

Art and the Common Man

I visited the free show of Mapplethorpe photographs at the Washington Project for the Arts (400 Seventh St. NW) and dropped some cash in a glass jar they have down there for free-will offerings, hoping to encourage them.

But the main thing I got from the show was a renewed bafflement, the same the Founding Fathers wrestled with, at how far an elite should rule and how far a rabble should.

Rabble is an un-American word, of course. Here we have yeomen of virtue, often leading hard lives but fully reliable in self-government and general goodness.

Those yeoman farmers won American liberty in the first place, and framers of the Constitution were not likely to start calling them a rabble. Still, there was uneasiness in Philadelphia that the government might pass into the hands of uneducated men, quick to seize any temporary advantage to themselves and careless of the ultimate freedom and honor of the state.

They concluded the common man should rule but only at a discreet distance through the ballot.

Men at the Constitutional Convention did not exactly distrust the ordinary bloke so much as they trusted him in quite limited ways. Your small farmer should not have much say in negotiations with France or setting monetary policy. They were settled that an elite should rule, but the common man should choose the elitist. They were uneasy how to do this, and some of them (all of them, at the last) wanted guarantees for the commonest of men, lest the ruling elite go too far and threaten liberty instead of defending it.

Literature is singularly happy that its protection is acknowledged. You can say or write what you please about the president, a senator, a mayor or a village idiot. But the lesser arts, painting, sculpture, photography and so forth, have not fared so well, mainly because relatively few people care about them.

When the two National Endowments, for the Arts and for the Humanities, got off the ground in the Nixon administration, there were many who said that if the government got into the arts field the state would soon be supporting art as sterile and trifling as that of China today. But others said no, the endowments would have distinguished boards that would pass on the quality of the art and the need of the artist, free from government control. People who were not born yesterday said Ha. That will be the day.

Naturally, when the Mapplethorpe show came along, which had some trifling investment of tax dollars, the shout was raised that we should not be taxed to support pornography. Never mind that presumably competent boards had passed on the little support the Mapplethorpe work ever got from the state, and never mind that the Corcoran Gallery of Art had proclaimed the pictures important art worthy of a major show.

Pictorial art has not gone through the fights that literature has, and few care to defend it.

Why should anybody defend it? The Corcoran, after all, canceled it at the sound of the first firecracker, not even waiting for the first shot. Museum directors, not wishing to be beastly to the idiots of the Corcoran, mumbled a little and let it pass. Even artists intend to keep right on cooperating with the gallery. They all think they will sustain freedom by supporting those who would squelch them.

Supporters of the endowments said the quality of their boards would be proof against political tampering, and both artists and lovers of freedom would man the barricades at the first sign of state meddling.

The Mapplethorpe exhibit illustrates how little power the arts have and how little energy, let alone passion, their formal protectors can summon.

The Constitution is silent on painting and photography as it is on so many other matters, leaving it to citizens at large to work out. So it's working out, and the rednecks are way ahead. If even the arts community doesn't go to bat for the artist, why should the ordinary bloke who doesn't see any art at any gallery?

One amazing argument is that the artist's freedom was not touched since, after all, you can see it at a better gallery than the Corcoran. Or, another imbecilic argument, he was free to make his art, it's just that no tax dollars should help in the cost of showing it. This argument is never used for the National Academy of Science or NASA or universities. It

The ruling elite go too far and threaten liberty instead of defending it.

can be used against art because few believe art amounts to a row of beans.

And this art in particular can be safely trashed because, first, it's just a photographer we're talking about, and besides he's dead, and besides he was gay, and besides he embarrasses me. (July 1989)

Buckingham

Because Buckingham always seemed happy it was assumed something happened to his brains as a child, but even at the time, 40 years ago, I noticed he managed a career of complete leisure with virtually no cash.

At first I felt sorry for him, as for people in asylums who thought they were Napoleon, but within a year I saw he was content with his food, his shelter, his whole way of living, and while this was distressing to all steady citizens, still there was something in it.

For one thing, he seemed to have chosen his life, not to have fallen into it, and he was almost the only human I knew who held no grudge against God or government.

We had moved into a house we inherited, ugly till you got the knack of it and then lovable with oak cornices and plenty of retreats for dogs and mice. As a young married couple we did our damnedest to be enlightened, responsible, and rich enough to pay for a new roof.

Buckingham arrived one day to ask if he could rent the servants' house out back and I said certainly not. It was in disrepair, no heat except an iron stove, only cold running water, and a john that made English plumbing seem grand.

He said nobody was allowed to sleep on a park bench. Well, all right, just for a night.

Within a dozen years, however, Buckingham had accumulated a whole thrift shop of impedimenta. He said he lived on a painshun, but as he had never had a regular job this must have been insufficient to maintain a dog, but then Buckingham was not a dog.

We had two black hounds that lived in the garage and jumped through a permanently open window to their wired run. Sometimes Buckingham fed them and daily sat down to visit them, and almost as frequently left the door open so they got loose and had to be chased, not that even the Second Coming could prod him past slow amble.

Once he was run down by a truck and taken to a hospital where he told one social worker he was our butler and another one that he took care of our kennels. We paid his electricity and water bills, which were nothing, and he visited the mutts every day, which was also nothing, so it seemed a fair swap.

On holidays he helped the cook by sitting down with a glass of wine and flattering her while she scrubbed pots. He got hot water and sometimes drank claret in the kitchen but other than that he never set foot in the house. He had nothing against servants but he was never one.

If there had been justice he would have got something from those free-enterprise groups that like to give each other awards, or from some church, for he was, as recommended, wise as a serpent and guileless as a dove.

He had white hair and a refined sister who had taught school. Once she got him an apartment in a public-housing complex but he declined to accept it.

He was the only man I knew who held a daily salon of some sparkle. At an age when many are lonely, Buckingham was not. He had a window on the alley from which he could call to people and ask them in for a glass of sherry at 25 cents, reasonable even then.

At 8 every morning he marched down the cobbled alley, crossed a big boulevard (which is how he got run over that time) to a whiskey store. There he bought two quarts of sherry. By charging a quarter a glass, he financed his own need of a quart a day and enjoyed his guests.

A snoopy and rather vicious neighbor who once cut a hole in our shrubs to keep an eye on our kennel master phoned the police. It got to be a thing with them. From time to time they descended to arrest him but they never could find any evidence and contented themselves with throwing things on the floor.

Buckingham regarded this as one of life's irritants to be risen above. He hid all but a pint of wine across the alley in a dilapidated garage smothered with a pink and thorny rambler rose.

In those years, as formerly, he never worked, except about four days a year he would walk a mile to the house of a woman we knew. Once I answered the phone and she said Buckingham must come instantly as the caladiums were wilting. Once my wife saw him with the hose turned on full, typhooning the colored leaves.

Like his sister before us, and I guess like his parents before her, we tried to get Buckingham a job or decent housing so he would have self-respect and no sense of persecution. He was lord of his manor, asking no help but taking no guff. Every year or so he was jailed for emptying his bladder in some alley. Once away from his house, there were no toilets he could use. His fines were modest and I paid them. This was his due.

When we moved, his sister got him an apartment. We lost track of him, but we heard he never liked it. He lost his salon friends and I think he was lonely. A compassionate society managed to do away with his privacy, his stimulating circle, his excursions down the cobbles, his hot iron stove and most of his world.

He missed the cook and maybe us. I know he missed the dogs. (December 1989)

Why the Bear Slides
Down the Hill

For a long time I tried to learn (by reading books) the reason or the mechanism that makes some people believe in balderdash, until it occurred to me I have enough to keep me busy just trying to be sane myself.

It no longer bothers me that so many believe in ectoplasm and messages from other worlds, commonly through the teeth; it doesn't even bother me now if important institutions promote hogwash because as I now see it the average human lives a number of years with nothing much to do but (this is true of most) can only eat, drink, sleep and get into mischief 16 hours a day.

To fill up the otherwise empty hours, sensible people (and there are some still) make it their business to understand coral reefs or beetles, or set themselves such problems as why vines twine—where did they learn to spiral?

But if you get through compulsory school without the slightest sense of wonder or curiosity, there is no deep end to go off of, no bees to inhabit the bonnet. The void is filled for many happy folk by professional sport, provided its riches may be savored from an easy chair with adequate Budweiser and ham sandwiches, which the upper classes smear Grey Poupon on and which the majority of men eat plain in the presence of other men but put mayonnaise on if alone.

Thus life passes for a good-sized minority. But women lack the Raiders gene in the majority of cases and the main thing they get from pro sports is having the slob out of the way for three and a half hours.

How women fill up the void I neither know nor wish to speculate on, but I now see that both sexes still have the time left over and no curiosity about beetles to fill it up.

They turn, therefore, to sighting Elvis in Mobile—he is never spotted in Memphis, which is worth mentioning—or else invest time and coin trying to reach Aunt Maud in the other world, probably to find out where she put the emeralds, as (considering their treatment of her in this life) there is no reason to suppose she has much to say to them now.

In August in the country where I grew up it is hot enough to melt egrets, and the cotton is laid by (the plants shade out the weeds and there is no labor in the fields till picking begins in the fall) and the leeches are so thick in the pond that swimming is not what it was, so everybody turns to monsters or miracles or other gee-whizzeries.

I have spent happy hours as a boy reporter investigating a snake, estimated by sober folk to be 30 or 40 or even 65 feet long and thick as a tire or a nail keg or a whiskey barrel, and sighted from a tractor or a farm porch or through a copse. But soon September comes and kids go to school and there are cooler nights and anxiety about the crop rises and you hear no more about giant snakes. Nice while they lasted, and I particularly enjoyed interviewing learned professors on the topic of anacondas and they enjoyed, I guess, trotting out statistics and the temperature of sewers and alligator dens and the number of rabbits reasonably required to get a tremendous snake through the winter. Chickens? Oh, indeed, chickens would do.

If you are fortunate enough to watch bears (and a sorrow of my life is that I have not been able to) you will see them sliding down hills not to ameliorate an itch or to reach a stream with fish but simply to amuse themselves and kill time.

And anyone with dogs is aware that most of their waking hours are spent (until advanced age turns them to twitchy dreams under the pecan tree with one eye half open in case a squirrel should charge into their teeth) in romping and Walter Mitty–type battles or a vain energetic search for treasures known to be buried four feet deep.

With animals the illusory search is innocent enough and uses up the energy that humans spend otherwise in passing tedious nights.

But with humans it is innocent, too, at least in original impulse. Farmers who once pointed to the track of the giant serpent now point to the blasted earth where a space capsule landed, and news agencies that once reported on Lake Ness now report on eight-foot-tall creatures from outer space.

Daffy folk who formerly had visions of the Lord in the river bottoms—perhaps I should say we once had a yard man who heard a celestial voice cry, "Stop, Vernon," so he stopped and behold a Bible fell out of the sky at his feet open to some passage I no longer recollect. Anyway, there aren't so many Bibles falling out of the sky nowadays but people still see the sun stand still in remote places such as Mexico and Yugoslavia where I suppose it is very hot.

In line with the modest aspirations of our own day there are fewer

The empty head is the visionary's workshop.

sightings of amazing monsters in the fields, but even more than ever people get phone calls the instant it has come into their heads that Irma fell off a cliff and sure enough, "I hate to tell you, Irma fell off a cliff and is smashed to bits."

Now some say all these strange things come about through shorts in the wiring of the brain, and God knows almost any malfunction seems possible there, while others say bodily chemicals upset the eyeballs and show, clear as day, Elvis wrapped in a blue and rose cloud on top of Sturdevant's gin.

But I say we need not go so far to explain it. The empty head is the visionary's workshop. It's as simple as that.

I have surveyed 1,623 entomologists (to prove the point) who have been usefully employed for an average of 11 years in assorted studies of the dragonfly, the crane fly, the lightning bug, the azure butterfly, the parasitic wasps and so forth. Not one of them has ever seen the sun stand still in the sky. None has ever seen Elvis. None has ever ridden in a spaceship, tied down by small or giant green men.

They have found the natural world enough (to use the poet's phrase, though in a different connection) and they get no phone calls about Irma's cliff.

So there you have it. If there is no wonder (such as the lightning bug or the blue tree toad) to invest a lifetime of work upon, then there will be ghosts and visible demons and fires in the sky. If there is not pro football or (assuming ursine proclivities) a grassy hill to sail down on your butt, then there will be signs in the sky or on the telephone.

It's that simple. Something has to fill up time and something does.

Now many deplore the stupid (as they say) fantasies of Mars in Jupiter's house and, as you could read on the front page of Russian newspapers recently, giant creatures waddling about the field from outer space.

But I say every man has to fill up time. God, after all, made the Elvis-sighters and it seems a trifle wrong to complain of divine handiwork. So I do not call such people idiots, imbeciles, cretins or any other impolite thing.

I do regret they have found only such poor coppers in a golden world, and regret their spaceships and sun-stoppings are so brief.

They acknowledge the sun only stands still for a few minutes. They acknowledge they see Elvis only a fleeting second. Something falls out of the sky on Tuesday but only takes a minute and never happens (to that person) again.

Whereas the study and the wonders of the dragonfly last longer than life does. (December 1989)

Tripping on the Mother Tongue

I think you call a bathtub a bathtub or a tub; I never heard anybody call a bathtub a bath.

English is odd because people are. Even so, I think the tub is one thing and the bath is another. You can have a bath without a tub and a tub without a bath.

We used to be warned not to throw out the baby with the bath. Now we are warned not to throw out the baby with the bath water. If you throw out the bath (with or without the baby) I always supposed you threw out the water—not the tub. It's not necessary, then, to say "bath water."

The same kind of unnecessary noun has got into the dining room. People say "dining room table" but why isn't "dining table" enough? Is it so important for it to be in a dining room?

You've probably also heard of "operating room table" at a hospital. "Operating table" would do the trick, wouldn't it?

Soon we'll be writing about diningroomtables, in line with the trend to lump words together. This is the penalty, no doubt, for all those German settlers who came over—they and their descendants were born with a gene for conglobulating words; they hate short ones. It all started with "good bye" which is now, in many books, written "goodbye" or even "goodby." When I see "goodby," I want to say "goodbee."

The whole point of spelling is to give the poor reader a fighting chance at guessing how to pronounce the word, on the theory that if he hears it he probably will recognize it.

But we have a lousy language for that. My wife still says "yelk" when speaking of the yellow nucleus of an egg. Everybody used to say it, but since it's spelled "yolk," people started pronouncing it the way it's spelled, instead of spelling it the way it's pronounced.

Already people have started making odd noises when they say "aren't." The word is pronounced "arnt," of course, but increasingly you hear "ar(huh)nt." This is particularly likely on TV and is the result, probably, of having discovered only late in life that there's an "e" in there and figuring a silent "e" is a day without sun.

Ever since World War II people have been gardening more, and the craze for herbs has led to the sudden general revival of the ancient word, "wort," which is pronounced "wurt." You find it in many herbs, as in starwort, mugwort, sneezewort, figwort, pigwort and so forth. All pronounced "wurt." But you now hear "woart" to rime with "court" and "port."

The word "horticulture" means the growing of plants or worts. You say "whore-teh-cull-sher" and you might reasonably ask, if "wort" is pronounced "wurt," why isn't "hort" pronounced "hurt?"

It isn't because it isn't. That is the first rule of English.

Within a decade you may expect all other words in which "or" is pronounced "ur" to be changed in daily speech. World will become woarld, worthy will become woarthy, Jordan will become Joardan (as it already is, except the Jordans who are determined to keep calling themselves Jurdans, and some who still cleave to the Jurdan River).

Few people who speak English will acknowledge that "or" is commonly, or even usually, pronounced "ur" following the letter "w," except you are supposed to know that "worn" is pronounced "woarn" while "worm" is pronounced "wurm."

It's that way because it's that way, just as Wednesday is called Wennsdy —and that's another word that people are beginning to stick an extra grunt in.

What's to be done about all this?

I suggest nothing be done about it. My own rule is to pronounce all words I grew up with the way I grew up pronouncing them, on the theory that there were no affectations of speech, no oddities of pronunciation anywhere in the family. Words new to me I look up in the word books.

If you pronounce words as the dictionary says you should, of course you will find yourself uttering a word one way while the person you are talking with pronounces it another way.

Let him. It's no crime to mispronounce or misspell a word, and in the strange language of English everybody does, sooner or later. I have never presumed to correct anybody.

But I do not believe in deliberately mispronouncing a word simply because somebody else doesn't know any better. No need to say "Murka" just because "America" is a bit difficult to get out. An accountant is not expected to accept my addition on my tax form out of politeness, when he knows his sum is correct and mine is not.

Wednesday is another word that people are beginning to stick an extra grunt in.

No need to man the ramparts. But no need to join the barbarians, either.

Sexism in language is, needless to say, a topic too vast to deal with here, but perhaps I should say I got a letter from somebody about "Man that is born of woman . . ."

That writer complains this is outrageous and demeaning to women. A lot of women, it is clear, think any allusion to females is demeaning. They want it to be a secret, at least in polite society, that they have breasts and give birth and all that sort of disgusting stuff that men keep noticing. So I report the complaint. But now that women are increasingly permitted to get their heads blown off in war, surely they see that men support them all the way? (January 1990)

The Razor and the Raucous Scene

It popped into my head during the Triumphal Scene of "Aida" that less is more, and I thought of my grandfather's old razor in its velvet case, a pretty example as we shall see.

The opera, notable for beautiful choral work and a rightly self-satisfied Amneris, had six real trumpets on the stage, and much humanity and gold, along with decibels to make Guns N' Roses blush.

Coleridge, one of those poets who grow on you with the years, says of a big wedding (which I imagine is much like "Aida"):

"What loud uproar comes from that door?

"The wedding guests are there."

And of course the wedding guests should be all whooping at once; it's time to celebrate loud.

Then he goes on:

"But in the garden bower the bride

"And the bride-maids singing are."

Magical lines. The central actor of the scene, the bride, is alone with her maids in a garden and the girls are cheeping young and innocent. But over yonder is the non-magical world of everyday life, all the guests glugging down the wine and catching up on loud jokes.

For the bride it's not a scene of roaring mirth but a time of wonder and wondering. She's a little scared (it's a 19th-century poem) and a little doubtful, and she's waiting in a quiet place for her prince to come.

I mean nothing against "Aida." It would be hard to do the Triumphal Scene with kings and princes and shabby prisoners and gorgeous folk and trumpets and processions and zub, zub, zub—it would be hard and possibly wrong to stage such a scene in a garden bower with a few birds twittering in the jasmine.

Still, while there is a place for grand uproar and gold and people so thick that half of them are plastered in high wall niches, a little of it goes quite a way.

My grandfather's razor (which along with an old silver belt buckle was my inheritance from him along with his name) I long since lost along the way, but I think of it at absurd times, as in the middle of "Aida."

Any Day

It came in a brass nickel-plated case with grapevines in low relief, and inside it was lined with purple velvet. You might think that over the years the velvet would get wet, but then if you dried the razor carefully before putting it back every day, it wouldn't.

The razor itself had a silver-looking shaft with grapes sculpted on it and you twisted a disk at the bottom to make the blade shields open.

It was like the opera in that it was absurdly (and agreeably) ornamented with grapes and never mind their relevance to the art of shaving.

But then it was unlike the opera too, and more like the quiet bride in the bower when you actually used it to shave yourself. Certainly there was no thought, when you used it, that you would shave before the phone rang again. You pushed a tab to open the case, you removed the silver stem then screwed on the top. You got out a blade and turned the disk. Meanwhile you softened the badger-hair brush in water, worked up the lather in a mug that was also decorated with irrelevant flowers. You heated the towel and steamed your face a bit and when you were finally done shaving, you started unscrewing and washing and drying and putting all the machinery back in its case just so and snapped it all shut.

There was time, when you shaved with it, to think about Bismarck and Victoria and whether to try that new 'Ponderosa' tomato.

But now I allow no more than a minute and a half to shave, start to finish. I have time now to go to the opera. I have time to return a lot of phone calls. Time to get to the parking garage even if a wreck has blocked the entrance to the parkway.

I think often of the bride with her bride-maids in the bower, while the wedding guests are elsewhere in a loud uproar.

"Hold it a minute," said a lively woman on the phone this morning. "Gotta open the door for the squirrel."

Is this what life comes to? A woman says hold it, she has to go play with the squirrel. It does little for one's vanity, though this is by no means the first time women have put me on hold while they prioritized squirrels.

The time you save shaving you spend holding on for Rocky. And then I thought, well, the bright woman is right. For her I am the loud uproar, in a hurry to discuss newspaper stuff and get to the office, running for the subway because another train will not be along for four minutes.

I'm her opera with trumpets and horns and split-second timing. But she has more sense that I. She's out in the garden bower. Not with the bride-maids singing, perhaps, but feeding peanuts which is much the same thing.

Take your garden bower where you find it. Put the loud world on hold. (February 1990)

Gentlemen and Scholars

The honor system at the University of Virginia is under attack again.

It was started about 150 years ago following the killing of a professor, but as I recall you don't have to promise not to kill professors when you subscribe to the honor system.

Its main use is to discourage cheating (on exams, for instance) by invoking a heavy penalty—expulsion from school.

Theoretically, every student feels bound to report any student he sees cheating, and the case is heard by a committee or court of students. Sometimes the evidence is too flimsy, but sometimes students are found guilty and asked to leave.

The arguments against the honor system are that it invites a police-state mentality, that the student judges are too inexperienced to be entrusted with such rigorous penalties, that the system may not be applied impartially, and so on.

As far as I know, nobody has argued the system should be abolished simply because cheating in school is fine and prepares you for adult life.

Those who support the system argue it has worked well for more than a century, that there is less cheating at Charlottesville than elsewhere, that a guy who cheats is unfair to those who don't. Besides, there are plenty of colleges without an honor system and that's where cheaters should go.

Underlying the arguments now, however, is the concept of "gentleman." I'm not sure the word is ever spoken in public, but the concept is there all the same.

You could take the most important exams at Charlottesville without a professor or monitor in the room. You could go out and get a coffee and come back. Students were proud they were not watched like kids.

Especially in the past (and the middle and late 19th century was a time when ideas of knights and loyalty and purity were fashionable) men liked to think of themselves as gentlemen—people above cheating, above lying, above petty, mean behavior.

What people pretend to be has a great bearing on what they are. I don't doubt that if you get it in your head that people like yourself don't cheat, then you won't cheat.

My claim to virtue is I have never read other people's mail. That I recall. I have also refrained from writing anonymous or falsely signed letters to bookstores inquiring about some book I may have written (to persuade the bookseller there's a groundswell of interest).

I never cheated on an exam because I never was tempted to. Even if I flunked (as I did occasionally) it never bothered me much. The student of today has only to look at the Reagan White House to see that scholarship is not a requisite to success. It was the same when I was young, and the same in 5000 B.C.

Some people don't cheat because they are too arrogant to bend. Others value learning for its own sake—just for knowing about the world—and to them grades are not important.

Nothing infuriates some people more than the concept that one is too good to cheat. They think everybody is born a bastard and that nobody should give himself airs about being better than the average run of folk.

That is the anti-elitist position, and very popular it is, especially with those who cannot think of anything to be elite about.

Then there is our present century's deeper understanding of behavior. The insights of psychiatry have done much to take us all down a peg or two. Besides, great events have had a sobering effect on the knights-in-armor folk. The Great War did much to assure even numbskulls that humans are barbarians, once you take away the Evian water, and the Hitler regime made the same point. The proud clean youth of Bach's and Goethe's nation were seen to be as malleable, as flexible, as vicious as rats in a training maze.

All of a sudden, then, you stopped hearing about gentlemen. After all, gentlemen found it quite possible to officiate at gas ovens, so let's have no more baloney about gentlemen.

All this is just beneath the surface when Virginia's honor system is discussed.

Of course every school changes over the years. They no longer wear jackets down there. They live in dormitories. They no longer bring their dogs to college. Miss Booker and Miss Cocke no longer house first-year men, partially taming them. Students don't smoke in class any more. Not many live on the Lawn, and those who do are

In the past men liked to think of themselves as gentlemen - people above lying.

packed in like soldiers on a troop ship. It's part of the world going to hell.

The world is always going to hell, which does not alter the fact that one is alive in the middle of it. Whatever the world does, whatever it is, you don't have to applaud or join the guys who cheat. You live with what you are, and I doubt cheating on exams does much for the ego. A nation, a city, a school where cheating is sort of okay is not so dandy, either. (April 1990)

Wallowing in Sweet Swelter

Air conditioning is a wonderful advance in national comfort, no doubt of it, but like most good things it has drawbacks that can be serious.

I don't mean simply that idiots will of course use air conditioning to get a room to goose-bump levels of cold that would not be tolerated in winter.

The bad thing about air conditioning is not that it can be abused but that it can be used reasonably and correctly. Its very virtues can be an obstacle to deep understanding.

To work comfortably all day in a modern office is such a benefit that nobody would want to return to the days of sweat-soaked shirts, wilted seersuckers and edgy tempers, so what good can possibly be lost, you may ask, by turning on the air conditioning?

I remember some years ago living at Dupont Circle on the fourth floor of an old house that had high ceilings. We had only one room, a huge one into which a kitchen and bathroom had been fitted. A Palladian window framed a superb view of the fire engines that came about twice a week to put out small fires in our basement. Everybody would go out on the street, then return when the firemen left. Because the roof was not shaded it never quite cooled off, though usually by 10:30 P.M. the room was cool enough to support life. Before that, one could sit on the fire escape.

There was a wooden chest in the kitchen that held a 50-pound lump of ice. It was called an icebox, children, and it kept milk cool enough to prevent souring, usually. The iceman lugged the ice up the endless stairs and put it in the icebox once a week. On Friday evenings the ice lump was about the size of a fist and, as the new block of ice had arrived earlier, the small lump could be cracked, put in two glasses of tap water and, wow, you had instant ice water.

It was something any young married couple could look forward to all week.

But now I just reach into that plastic box in the freezer and grab a few ice cubes. It's been ages since I looked forward to Friday night ice

Summer is best surrendered to and, within legal limits, wallowed in.

water. Much has been gained over the years in the ice department, but also something has been lost quite apart from youth.

Also, I noticed ages ago that if I worked all day in farm fields along the Lower Mississippi I was surprisingly comfortable. Everything was cotton, and even without a breeze the air continually cooled the sweat. When the sun got low it was a sensuous matter to swim in the farm lake, even if the water was 86 degrees and the lake surface covered with fuzz from cottonwood trees.

Not for a minute do I say there is total merit in a life of physical discomfort. If I thought so, I'd pitch out our electric icebox and get a job in the fields of Southside Maryland.

But I cannot help noticing summer is different now. It goes too quickly.

All too soon, about Aug. 20, something new is in the air, even if the weather is still hot. A hint of fall is about, and the best bugs stop singing in the sundown air. By Labor Day, which is often hotter than hell, you realize summer is over. Summer is opulence, not just heat, and it ends in August.

And what if you have not really experienced it? Even with air conditioning, everybody experiences uncomfortable heat in summer.

But we no longer have that long spell when our formerly protesting body has finally yielded to July. We dabble with summer nowadays and sometimes fight it, sometimes try to sneak past it, but no longer sink deeply into it.

I think one can try, at least, to strike a mean by which you accept cold grocery stores, cool offices and public buildings, but still experience much of the summer when not in those places.

I once had a big convertible that had air conditioning. Of all dumb things. And that dumbness is spreading in America. Now I would not have, and don't have, air conditioning in the car. Nor have we turned on air conditioning in the house thus far. Sometimes we do, in summers, usually for a couple of days at the end of August.

We sometimes sleep with the ceiling fan going all night on low, sometimes even on high, though that usually means you have to get up about 2:30 to turn it off. The ceiling fan has a long green string you pull to start or stop it. I could make the string longer and work the fan from bed, but that has always seemed wrong. So many ethical choices in summer.

In our cities, entirely too many citizens are not only estranged but bitterly divorced from the natural world. They are no longer good animals. They live inside their heads.

"The life of the mind," as it is called, is all very well. The glory of human life. But the danger is always there, and all too often dominant, that living in just the human mind means living in a fantasy world. My wise father used to say a lot of human angst could be cured if more people sawed wood and cracked rocks, by which he meant a return to natural things.

We should go far beyond the primitive need for food and fire—and, God knows, ice—but at the same time we ought never forget we evolved in real summers. My grandfather used to say summer burned the impurities out of the blood. I doubt it. But I am pretty sure there is some benefit from the natural heat of summer when it is experienced for prolonged periods. Experience suggests that summer is best surrendered to and, within legal limits, wallowed in. Joseph Conrad said, "In the destructive element immerse," and it will hold you up. Something in that. You might want to turn off the cold for a spell and see. (July 1990)

Jim the Wonder Dog

Look, everybody knew Jim the Wonder Dog was something else, but I still don't believe he could read Greek and shorthand.

Still, his story makes a diversion for those weary of Marion Barry. Jim was whelped in Louisiana in 1925 and went to God from Missouri 12 years later.

As a pup he was backward. He was no good at all in those schools that teach dogs to hunt birds. He just sat there. Then it was noticed that while all the good students were quartering the field, back and forth, back and forth, Jim just trotted directly to the covey.

His master, the late Sam Van Arsdale, was hunting one day with Jim and said, "Let's take a break over there under that hickory." Jim took off and sat under the hickory. His master thought well, it's a coincidence. So he told Jim to go to an elm, which Jim did, and a black oak and a cedar. Jim did all of them.

Sam told his wife about this—they'd had Jim three years before they'd noticed his gifts—and she said well, yes, but don't tell anybody else or they'll laugh us out of the county.

But how can you keep genius hidden? Soon everybody in Missouri, in Marshall, Sedalia and all, was talking about this wonder dog who could point out the lady in the blue dress, the man in the red tie, the guy with rolled socks, a strange postman named Wagner, and much else.

Sam ran the Ruff Hotel, and traveling men from all over soon told other people the marvels they'd seen Jim perform. Sam would say, "Jim, go find this man's car," and he'd run down the street and do it. Then Jim was told, "Go find the car with the license plate G73-814," and he'd do that.

He appeared before the Missouri legislature and listened to a Morse code message tapped out for him directing him to pick out a certain member. Jim did it, as the solons of Missouri watched in dumb surmise.

A Greek professor brought his class and wrote some Greek on a paper. Jim did nothing. Sam said, "What's the matter, Jim?" and the professor said he'd just written the alphabet, alpha, beta, gamma etc., and that's why Jim just sat there. He had not been asked to do anything.

The St. Louis Post-Dispatch published a long article on Jim, and so did Outdoor Life, written by its authoritative Larry Mueller, hunting dogs editor.

When Jim died, Sam damned near did.

In 1942 Clarence Dewey Mitchell wrote "Jim the Wonder Dog," in the first person, as if dictated by Jim, and the soft-cover edition is still in print (Jim The Wonder Dog Inc., 906 Royal Blvd, Sedalia, Mo. 65301, $8.50 ppd.). H. J. Hausam, copyright holder, says all proceeds go to the College of the Ozarks, where students work their way through school.

Hausam is in Washington trying to persuade the Postal Service to issue a stamp with Jim on it. No luck thus far, "but if the department will do it up right," he says, "then old Jim will have done it again. Done what? Erased our post office deficit, that's what."

A church minister, a newspaper editor, a former president of the national veterinarians association and others all testify to Jim's incredible powers.

My view is that Jim didn't comprehend foreign languages any better than the average Lousiana whelp, and I don't believe you could give him a license number and he'd race off to set his paw on it. Perfectly sane and honorable people see flying saucers and get messages from outer space through the fillings in their teeth, but just because they're honorable doesn't mean their accounts are factual.

The answer is simple enough. Jim the Wonder Dog was beyond doubt a singular specimen, toward whom almost everybody felt a strong emotional surge. Anybody who ever had a dog can comprehend that. Once the emotional commitment is made, humans will believe anything, based on what they think is proof right in front of their eyes. Thus many dog lovers think their dogs can sing "Carmen."

Everybody knows that when you think of taking your mutt for a walk, he knows it even before you stand up. He pads over to his lead. If you *think* of giving him a bath, he knows it and vanishes.

Those are curious things, and why doubt that Jim was even more sensitive and aware than, say, my wonderful hound, Luke, though I doubt it, actually.

You get an outstanding dog—the fabulous one in our family in the past century was Jack, an American bull terrier who flourished in 1908 and is still talked about today—and you yourself become hypnotized. You are too sensible, too reserved, to fling your arms about him and hug him 86 times a day, so your love and wonder are translated into awe at his supernatural gifts.

I still don't think Jim could read Greek or shorthand.

Some dogs bring this out in people more than others, and Jim must have set an all-time record. The wonder he inspired in people is at least as remarkable as his alleged gift for shorthand.

So what was there about Jim that made otherwise sober folk go off the deep end?

Well, one nature writer of the 1940s said dogs had ruined most of the population of England, reducing them to blathering, infantile nitwits, unfit for science or sound learning.

But then the Royal Society's Sir Robert Ball pointed out that "humanity's greatest benefactor was the first savage to tame a litter of wolf cubs," and Schopenhauer complained that the "real trouble with humanity is that it is descended from monkeys and not from dogs." Furthermore, in "Thus Spake Zarathustra," we learn that "the world was conquered through the understanding of dogs, and the world exists through the understanding of dogs." And before you bad-mouth one, Mohammed said, "Dogs will be witnesses at the Last Judgment."

Finally, if you must know why all those people went bats over Jim, get yourself a dog, take good care of him, and see. (August 1990)

Shuddering at the Mere Thought

Today a note on prurience, without (I assure you) providing any.

In obscenity trials one test of the offense is prurience, which is lewdness, lasciviousness, lust etc., and which is brought about by words, images, body movements and thoughts.

Prurience is widespread in the republic. Elements of it are to be found in many naughty persons such as Franklin Roosevelt, John Kennedy, Jimmy Swaggart, Gary Hart, the archbishop of Atlanta, Marion Barry and the Lord only knows who else.

Many people who have prurient thoughts and desires do not come to them through pornographic literature, however, but seem to be, as you might say, self-starters.

Since so many people have prurient ideas all on their own, without the assistance of publishers or broadcasters, it's hard to see why it is thought so shocking for prurience to be expressed in literature, drama or speech.

When Jimmy Carter confessed he had sometimes lusted in his heart, are we to believe he should therefore be locked up in the cause of public safety?

The general view is that lustful thoughts are so easily aroused and so often lead to everything from rape to drunken singing in the middle of the night that we should nip the first signs of prurience wherever we find it.

The law is supposed to prohibit or punish acts dangerous to society, and is therefore keen on the trail of theft, mayhem, kidnapping and much else.

But law does not concern itself with thoughts or words as a rule. You can think the most frightful things, or dream them, without going to jail. And to a large extent you can say them. Words are not deeds, though vigilantes and thought police are forever arguing that words are black magic with frightful power to destroy.

Thus there is confusion between words and acts in many of those areas that make us embarrassed or uncomfortable or uncertain. The more uneasy we are, the more likely we are to equate words with acts.

Many people who have prurient thoughts seem to be self-starters.

A Cabinet member may be ejected for telling a dirty joke about blacks, a good example of the surface charade of politics.

A university president may be bounced out for a "sick fantasy" about sex with children, just as if he had committed sexual acts against children.

Suppose there are seven hours of taped phone calls that such a man made to a woman he didn't know.

Suppose the case comes to court and the man is heavily penalized. Would that be for terrifying a helpless woman or would it be for having a fantasy we dislike? It should not be against the law to have thoughts, however heated, depraved, perverse, disgusting etc., and it should not be against the law to express those thoughts in words to someone who listens by the hour, even if she is doing it to facilitate his arrest.

Men are known to have shocking and disgusting thoughts, and now that they're liberated, women do too. The danger is not that some timid, helpless creature whose phone has rung will be subjected to mental torment (because of the inability to slam the receiver) but that the courts, the police, the powerful state, will start saying words are crimes. If it is actionable to say something dirty on the phone to a person who repeatedly listens to it, then perhaps it is also illegal to say something political that is equally offensive to the state.

We have already gone far with the list of words that may not be uttered in America. We have gone too far in our terror of ethnic jokes, too far in our distaste for all words that we think may conceivably offend us or somebody somewhere somehow. Outlawing words does nothing to stop prejudice and harm but does a good bit to weaken freedom of speech.

A nation that appears to care less and less for the weak is nevertheless a nation that goes into a tailspin at a joke or a dirty phone call. It may be hard to remember that the brisk and vigorous defense of virtue (starting with naughty words) is the common ploy of tyranny. (August 1990)

Bushy-tailed Symbol of the Nation

You think instantly of the horse, but when it comes to proclaiming a national mammal (to go with the national bird, the bald eagle) you must look deeply and consider wisely.

The squirrel, in other words. An ideal beast, familiar to and loved by all. An animal that is not endangered, not becoming extinct. And not possessing a famous rear end.

The buffalo has its claims. But it became extinct in the East quite early in the last century. It is easily stampeded, which is a heavy claim for choosing it, but not a good one. As a people we are easily stampeded but I doubt we should boast of it.

The mountain lion is noble and would be a perfect choice except there used to be one on every hill but now it survives only in the middle of nowhere. That is not the message we need.

As everybody knows, Benjamin Franklin objected to the bald eagle as a bird of bad repute. The eagle is now so rare that few Americans have ever seen one in the wild. It is moreover one of the first things to vanish if lesser fry are poisoned with chemicals, as it eats them all.

Franklin wanted the wild turkey, a better choice, but why argue now over lost causes.

Instead, let's get on with a national animal, one that rightly symbolizes the great republic but does not sentimentalize it (my objection to a basset hound puppy, irresistible but certain to make the world go awwwwww) and that does not mock us, as the wild asses of our Western states would do.

No sir, once you give the matter as much thought as I have, you will come up with the squirrel. The name derives, of course, from the Greek words for shadow and tail. We acknowledge, in the national squirrel, our heritage from the classical world, with all that that implies of the first democracy, the love of learning, the execution of Socrates and so on indefinitely.

As the name implies, there is something veiled or formless—now you see it, now you don't—about us as a nation. Shadow tail indeed.

Hard to say what its bulk and substance are, yet the tail is surely there and is glorious.

The charm of the squirrel is undeniable and a chief reason for its prominence in all our great cities. People cannot resist feeding squirrels, though our manly containment of emotion causes us to say we're "feeding birds."

Most Americans remember the squirrel as savior of starving frontiersmen and, later, as the critical ingredient of Brunswick stew. Squirrels will always be associated with the rifle named for (and used against) them. Like us, the squirrel has a bloody history and has now entered a new era (at least for squirrels) of peace and acceptance.

The squirrel is craftier than the fox. Some call him a thief, merely because the little fellow has to eat. He is thrifty, burying acorns and peanuts everywhere. He is an inspiration to us to save for the coming winter; he is patron of oak forests and a born ecologist.

More pioneers wore squirrel hats than coonskins and more coats were trimmed with squirrel fur than with ermine. In our savage moments as well as our good ones the little squirrel has been right there with us.

His name suggests not only thrift, as he squirrels things away, but also (and I face this head-on) a sort of daffy imbalance. Squirrelly. Well, that's us. But squirrelly is not the same as paranoid or sociopathic. As a nation we are frequently off our rockers but, like the squirrel, we usually recover before all is lost.

Our native squirrels have enormous ears (in the western fox squirrels) and come in gray, reddish, white and black. Our squirrels fly through the air in some species, and in others they leap with a dazzle that commands amazement. They do not fly as well as bats, or see danger ahead as well as bats, but for reasons we need not go into, bats did not make the second cut.

You might ask why we need a national beast to display on our shield. Well, why do we need anything, if you want to start arguing. I am uneasy at the growing number of references to Millie, a White House spaniel, as First Dog. A slippery slope. There is some danger Millie will be proposed as national animal. We had a narrow escape from Falla, a previous White House mutt, and from Rin-Tin-Tin and Lassie. Now I love dogs but would never countenance any dog as the national mammal because nothing raises hackles quicker. If a dog were

As a nation we are frequently off our rockers like the squirrel.

chosen we'd be in a civil war or a general riot as the Hound People chased the Friends of the Poodle and the Terrier Contingent would never let go.

Beside, we want something native, not imported, and something wild, not pampered. The free-roaming, modest, I'm OK, Jack nature of the squirrel is what we want. Write Congress. They have more time than they know what to do with. (October 1990)

On the Curse of AIDS

As every good Puritan knows, God sent a plague on the New England Indians to clear them out shortly before the Pilgrims arrived in 1620.

Smallpox was the divine agent in that case, and for the next century or so the Pilgrims, who were not of a naturally thankful disposition, at least gave thanks for that.

John Winthrop, the great Puritan leader of Massachusetts Bay, said it was God's way of "thinning out" the heathen (in 1616–1618) just in the nick of time. Otherwise, no doubt, the virtuous Puritans would have had to kill them at considerable investment of gunpowder.

The plague came again a few years later, enabling Winthrop to write that "the natives are near all dead of the smallpox so as the Lord hath cleared out title to what we possess."

An important function of God, as millions of His worshipers see Him, is to curse or send plagues upon other people who are troublesome.

The Book of Mormon—though I do not hold Mormons responsible for what is written in their book any more than I hold Jews or Christians liable for some of the things in the Bible—says that blacks used to be white until God cursed them for their sins.

God appears to have been busy through many generations cursing this group and that, so we should not be surprised to hear today that AIDS has been sent to wipe out the gay population. This is only said or believed by the ignorant, the naturally vicious and the generally Hell-bound part of the American public, but it is a sufficiently large group to make itself heard. The same idea of a divine curse is sometimes altered slightly. Thus you may hear that "they brought it on themselves," or "what could you expect from the way they carry on," or "they wouldn't be in trouble if they lived decent lives."

The "decent lives" that the straight population leads may not be perfect, what with a few divorces and murders and broken homes, etc., but the lives of gay people must be far worse, else God would not be killing them.

It's hard to believe anybody believes that, no matter how benighted

An important function of God is to curse or send plagues upon other people who are troublesome.

he is, but plenty of people do believe it, just as they believed God killed off the Indians for the sake of some Puritans.

The sane person is always on guard over his own prejudices, knowing how easily a human finds high authority for any convenient belief he may hold. The human (as distinct from the more enlightened and more innocent animals, such as the dog) first notices some circumstance or some person or group that he could happily do without. After mulling this over a few hours or a few years, he concludes it must be God's will for that group to get out of the way. Often enough it occurs to him it would be a service to the divinity to act as agent, to rid the world of (depending on which century and nation we're talking about) Jews, Roman Catholics, Anglicans, Christians, Quakers, Baptists, blacks, Japanese, Presbyterians, Moslems, bankers, aristocrats, lawyers. Lawyers—but never mind. Not all of them.

The human brain, even if it is brought up short and does not allow itself to go quite as far as discovering divine curses, still finds it easy to believe whatever is most convenient or profitable to believe.

I remember when the three civil rights youths were murdered and buried in a dam at Philadelphia, Miss., the prevailing rumor down there was that all three were living in luxury in the Plaza Hotel in New York, laughing their heads off.

It was almost certain from the beginning that they were murdered, but as it was more comfortable to think they were in New York, that's what people decided to believe. As if that absurd belief could deflect the guilt that would otherwise be felt.

We'll all go to our graves as irrational as the day we were born, and the best we can do is watch out whenever our personal interest seems to coincide with celestial virtue.

It's better, surely, to say it was lucky the Indians got sick and died and left the land vacant, than to say God killed them for our benefit. It's better to say (if it comes to that) that greed or fear made us do somebody in, rather than to blame it on God.

There was a preacher once who had some particular knowledge of what went on in Hell, and told his flock about a batch of sinners down there. He said they hollered considerably and cried out, "Lord, we didn't know, we didn't know."

Then a whirlwind voice was heard (the preacher went on) that said, "Well, you damned well know now."

Of course, nobody can say with certainty but it's a pretty point to argue, how many of those who say or hint that people with AIDS had it coming, will one day hear it from on high:

"Well, you damned well know now." (December 1990)

Putting Technology in Its Place

Nobody, to fulfill his animal obligations, needs to fling off clothes especially in winter and race about the forest subsisting on tree bark. It is natural to cows, dogs and other animals to learn from experience and to devise clever ways to make life easier.

All the same, it is worth keeping in mind that we are not gods but animals, however sophisticated, and we do not inhabit a realm of disembodied thought, but think in a quite real world of water, earth, air and the creatures visible and invisible within it.

Civilization, in other words, is as natural as savagery and more desirable. But civilization is not just another word for technology. Civilization is far larger than technology and more important.

The gap between the two may sometimes be narrow, but the emphasis in public policy as well as private thinking should always be on the natural world and a good life for humans in it.

Some think the natural world exists in order that IBM or Ford may be born. But that is shocking to me, and dangerous to believe. Instead, Ford and other high technologies exist so that man can live with delight in the natural world.

If the main point of life is to gross out the national product, to put rockets in outer space and in general to ensure further technical tricks and amusements, then there is no good argument against doing whatever is necessary to reach that goal.

But it is a stupid goal. The sane goal is to devise technology that permits humans to live without hunger and to have shelter and leisure and education and room for play and for wonder.

To a great extent technology has made all that possible for humans of favored geography and who belong to favored classes. But there is no need to run down the litany of failures in a society of high technology—the poor, the bored, the frantic, the sick in physical pain, the anxious and the fearful.

What real point is there to life if it means only regimentation and work so simple-minded and boring that it may rightly be called deadly? It is the lot of many, and worse than that, the charms of high technology have seduced far too many humans to the view that the good things of life are possible only if technology is pressed harder and faster.

When I was a kid I marveled at subsistence farmers, who yearly lost money until at last they lost the farm, but one reason they persisted was the addictive effect of weather, plants and animals. You are loath to leave it, when the alternative is a subsistence wage and a hovel in the nearest city.

The horrendous sorrows of society will hardly be redeemed by turning everybody into small farmers again, letting the kids feed the calves their milk from buckets. (Which is, of course, one of the few totally exquisite joys of life.) We do not get far dreaming of pastoral Arcadias inhabited by fellows like Jefferson and Johnny Appleseed.

But we will get much further if we rethink the cost of technology. The spotted owl, to mention a current idol of conservationists (the so-called butterfly net bunch), in itself does not do all that much for civilization, you might argue. But then neither do oil spills, land ruined in a thousand technological ways, or sulfur-heavy air.

How is any great change to come about, away from the often too-high-cost technology that we worship? Not by trashing telephones (admittedly a temptation) and smashing even more cars than we do. But by the force of millions of people rediscovering the natural world. Every human should have a piece of his own land (if only to use) where if nothing else he can watch the weeds grow. Or, even better, to have his own fig tree and grapevine, if only on an apartment balcony. Everybody should have an animal to take care of, even if it's just a pigeon, though ideally that dazzle of the animal kingdom, the dog.

It goes without saying that these are currently impossible goals for millions of Americans. If you have to live near the office or plant where you work, and where your income dictates a small apartment in a physically ugly place, it is absurd to say that what you need is a colt and a patch of corn and a good hound. And it is no easier if you have no place to work at all.

But it is not absurd to keep in mind that close ties to plants and animals ought to be possible for every citizen. Any policy that tends toward Joe Blow having a few tomato plants and a mutt is worth encouraging. Any policy that encourages or obliges him to live in some damned rabbit warren should be discouraged.

All of which is obvious. Then why do so many policies, so many

Any policy that tends toward Joe Blow having a few tomato plants and a mutt is worth encouraging.

national priorities, tend to a contempt for the natural world and a demeaning of those who would like a few good things—some privacy, room for the kids, resources to keep a dog, to grow a grape—but who are not rich enough or aggressive enough or sly enough to seize those good things for themselves?

Our civilization has gone so far in paltriness that in some classes the aim is to spend $125 for supper and to drive a painted tank, while in other groups the *beau idéal* is to get a gun.

And while it is gratifying to discover that a coalition of half a billion people can defeat a nation of 17 million in a war that cost nothing much, the true hazard to the nation remains the same: a large and increasing class of the poor starved for much more than food, and a large and increasing class of rich, who are into roast crocodile for lunch. (March 1991)

Wonder Bread

I've often thought the value of Wonder Bread as a sponge has yet to be explored, and when you consider the cost of cleaning up oil spills in the sea you must ask if Wonder Bread is not fully competitive.

Just this week I was on jury duty and retired briefly to the cafeteria of Superior Court, where, in a mad fit, I ordered two pieces of toast. I believe they were Wonder Bread, as they had that limp look when flung into a toasting machine. They came out somewhat firmer and when painted with melted butter they absorbed a full quarter of a pound.

I thought it a good buy for 20 cents.

My other most recent experience with this famous product was a few years ago at Sibley Hospital, where some steroids produced a frantic appetite. Once at 3 a.m. the floor nurse, seeing me drool as I watched nurses snacking heavily at their station, said I could go right on down to the lunchroom and get me something.

All they had was macaroni left over from supper and a good supply of Wonder Bread. I ate both with a pleasure so intense that the memory is still sharp. On only one other occasion, walking into the great yum-yum town of Lyon late at night to find a three-star restaurant still open—only on that occasion did the pleasure of food equal the Wonder Bread–macaroni feast of Sibley Hospital. And at Lyon it took crawfish bisque and much else to produce the ecstasy so easily coaxed from a balloon-spangled squashy wrapper at any grocery store.

But get this. Recently Wonder Bread was held up as an example of what's wrong with American business and, by implication, what's wrong with America. Some Harvard egghead said so many compromises had to be made in order for Wonder Bread to be mass-produced and marketed that it lost all its taste and food value.

Imagine the chairman of Wonder Bread reading such a thing at breakfast in St. Louis (Continental Baking is at St. Louis). It must have taken all the superior food value of Wonder Bread to keep him from having a stroke on the spot. He wrote a public letter, published this week, to point out that Americans have made Wonder the leading bread of the republic, and this could hardly have come about if the

I thought they just blew up library paste with gas and sent it to the oven.

bread were tasteless and nutritionally sterile. Ha. What do you say to that?

Furthermore, this vigorous defender of the Wonder faith went on, it is the very taste of this product that has made it preeminent on our continent.

I had not known that Wonder relaxes and rises three times during a four-hour process of manufacture. I thought they just blew up library paste with gas and sent it to the oven. Imagine all that rising and falling that results at the last (the spokesman concludes) in Wonder Bread, "an example of American food manufacturing at its best."

You would think, reading the brisk defense of this product, that little old Mr. and Mrs. Wonder began whipping the stuff up in St. Louis, probably with all the special vitamins of a Missouri environment. And then all the neighbors had to have some and then the Great American Palate heard of Wonder and now, a few years later, the nation will have no other bread to receive its peanut butter and/or jelly.

Nothing is said, you notice, of marketing strategies, advertising, distributional arrangements or other factors relevant to the No. 1 position of Wonder Bread.

It may not, in other words, be just the delicious taste of Wonder Bread that got it where it is today.

Well, I make do on a peasant bread of stone-ground whole wheat. You get five loaves start to finish in less than an hour, though I admit you can't run a loaf of it through the eye of a needle. Still, this brown bread suffices the likes of me.

I have no argument with the spokesman for Wonder Bread. The depressing thing is not that he speaks with forked tongue, spreading untruths. The thing that sinks me to the depths is the awful suspicion that when he says Wonder Bread is "American food manufacturing at its best," he is telling the truth. (March 1991)

Heroes

A hero doesn't have to be perfect. He can have an ax to grind. He doesn't have to be disinterested. He doesn't have to be an immediate candidate for Paradise. But he does have to be a hero.

Nothing is more offensive than the debasement of the concept of hero. Any day now I expect to find Donald Trump, Michael Jackson and Bob Hope on somebody's list of heroes on the grounds they have either been around since the Flood or have made tubs of money or have persuaded surgeons to give them a noble nose.

Even among true heroes there are different kinds. There are Achilles and Arjuna, great warriors who so despised death and danger that their lives were always on the line in face-to-face battle for what they thought was the highest honor.

There are others—Albert Schweitzer, Mother Teresa and Martin Luther King come to mind—who accepted a humble station in circumstances of great danger to serve the poor. No doubt they were highly paid in psychic satisfaction, but their gifts were so substantial and their effect on the world around them was so beneficial that nobody could refuse them hero status.

Closer to home there are firemen and cops who risk life and often enough give it to protect others.

I would also call some whistle-blowers heroes, especially such an example as Walter Stewart, say, who hung on like a bulldog for years in exposing fraud in the scientific community, not hesitating to go after even Nobel laureates, and not cracking under fierce pressure from famous people, and freely enduring the contempt of many and the endless petty indignities pitched his way.

In all cases, however, the hero sacrifices a great deal, far more than prudence would recommend or than the rest of us would find necessary.

The hero has to be expansive, as if splendor had to burst out from inside. It may be a sudden glory, as in a man who dives into an icy river to rescue the drowning, or it may be the slow work of years. Always it involves a personal risk so great that the rest of us are in awe that mere mortals could conjure up such courage.

Classically this was explained in ancient times by concluding the hero was a child of some great god, and worthy of divine honors after his magnificence on the earth was done.

In all cases, the cause must be noble or perceived by the hero to be noble, and the perception must be reasonable, not psychotic.

So great then is the luster of the hero that the temptation is irresistible to insolent men to pose as heroes when they have risked too little for that exalted status or who have crept and intruded into the fold, so to speak, or have crowned themselves with the laurels of their betters.

You see this occasionally. Sometimes a man who does no more than fulfill the legal requirements of citizenship can embellish his story. Sometimes a guy with a couple of battle stars on his ribbons who did nothing more than sleep through a rain of antipersonnel bombs (I speak of myself) can encourage or allow others to think he did great things in war.

Or in great movements such as civil rights there will always be some who, by virtue of having known the Rev. King or who were within shouting distance of Mississippi at some point, have gradually promoted themselves to heroes in the fray.

Not since American might was able to prevail in Grenada has the nation known such excitement as the war of the Persian Gulf. The commander announced to begin with that it would not last any time, that there would be no casualties to speak of, that it would not cost much treasure, and that its results would be a new order in our troubled planet, the initiation of a Pax Americana.

We shall see how it turns out. I believe an imitation war with an imitation victory will merit no more than a footnote in the history of the republic, and that those like the commander in chief who stood so proud and proclaimed so impressively that this was the mother of victories will wind up in our history books with Presidents Fillmore, Harding and the others who undoubtedly did something but nobody can quite remember what.

The gods are not lightly mocked and pretend-heroes fade quickly. As for our troops in the gulf, there is no doubt that many would have been heroes when called on to risk everything and to stand their ground against Hell itself. After all, the budding flame of heroism lives in every human, but not every human encounters circumstances that fan it to overwhelming fire, and not every human (who might have

The hero has to be expansive, as if splendor had to burst out from inside.

been a hero given ample preparation and ample warning) rises to the heights in the flash of one immortal second.

If you talk to people you know well, you find very little of that exultation or that bone-tired relief that followed, for example, the Civil War.

Then where does all the public mode of triumph come from? Mainly from television, whose chief job is to sell soap, and from the assortment of snake oil promoters who find cures in every meadow and who well know the easy tricks of persuading the thoughtless that they are an elite to end all elites. They are commonly to be found near the powerful, whose hides can absorb more flattery and general slop than any Biloxi sponge.

It makes no difference what is trumpeted in the streets. It makes a difference what we believe, however, and how we judge. It makes a difference how we use the word "hero," and whether we limit it to the sons of the gods or bestow it grandly on anybody who fulfilled a contract.

I know a mongrel named Beau who came from a humane shelter. At first his owner accepted him as a mutt that should be allowed to live. Then the owner thought by golly old Beau looks like a fine dog. He didn't have long fur or great ears or anything to make you catch your breath. But at the last you heard the owner say, "You know Beau, our Staffordshire terrier?"

I greatly enjoyed Beau's promotion from mongrel to purebred, because the promotion was based on a chronic love that, as you know, sees nobility where it feels affection and is otherwise somewhat near-sighted if not totally blind.

I like to think, but have serious doubts, that our promotion of ourselves to the rank of the heroic also springs from love and not from cunning bellywash. (March 1991)

Tidbits Dropped from the Table

Before coming to the important and interesting topic, What Dogs in Fact Eat, we should get Nancy Reagan out of the way, especially her rumored affair with Frank Sinatra.

The only evidence of such an affair at the White House seems to be that Sinatra was admitted to the living quarters on various occasions with the strict orders of Mrs. Reagan not to disturb her.

Nobody, as far as I can tell, has any better evidence than that.

My estimate is that the two were old friends from Hollywood. There would be much gossip to catch up on, and all the other topics that Sinatra and Mrs. Reagan would wish to chat about. At their respective ages—they were both born in the Jurassic—why would they want to carry on with each other? In their exalted positions they could find starlets and male models aplenty, if lively sex were what they wanted.

The thing about this kind of baloney in a book is that people suspect that where there's smoke there's fire. The fact of the rumor is grounds for the rumor. It feeds itself.

Now then, today's contribution to science deals with my terrier's diet. I would not have risked embarrassing him while he was alive, but now that he's safe in Abraham's bosom or what the philosopher called a fair and shady place, full of the sounds of summer, I will say that along with the various unmentionable substances that all dogs eat he was peculiarly fond of Brussels sprouts.

We are agreed at our house that nothing would bring him into the kitchen quicker than the smell of Brussels sprouts cooking. He also admired cabbage in all forms except sauerkraut. He was fond of spinach for some years but took against it three years ago unless it had Parmesan cheese. Broccoli was a Great Good Thing, and in this (as in so many ways) Max proved superior to men one can think of.

Needless to say he liked every kind of cheese, though he could not bite into those foil-wrapped soft cheeses and get it out through the tooth holes as old Jack could do. He liked low-fat cottage cheese, and preferred it with a little onion and green pepper cut up in it. There was no kind of meat or bread on his hate list. He went wild for homemade pizza with plenty of garlic, and he never met a potato he didn't like.

Sweet corn was a favorite, though he never mastered eating it from the cob, and if he found cobs with a few kernels left, he ate the cob and got sick. He tried it several times. But if you left cut corn on your plate while answering the phone, he downed it promptly. He thought well of tomatoes, fresh and canned, with or without oil. Turnips, celery, beets, lettuce, soups of various kinds, especially vichyssoise when he could lick bowls in summer. He would not, however, eat collards, being a Yankee dog I reckon.

You should not suppose we deliberately fed him all this stuff at first. As a youthful dog he just ate his dry chow, but when things dropped on the kitchen floor he investigated, so that over the years we came to know his taste. Never to his dying day did he eat an anchovy or an oyster, either raw or cooked. He eschewed pickled peppers, though hash on waffles with hot sauce was okay by him.

In his last three years of grievous illness (heartworms) and in and out of hospitals, the vet feared he would eat so little as to starve. That was not the case. We supplemented his diet with all the vegetables and other things we knew he liked, so he died fat as a bishop.

When he came to us from a kennel in New York years ago we were dismayed to notice his fondness for coffee, with or without cream. Clearly he had got this bad habit at the handler's house where he lived his first 3½ months. Took us half a year to break him of that. Toward the end we let him have coffee again, and the morning he died he had a little bowl of it.

People sometimes say I am forever writing about my dog, which is untrue. A review of several years of columns shows virtually nothing about my personal dog. I believe this error came through the drawings by Susan Davis, which are full of dogs, but she is independent in her drawings, which rarely—no, make that not always—have anything to do with the text.

As Michelangelo, who had not the foggiest notion what Moses looked like, sought to capture the spirit, some of her terriers looked like Max, once she comprehended that the ears of the Welsh stand up then flop down at the tips, and some did not. She is an artist, not an archivist.

What I should add is that this amiable beast continued to grow. He did not get crabby or vicious as some old animals do. He did not say Brussels sprouts it is and refuse everything else. On the contrary his interest in the world grew even as the mortal body declined. A week

He admired Brussels sprouts and cabbage in all forms except sauerkraut.

before his death I was eating a hamburger and dropped a dill pickle on the floor.

"You don't eat dill pickles," I reminded him, but for the first time in his life (as I believe) he took a bite. Then ate the whole thing. He had another pickle or two before he died. What I want to know is how many animals adventurously try new foods in decrepit old age? Most of them retreat to boiled cornmeal.

He would not eat fish eggs in any form. He was uneasy with smoked salmon (as God knows I am) and we never happened to drop any snails, since we never had any in the house to drop. A very catholic, very sophisticated, very outgoing dog, as of course all terriers are. In the interest of science perhaps I should add that we think he came to dill pickles at the last by way of deviled eggs which he discovered in puphood. The pickle relish in them did not bother him.

As in all great developments and breakthroughs, you can often see the signs early in life when you look back. (April 1991)

HENRY MITCHELL, who died in 1993, was a long-time columnist for the *Washington Post* and the author of two famous and beloved gardening books, *The Essential Earthman* and *One Man's Garden*.